STAMP COLLECTING

*This is the first ever paperback edition of the
Stanley Gibbons standard work on its subject,
recognized now as the finest, sanest, and most
comprehensive general guide to the hobby of stamp
collecting.*

*This edition contains the original text, revised and
with some new up-to-date material.*

D0928340

STANLEY PHILLIPS

Stamp Collecting

KNIGHT BOOKS

the paperback division of Brockhampton Press Ltd

SBN 340 03827 6

This revised edition first published 1968 by Knight Books,
the paperback division of Brockhampton Press Ltd, Leicester
Second impression 1968

Printed and bound in Great Britain by
Richard Clay (The Chaucer Press), Ltd, Bungay, Suffolk

© *1965 Mrs Emily Phillips*

Eighth edition published 1965 by Stanley Gibbons Ltd,
Drury House, Russell Street, London WC2,
by appointment philatelists to Her Majesty the Queen

CONTENTS

PART ONE · POSTS AND THE POSTAGE STAMP

		Page
1	The story of the post	8
2	The coming of the postage stamp	15
3	Stamps and their uses	19
4	Commemorative and charity stamps	28
5	The life and anatomy of a postage stamp	39
6	Stamp printing	59
7	Errors and varieties	69
8	Overprints and surcharges	88
9	Designs and inscriptions	96
10	Stamp colours and their names	107
11	Stamp sheets and booklets	114
12	The other side of the stamp	120
13	Postmarks and obliterations	123
14	Forgeries, reprints, and fakes	134

PART TWO · THE COLLECTION

15	The outfit	145
16	How to get stamps	153
17	The question of condition	160
18	How to identify stamps	163
19	Arranging the collection	173
20	The specialist	182
21	Thematic collecting	189

		Page
22	Sideline collections	200
23	Air stamps and covers	211
24	The money side of stamp collecting	216

PART THREE · THE HOBBY

25	The stamp world	223
26	Great collections and famous collectors	231
27	The stamp library	237
28	Behind the scenes	244
29	Treasure trove	252
30	The hobby of a thousand faces	260

APPENDICES

A	*Stamp currencies*	263
B	*Philatelic terms in three languages*	274
C	*Stamp inscriptions translated*	280
D	*The meaning of overprints*	286
	Index	292

PART ONE · POSTS AND THE POSTAGE STAMP

STAMP COLLECTING

The individual who decides to make collecting of one sort or another his choice as an amusement for leisure hours, finds, when he comes to make inquiries, that there is one hobby which stands out above all others. It overrides the barriers of race and class and age, linking black and white and king with schoolboy. It appeals to nearly every type of mind, and is within the reach of every purse. It has, without a shadow of a doubt, the largest number of followers that any collecting hobby can claim. Around and about it has sprung up a world press and a world trade, which in the operation of the law of supply and demand has created out of nothing a stable value of hundreds of millions, and gives regular employment to many thousands. While other hobbies have waxed and waned in popular favour, this has gone from strength to strength, and is now more highly and widely esteemed than at any previous period of its history. This hobby is postage-stamp collecting.

Its basis, inception, and growth, and the varied attractions which have raised it to its present position, are described in this volume, together with the practical methods by which the collector may best approach his enjoyable task. It is hoped that the work here presented may be of real value to many who are already enthusiasts, and that its perusal may be the means of introducing many more to the pleasures now enjoyed by the great army of stamp collectors throughout the world.

Chapter One

THE STORY OF THE POST

To appreciate fully the pleasures of stamp collecting it is necessary to realize that the postage stamp is merely the symbol of the working of the postal systems of the world. A postage stamp, as a single item in a collection, may, as we shall see, have intrinsic features of interest, but these are nothing compared with the fact that behind the postage stamp lies the post, that means of communication by which messages of joy and sorrow pass from one end of the world to the other, utilizing every known means of transport, often in circumstances of adventurous difficulty.

The story of the post takes us back to the vast empires of antiquity, whose rulers, for the preservation of themselves and their dominions, were forced to establish courier services by which messages might be carried surely and rapidly, over great roads adequately provided with relay stations, whence untiring man or beast set forth on stage after stage of a journey which might take the ruler's message hundreds or even thousands of miles.

If such posts had not existed, and even in some cases where they did, the emperor might find himself dispossessed of an outlying province either by invasion or revolt before his central authority could take steps to meet the emergency. Letters impressed on clay tablets and in some cases enclosed in clay 'envelopes', have come down to us from Babylon, and Cyrus the Great is credited by the early historians with the establishment of a scientifically worked out system of posts by horse-relays, which was taken up by the Romans and remained the basis of many postal systems until comparatively modern times. Egypt, too, had its postal system, but all these organizations were, of course, for the carriage of official mails alone, and in most cases the government couriers were strictly forbidden to carry private messages, and were severely punished if they broke the rule.

Private correspondence had to depend for transport on the servants of the writers, or, for more distant journeys, letters were entrusted to the hands of traders or seafarers who, in the dangerous conditions of those early days, might, or might not, arrive safely at their destination.

It is not possible to divide the history of the world's posts into periods according to the means of transport employed, for some of the most primitive methods of transportation are still in use in developing countries, but the letter carrier who walked gave place to the running courier in those official postal systems where speed was of the greatest consequence and he, in his turn, was replaced by the mounted man. Then came the horse-drawn chariot or other vehicle, followed, after many centuries, by the locomotive and the motor-car.

On water, the vessel driven by paddles or oars was succeeded by the sailing ship and later by the steamship. In the air, the pigeon holds pride of place, for this useful bird carried messages for the early Greeks and Romans, and possibly even before their time. Again a long interval, and we find the balloon being used as a mail carrier in exceptional circumstances, often with very uncertain results, and today we have a world-wide development of the use of aeroplanes for letter-carrying across continents and oceans, while rocket-posts have been tested and will eventually find a place among systems of rapid communication.

Some of the elements of this progress may be found illustrated on postage stamps, such as those of Mexico, issued in 1895, which depict the carriage of mails by foot peon, by pack mule, by coach, and by rail. Bosnia, also, took up the same idea on three stamps of the handsome 1906 series, where the pack animal, the horsed wagon, and a postal motor may be seen; and the United States had the same theme in mind when designing the Buffalo Exhibition stamps of 1901 and the Parcel Post series of 1912, the latter showing no less than eight scenes connected with the delivery of mails.

A similar series of later date comes from India (1937) which depicts the runner, the bullock cart, the camel, train, steamer, lorry, and aeroplane as postal carriers, representing all stages of progress in the carriage of mails, yet all in use at the present day in various parts of the country. Many more stamps illustrate the theme.

As the great monasteries and universities of the Middle Ages were the repositories of learning and therefore, apart from the rulers, the first to make frequent use of letter-writing as a means of communication, it is natural that we should be able to trace to them the beginnings of our present-day postal systems, by which not only official correspondence but the communications of the general public are carried.

Regular communication was kept up between the various monasteries. The universities, whose pupils came from many lands, found it necessary to employ messengers, by whom letters from the students to their parents might be carried and, human nature being the same then as now, these messengers doubtless added to their perquisites by carrying correspondence for persons outside the universities.

As trade and commerce increased their range from the purely local to the national and international fields, regular private services for letter-carrying were established, some of them growing up quite by chance, while others owed their existence to the efforts of wealthy trading communities, such as the merchants of the cities of the Hanseatic League of Northern Germany.

Extraordinary journeys were made by some of the messengers of the Middle Ages, the routes extending as far as Venice in the south and into the interior of Russia in an easterly direction. We have to remember, too, that roads, as we understand them today, were practically non-existent, and for the most part the courier had to make his way across country in the face of risks of all kinds.

In England we find King John maintaining a corps of royal messengers, but though there are indications that Charlemagne met with some success in reviving the old Roman posts, these decayed with the break-up of his empire, and we have to come down to the time of Louis XI to discover the royal messenger service which was the forerunner of the French postal system of today. As might be expected, so wily a monarch as Louis fully appreciated the value of a quick and reliable official postal service, and he organized it on an elaborate scale. For a heavy fee his subjects were permitted to use the 'Royal Mails', but, trusting no one, the monarch insisted that all letters so carried should be censored.

Though they were of course used at a much later period than that of which we are speaking, the stamps of Thurn and Taxis recall the story of a family which from the fifteenth century down to quite modern times, held a leading position as postal organizers in Europe. Counts of Thurn and Taxis covered the Continent with a network of posts which, in spite of competition, the risks of war, and a host of other difficulties, did wonderful service, though in a gradually decreasing area, for something like five hundred years. Even as late as the middle of the nineteenth century we find the Thurn and Taxis posts covering a territory of 25,000 square miles with a population of nearly four millions, and it was not until 1867 that Prussia bought out the last remaining rights, and this great service disappeared.

Their activities did not, however, touch France to any great extent, and that country was indebted for its first really public postal system to the vision of Richelieu who appointed a postmaster-general, who in course of time built up a courier system which functioned very efficiently and which even included provision for registered letters. The good work done by Richelieu was continued by Mazarin.

The most interesting French post, however, from the

stamp collector's point of view, was that instituted in the city of Paris about the middle of the seventeenth century by one de Villayer. With the royal authority these posts carried letters and parcels throughout Paris, and boxes were set up in various parts of the city where letters could be posted – the forerunners of our modern pillar boxes.

A most fascinating feature of the service consisted in the fact that de Villayer sold wrappers bearing a special mark, which when wrapped round the letter entitled it to be carried by his postal system. The wrappers were torn off by the officials of the post before the letter was delivered, so that they could not be used again. Here we have the earliest form of stamped postal wrapper, which eventually gave rise to the invention of the adhesive postage stamp.

The post of King John in England, to which we have already referred, consisted merely of a staff of couriers 'standing by' to carry royal messages as and when required, and we have to pass on to the reign of King Henry VIII to trace the establishment of relay stations for the royal service. Queen Elizabeth laid down formal regulations for the conduct of the service and references have come down to us which show that a certain number of private letters were carried by the post. The very elementary nature of the post, so far as outlying districts were concerned, is shown by the fact that while King James of Scotland received news of the death of Queen Elizabeth in three days, parts of Devonshire and Cornwall had not heard the news until after the court had ceased to wear mourning for her. The speed with which news travelled depended largely on the condition of the roads and how near a particular district was to the main routes of travel.

The period of the Stuarts was the birth era of the British post as we know it. The posts were thrown fully open to the public (those who could write and pay) in 1635, and the first Post Office Act was passed by Cromwell.

The posts were largely farmed out, and the system of rewarding court favourites by remunerative appointments meant that the postal services were often at the mercy of persons who were more concerned to line their own pockets than to give the public satisfactory transport for their correspondence.

Enterprising individuals worked out schemes for improvement, but had to fight the monopolists so that when a famous pioneer, William Dockwra, set up in 1680 an admirable penny post which covered the whole of London, he came into conflict with James, Duke of York, to whom Charles II had allotted the profits of the Government postal service, and the absurd attempts of Titus Oates to link the Dockwra post with the Popish Plot led to that organization being taken from its creator and incorporated in the official postal system.

Dockwra's post is of special interest to the collector, as he used postmarks showing the date, time, and place of posting, very much as they are used today.

The carriage of mails was improved in the years that followed, but the cost of sending letters, which was calculated on distance, remained very high and it was not until inland penny postage, a privilege of which the First World War robbed us, was established in 1840, that the truly popular post could be said to have arrived. As an immediate result of the introduction of the new system, the number of letters carried was more than doubled and cheap postage, one of the great benefits of modern civilization, had definitely arrived.

Meanwhile the posts of Europe had been improving with the building of new roads and the spread of learning, and the new worlds which were being opened up overseas were going through the primitive stages of their organization. It is noticeable that, from the very beginning of history, it was always the most enlightened rulers and statesmen who gave attention to the subject of intercommunication. It only remained for the development of the locomotive, the motorcar, and the aeroplane to bring the postal systems of the world to the high standard of the present day.

The collector who is content to look at his stamps as pieces of paper interesting merely because of their design or some technical detail or defect will undoubtedly derive much pleasure from his hobby, but the man of imagination, who sees behind every stamp the romantic story of the post, will have a background such as few other hobbies can offer.

Think of those early couriers struggling across Europe for weeks and months exposed to attack by robbers or wild animals, or to danger from the elements and the country they traversed. Look at the mail coaches rumbling over terrible roads, and often finding a resting place in the ditch, or relieved of their loads by highwaymen. Read the story of the early express services of the United States, whose messengers covered a rapidly growing territory, and who for three or four hundred dollars a year served their countrymen by carrying correspondence through lands infested with hostile Indians and often more dangerous white men.

Turn to our own day, and think of the men who serve in the great postal systems of the modern world, the seamen and engineers who drive our mail ships through all the dangers of the seven seas and the postmen of the air who cross the mighty Andes, or link Britain with Africa, India, or Australia by the quickest postal service yet devised by man.

The collector whose imagination is not fired by the romance of the mails is poorer for the fact, but he need not for that reason turn away from the hobby of stamp collecting. It has many other aspects of appeal.

Chapter Two

THE COMING OF THE POSTAGE STAMP

THE dictionary definition of a postage stamp reads 'an adhesive stamp for affixing to letters to show that the postal charge has been paid'. If we go further and ask for the meaning of the word 'stamp', the sense in which it is used in the above definition is obviously that of 'an official mark put on things chargeable with duty, as proof that the duty is paid'. Let us see how such adhesive postage stamps came into being.

The seals which were affixed to letters carried by the earliest royal courier services may perhaps be regarded as the germ of the postage-stamp idea. True they did not show that postage had been paid, but as the sight of the royal seal ensured prompt attention to the forwarding of the letter, the seal had in effect the power of a frank. The development of this idea may be found in the practice of 'franking' letters by means of the signature of a person, such as a member of parliament who had the privilege of having his letters carried free in the days before the establishment of the more modern postal service.

Until the arrival of the postage stamp, postage on letters carried by the services which the public could use was either prepaid in cash by the sender, or the sum due was collected on delivery. There are, therefore, many different kinds of marks to be found on correspondence carried in various countries before the use of the adhesive stamp, to indicate that postage has been paid. These are of great interest, and a few of them are often found in a collection of adhesive postage stamps where they serve as an introduction to the collection proper.

From 1835 onwards the subject of postal reform was being considered in England, and a committee was set up, which sat for three years, and issued numerous reports. Meanwhile Rowland Hill had been at work, and in January 1837 he issued his famous pamphlet on Post Office Reform, the result of which was the formation of a larger committee to examine his proposals. The most important suggestions were for uniform penny postage, and that all postage should be prepaid, and the natural corollary was the putting forward of a scheme for issuing stamped wrappers. Adhesive stamps were also referred to, but apparently without very much appreciation of how convenient they would be to the public, for they were mentioned as a possible alternative to the wrapper in the case of an illiterate person bringing an addressed letter to the post office not enclosed in a stamped wrapper. The adhesive stamp could, in such cases, be stuck directly on the already addressed letter, and would thus obviate the necessity for re-writing the address on the stamped wrapper.

In spite of the opposition which is usually aroused by any reforms which spell progress, the advocates of penny postage won their battle and from 10th January 1840 anyone could send a half-ounce letter anywhere in the Kingdom for a penny instead of at rates calculated by distance, which were so high as to render the use of the post too costly for the great mass of the people. Penny postage, coupled with pre-payment of postage, did away with the complications of collecting postal fees on delivery, and prevented the heavy loss of revenue caused by the carriage of letters by private persons in the attempt to avoid the heavy charges of the official post. This evasion was so general that Hill stated that though, from 1815 to 1825, the population had increased by about 30 per cent, there had been no corresponding increase in the post office revenue. The final guarantee of success was afforded by the issue of the adhesive postage stamp.

In September 1839 the Treasury had invited suggestions

'as to the manner in which the stamp may best be brought into use', and prizes of £200 and £100 were offered for the most useful proposals. In the event four prizes of £100 each were awarded (over 2,600 entries having been received), but the stamps that were issued in May 1840 were the work of Messrs. Perkins, Bacon & Co., as the result of negotiations with Rowland Hill, who had been attached to the Treasury. The designs for the wrappers and envelopes were the work of the artist William Mulready, who was invited to supply them, so that the Treasury competition, though it produced some very helpful suggestions, and also provided Hill with a valuable assistant in the person of Mr (afterwards Sir) Henry Cole, one of the prize-winners, cannot be said to have been directly responsible for the issued stamps, etc.

The adhesive stamps, together with the covers and envelopes, came into use on 6th May 1840, but the 'Mulreadys', as they are now affectionately called by collectors, were killed by ridicule of their design, while the practical and beautiful stamps at once found favour with the public.

So the adhesive postage stamp was born, and though its use is now being curtailed by the increasing employment of automatic franking devices, and the system of prepaying postage in bulk, it has such obvious advantages for private correspondence that we need not fear that it will disappear in our day.

It was not long before the success of the British experiment led to the issue of adhesive postage stamps in other countries, and it may be of interest to give a list of some of those pioneer countries, in the order in which their stamps appeared.

1843   Cantons of Zurich and Geneva (Switzerland) and Brazil.
1845   Canton of Basle (Switzerland).
1847   Trinidad (Lady McLeod local), United States of America and Mauritius.
1849   France, Belgium, Bavaria.

From 1850 onwards there were numerous accessions to the ranks of stamp-issuing countries and colonies, and although some of these no longer have their own stamps, others have taken their place, and today there are more than two hundred territories which issue stamps for their postal services and for the interest and delectation of the collector.

Chapter Three

STAMPS AND THEIR USES

(*For illustrations to this chapter see pages 98–9*)

LOOKING through an old-time stamp collection, we shall find that it contains many stamps – or labels that look like stamps – which are not mentioned in our modern stamp catalogues or collected by present-day enthusiasts.

The collectors of earlier days, like many juniors nowadays, placed in their albums everything they came across which bore the least resemblance to a postage stamp, and, in consequence, we find there many labels which have no connexion with the post at all.

Apart from these interlopers, however, there has been a progressive reduction in the size of the field which the ordinary collector attempts to cover, so that many kinds of stamps which were at one time generally collected are now of little interest, save to a few keen students.

This curtailment of the scope of a stamp collection has been due to the vast increase which has taken place in the number of stamps of a single group, the adhesive postage stamps, which, by themselves, are sufficient to provide the average collector with a lifetime's material for his hobby. As the number of adhesive stamps grew from year to year, collectors and dealers, finding their album and shelf space overtaxed, threw overboard one group of stamps after another, though, through an inconsistency which is not peculiar to this hobby, many of the groups still have a few representatives in the catalogues and albums of today.

Before we turn to the subject of how stamps are made, it will be as well to look at the various groups which may come within the ken of the collector, and clear from the field those with which he need, by present standards of collecting, have nothing to do. Though it is necessary to remark in this connexion that if the collector finds himself attracted by any of these forbidden groups, there is no reason why he should not study them.

The first distinction to be drawn is between stamps which serve a postal purpose and those which are used for revenue services only. A stamp whose sole function is to pay a tax on a receipt, to frank a customs document, or to represent the stamp duty on a contract, does not come within the scope of a postage stamp collector, to whom it is known as a 'fiscal' or 'revenue' – the word 'stamp' being understood.

A postage stamp must have some function in regard to the payment of fees for postal service, but many postage stamps can also be used for revenue purposes, in which case the collector will try to find out by means of the postmark or otherwise, in which way the particular specimen before him has been used, and will exclude from his album stamps which (though also available for postal use) can be proved to have served 'fiscally'.

On the other hand, revenue stamps which have, at one time or another, been used, *with official authority*, for postal purposes, are included in a stamp collection, when unused or properly postmarked, and are known as 'postal-fiscals'.

A sub-group of postage stamps which is included in at least one European stamp catalogue, consists of stamps issued for use on telegrams. Why this group should now be disregarded it is a little hard to say, as the conveyance of a message by telegraph is not so very different from its transmission by letter, and the stamp performs the same office in relation to a telegram as it does in regard to a letter, with the exception that it cannot accompany it on its journey. Telegraph stamps have, on occasion, been used, with authority, for payment of postage, and when such use can be proved, they are collectable as postage stamps, under the name of 'postal-telegraphs'.

Looking at the group of postage stamps, which is all that is left to us after we have discarded 'revenues' and 'telegraphs', it will be noticed that these fall into two main sections – the adhesive stamps, which are printed separately from the envelopes, etc., which they are intended to frank, and the impressed stamps, which are printed or embossed on envelopes, postcards, or wrappers before they are sold to the public. These impressed stamps, though of great interest and in many cases surpassing the adhesive stamps in beauty, are now generally collected by specialists and postal historians. Envelopes and other postal stationery bearing such impressed stamps are known colloquially to collectors as 'entires', to distinguish them from the impressed stamps cut from such stationery, which are called 'cut-squares'.

The collector of today who comes across stamps of this class, either cut out, or on the complete piece of stationery, might well keep them, not in his main collection, but in a spare album. They may, on occasion, serve to elucidate problems in connexion with the adhesive stamps to which he is more particularly devoting his attention. Telegraph stamps may, for the same reason, find a place in this philatelic 'overflow meeting', and as fiscal stamps are often printed by the same firms as the postage stamps, and by the same processes, they also have a claim to a place in the side-line collection.

Having cleared the field of these three groups, we find another which, though it has begun of late to find favour again with some students of stamps, has not been generally collected for many years. This group consists of the local postage stamps which, in the words of the official philatelic definition, are 'stamps whose franking validity is limited to a town, district, or route in any country or between particular seaports'. Some representatives of this group have retained their places in our stamp catalogues by reason of the spirit of inconsistency already referred to, but the vast majority of old-time locals never come the way of the average stamp collector.

Local stamps are historically interesting, as they often preceded the official government issues of their particular sphere. The fact that they were the product of more or less private individuals was the cause of their falling into disfavour with stamp collectors, for when stocks were exhausted and the collectors' demand continued, the temptation to make reprints of them was, in many cases, too great to be resisted. The forger also took a hand in the game. Actually, however, 'locals' are, as has been said, of real interest, and the work done by the comparatively small band of collectors who have studied them, has provided the necessary data for distinguishing between originals, forgeries, and reprints. Apart from the stamps of various steamship companies, such as the Pacific Steam Navigation Co., and the Danube Steam Navigation Co., the most interesting local stamps are those of the Chinese Treaty Ports, which have a picturesquely eastern appearance, and the quaint '*zemstvo*' rural issues of Russia. It may be added that the curious labels emanating from the United States and purporting to be stamps of various local posts and carrier services, which are often found in old collections, are nearly always valueless imitations.

The present-day, so-called 'locals' of Great Britain can only be described as 'Local Carriage Labels', while many of them, bearing the names of remote islands around the coasts of England, Northern Ireland, Scotland, and in the Channel Islands, do not even merit this distinction for they are not related to any kind of postal service or transport. With the possible exception of the islands of Lundy, in the Bristol Channel, and Herm, near Guernsey, both of which once had authorized post offices, these island 'locals' and their multifarious 'commemoratives' are produced by private (and usually anonymous) promoters for sale to unsuspecting stamp collectors, often, unfortunately, those of the younger generation. Some of the gaudiest labels purport to come from islands which are, in fact, uninhabited! This worthless rubbish is best left well alone.

Now the ground is clear for a consideration of 'postage stamps', as the term is understood at the present day by the majority of collectors, but before attempting to divide them into sub-groups, according to their various functions, the reader should note two more terms, which are applicable to the whole group. When, for any reason, a postal emergency arises, and stamps for temporary use have to be produced in a hurry, the collector calls them 'provisionals' (i.e. provisional, or temporary, issues). When these temporary stamps are replaced by stamps probably produced more carefully and intended for a more permanent existence, it is said that a 'definitive issue' has appeared. 'Provisionals' are frequently produced by over-printing or surcharging stamps already in existence, to make them suitable for the emergency which has arisen, and this subject will be dealt with more fully in a later chapter.

Postage stamps proper are usually considered to be those which are used for franking ordinary correspondence. In many countries there is only one series of postage stamps, which serves for paying fees in connexion with every available postal service, and which can also be used on telegrams, or for revenue requirements. In other countries some of these functions will be dissociated from the general issue of postage stamps, and in such cases special stamps may be provided.

As ordinary postage stamps, which indicate that postage has been prepaid, are naturally the most numerous group, we are not surprised to find that the next most important section is one which pays a tribute to the innate forgetfulness or carelessness of the human race, and indicates that postage has not been paid. Such stamps, referred to as 'Postage Due' or 'Unpaid Letter' stamps, or, more briefly, as 'Dues' or 'Unpaids', are affixed to understamped, or unstamped correspondence by the postal authorities, to indicate to the postman and to the addressee the amount which is to be collected on delivery. In most countries the addressee is fined a small sum, for the cost of collecting the deficiency in postage, so that a postage due stamp represents not only the payment of a charge for carriage but also a fine.

In countries where special stamps are not provided for this purpose, the initial 'T' will often be found stamped on letters, accompanied by figures showing the amount due to be paid by the addressee. This letter stands for the French word 'Taxe' which is in international use in connexion with insufficiently stamped correspondence.

Human frailty is catered for more kindly by another class of stamp, the 'Too Late' or 'Late Fee' stamp. This represents an extra sum payable in order to catch a certain mail, after it has been closed down for correspondence posted in the normal course.

Another useful stamp is the 'Acknowledgment of Receipt' stamp, which if bought, and attached to correspondence, ensures that the writer will receive, through the post office, a formal advice that the missive has reached its destination. Such stamps have not been very widely issued, the majority being found among the earlier issues of some of the South and Central American states. They often have the initials 'AR' as a prominent feature of their design, these standing for the Spanish words '*Aviso de Recepcion*' (advice of receipt).

A service with which all are familiar is the registration of correspondence. An additional fee is paid, which ensures that extra care is taken in transit, and also entitles the correspondent, if he finds the postmaster-general in a kindly mood, to compensation in the event of the contents of his letter going astray. Some countries have special stamps to indicate that the registration fee has been duly prepaid. They are often not unlike our own registration labels in Great Britain, except that they have the appearance of an oblong postage stamp with a rather more elaborate design than is usually associated with a label. In some countries a space is left on the registration stamp, in which the reference number of the letter it franks is written in ink by the postal clerk.

In most countries it is possible to secure more speedy delivery of correspondence on payment of a special fee. Many countries have, at one time or another, provided 'Special Delivery' or 'Express Letter' stamps for this purpose, and in some cases the designs of such stamps have been selected to typify the rapidity (often fictitious) with which delivery could be made, such as a running postman, a motor-bicycle, a motor-van, or an aeroplane.

In the United States, stamps inscribed 'Special Handling' have been issued. The use of these stamps and the payment of the special scale of fees which they represent, secured quicker handling of parcels. In Denmark, stamps overprinted or inscribed '*Gebyr*', were used to indicate that certain fees had been paid, among which was one for the registration of letters too late to catch the normal registered post.

The rapid growth of mail-carrying by air in the 1920s brought into being another class of special service stamps, known to collectors as 'air stamps'. They are not, in most countries, exclusively used on correspondence carried by air, but can also be used on ordinary correspondence, just as ordinary stamps can be used for airmail letters.

So far we have no special stamps for submarine posts, though collectors may find a few souvenirs connected with the use of German submarines for purposes of communication during the two world wars. Underground letters, are, however, represented in the stamp album by the special stamps issued for the pneumatic post in Italy.

Stamps of distinctive designs are sometimes appropriated to specific classes of mail matter. Newspaper stamps are sometimes met with, and Austria has had special stamps for newspapers carried at express rates. The earlier newspaper stamps of Austria and Hungary, however, really represent a tax, collected by the post office, on foreign newspapers, but as the newspapers would not have been delivered without the appropriate tax stamps the latter can be regarded, in one sense, as postage stamps.

Parcels, too, have their own stamps in some countries, and Uruguay has issued a series of triangular stamps for use on farmers' parcels. The United States carried multiplicity of special stamps a stage further and issued distinct stamps for payment of postage due on understamped parcels.

It may be asked why these different stamps are issued by various countries, when other nations contrive to get on very well with a single series for general use. It is, of course, a convenience for the postal clerk, who has to handle large quantities of mail very rapidly, to be able to tell, by a glance at the postage stamp, whether the letter, or whatever it may be, is to be dealt with in any special way. This is why many of the stamps we have been discussing are issued in distinctive designs or colours, or, sometimes, in striking shapes or sizes.

In the days when practically all stamps were used for their legitimate postal purposes, and only very small numbers were taken by collectors, the use of special stamps was helpful for accountancy purposes in connexion with the cost of and receipts from various services. Now, however, collectors take so many stamps of every kind that may be issued, that the number of stamps sold for a particular service may be no indication at all of the number actually used for that service. Attempts were made from time to time to maintain the principle, by refusing to sell stamps of certain classes to the public, but the demand from collectors was so great that leakages nearly always occurred.

The stamps issued by many countries, particularly in earlier days, for use by government departments, – as for example, the 'official' stamps of Great Britain and the 'departmental' stamps of the United States – were for a similar purpose, that of checking the use made of the postal service by the various state offices. Overprinting of the ordinary postage stamps of a country with the name or initials of the department was often resorted to in this connexion, but some countries issued stamps specifically for the purpose. They are known to collectors colloquially as 'officials', 'departmentals', or 'service' stamps according to their function.

A very interesting, though not very numerous, class of stamps consists of those which, instead of indicating that postage has been paid, show that no postage is payable. These are known as 'frank' stamps. They are found among the early issues of Spain, where we have two stamps which franked through the post copies of books which were considered of such public value that they were granted free transit. Similarly, Portugal has granted franking privileges at various times to the Red Cross Society, to civilian rifle clubs, and to the Geographical Society of Lisbon, each having its special stamps, while among the issues of France and other countries we find stamps specially overprinted or inscribed for use on soldiers' letters which were carried free.

In the Dominican Republic, in 1935, a special 25c. stamp was issued, which had to be added on letters addressed to the President, while in 1937 Czechoslovakia introduced 'Personal Delivery' stamps, which ensured delivery to the addressee only – a useful innovation for sweethearts!

Another novelty, this time from Argentina, was a service for the delivery of vocally recorded messages. In order that the public might have facilities for making these records, special mobile recording vans were employed. Special stamps were issued in connexion with this service, which cannot have been very expensive as the value of the three different stamps which were issued ranged between 2s. and 2s. 6d. A gramophone record figures in the design of each.

Chapter Four

COMMEMORATIVE AND CHARITY STAMPS

WHOEVER first had the idea of using postage stamps for commemorative purposes has deserved well of philately in one sense, for he has added greatly to the pictorial and historical interest of the hobby, but from another angle he has done considerable harm, giving the countries of the world an excuse for issuing many more postage stamps than they might otherwise have done, and also opening up the way to one of the worst forms of exploiting stamp collectors – the 'speculative' issue.

It was a natural suggestion that stamps, which are so widely circulated, and which travel far beyond the confines of the land which issues them, should be used to commemorate important present-day events or anniversaries. A picture attracts the eye and tells its story quickly, and stamp pictures, which go everywhere are peculiarly suitable for reminding the world of events which are worthy of its attention.

In the eyes of a stamp collector, a stamp, to be a 'commemorative', must be issued specifically for that purpose. A stamp in the ordinary postal series of a country, though it may bear the portrait of a famous man or the picture of a notable event in the country's history, is not regarded as belonging to the commemorative group. On the other hand, a special series of stamps issued in connexion with a particular commemoration may for a time take the place of the ordinary postage stamps at all post offices, but it will still hold its place in the 'commemorative' class. The distinction has no very great importance nowadays, as those who are interested in the designs and historical associations of stamps will arrange them without regard to their specific postal or other purpose, as we shall see in a later chapter.

It is a curious fact that, though Britain did not, until recent years, favour commemorative stamps (or, in fact, superfluous stamps of any kind) it was a British postcard which was the seed from which sprang two of the most numerous groups of unnecessary stamps, the commemoratives and the charity stamps. This card, which was issued in 1890, commemorated the Jubilee of Penny Postage (and thus, of the postage stamp), and though the envelope containing it was only franked by a penny stamp, it was sold at sixpence, the surplus being devoted to a fund for postal servants. All very innocent and laudable, no doubt, but let us see what has grown out of this modest beginning.

No one can deny that a sovereign state has the right to use its postage stamps in any way it pleases, and it is natural that, when a nation is rejoicing over some great event, or celebrating an important anniversary, postage stamps should be pressed into service to do their part. In developing countries, with a high rate of illiteracy, the postage stamp may thus become a valuable medium of education, particularly when it is desired to create, or revive, a national spirit and tradition in a race only recently enfranchised. Some of the new states formed as a result of the recasting of Europe after the two world wars are typical examples.

We must remember, however, that to many needy governments stamp collectors are of more importance than their own people, at least so far as stamps are concerned. A postage stamp can be attractively printed at a low cost. If sold to a member of the public for postal use, it carries with it a liability of the government to provide some form of postal service, to the franking value of the stamp; but when it is sold to a stamp collector, possibly at the other side of the world, the only cost to the country issuing it is the expense of printing it, while the liability to provide service need hardly enter into calculation.

The commemorative idea thus opened up the way to considerable abuses. Collectors became suspicious of a country which was always changing its ordinary stamps, and thought that they were being exploited, but when a country labelled its new issue of stamps as an 'Independence Commemorative Series', and linked it with an historical event which had happened one hundred years before, there was, at first, a natural tendency to consider such an issue as justified, and, in fact, it often was. The excuse was, however, too good to be used only occasionally, and in course of time nearly every country that wanted to increase its postal revenue, started issuing commemorative stamps. Competition between nations for the pence or shillings of the collector then became keen. Stamps had to attract his eye or appeal to his historical sense, or in some way specially impress themselves on his notice, if they were to stand out from the multitudes which claimed his attention. Thus all sorts of events came to be commemorated; many still, of course, on a purely national basis of genuine desire to issue such stamps for home consumption, but a large number mainly with the object of extracting money from the pockets of collectors.

Violent discussions have raged for many years as to whether the commemorative stamp has done harm to the hobby. It has certainly added greatly to the number of stamps to be collected, but against this must be set the fact that attractive stamps, with a 'news interest', are valuable recruiting agents for the hobby. The collector who is interested mainly in the designs and associations of postage stamps will not inquire too closely into the necessity of an issue which throws light on some person or period hitherto unrepresented in his album, while the enthusiast who is studying the stamps of a country in their relationship to the postal services, may omit from his collection any stamps which he considers to have fulfilled no particular function in such services.

If a test is needed as to the necessity or otherwise of a

commemorative issue, we can hardly claim to judge it from the national point of view. An event or personage whom we, with our often very limited knowledge of foreign history, may never have heard of, may bulk very largely in the story of the nation concerned. We can, however, assert with safety that a series of stamps, if it is to fulfil the purposes of a national commemoration, should be on sale at all the post offices of the country of issue, at least concurrently with its ordinary postage stamps, if not temporarily in place of them. When we find that, far from this being the case, many commemorative stamps are put on sale only at one or two special offices and then only for a very limited period, and that the bulk of the stamps very quickly finds its way into the hands of stamp dealers for sale to collectors, while the inhabitants of the country have hardly any opportunity of buying them or using them, then we may be sure that international robbery, not national propaganda, is the intention of the authorities concerned, though perhaps they would not give their action quite so strong a name.

The basis on which postage stamps are listed in our stamp catalogues, and attain the status of 'collectable varieties', may be expressed in the formula that they must be issued with the authority of a recognized government and must be available for postal use. If a government produces postage stamps, mainly for sale to collectors, it is an easy matter to publish the necessary decree, giving them official status, but 'issue' is another matter. If the stamps are placed on sale throughout the country, large supplies will be required and liability for service will be entered into, but the difficulty is avoided by placing quite small supplies on sale, either for a very limited period, or at only a few offices. So long as collectors accept such very limited distribution as 'issue' in the sense of our formula, so long will they be the victims of the system. It would, perhaps, be better to exclude from the catalogues all postage stamps which are not on general sale throughout the country of issue for a minimum period of, say, a week. Attempts made by editors of the standard catalogues to boycott some of the most flagrantly unnecessary issues of this nature are usually defeated, not by the governments who are at fault, but the collector himself, who insists that every postage stamp, necessary or unnecessary, should be listed, and that he should use his own judgment as to what he may collect.

There are signs, however, that the really unnecessary commemorative stamp is on the wane. Collectors do not object to a country like the United States issuing several different stamps of low value each year, in commemoration of events in her past history, but they quickly rendered abortive, by neglecting to purchase the stamps, a scheme by which Portugal was to issue a long series of special historical stamps annually for nearly twenty years. Dealers, too, play their part in the warfare against unnecessary stamps, by refusing to stock or advertise them, and in the case of great firms, which in the normal way may need supplies of a single series to the value of thousands of pounds, such action, accompanied by a protest in the right quarters, exercises a strong influence on a mercenarily-minded postal department. The world philatelic press gives publicity to each attempt to exploit collectors, and such publicity tends to reduce the demand for limited and unnecessary issues.

In stamps, as elsewhere, however, the flock must not be judged by the black sheep, and the commemorative stamp is always interesting, whether necessary or not, for the very reason that the issuing government must link it with a particular person or event, thus adding, as the field of commemoration widens, to the ground covered by a stamp collection.

Turning from the circumstances of their issue to the stamps themselves, we are faced with a most striking range of subjects which have been thought worthy of commemoration. Important dates in the lives of rulers and of nations are the most natural subjects for commemoration and celebration of all kinds. Such are the accession and coronation of kings, their jubilees, their weddings, the birth of an heir to the throne, the coming into power of a new president (or even, in the case of Ecuador, the triumph of a particular political party), and all sorts of minor events, some of which do not form the subject of a special commemoration, but are illustrated on the stamps of a royal wedding or jubilee series.

In the history of nations the commemorations include the discovery of their land by one of the early explorers, the revolutions or other means by which they gained their independence and the adoption of a constitution, with its not always beneficial corollary, the setting up of a parliament. The patriots who were concerned in these struggles for liberty provide, with the anniversaries of their births or deaths, a natural excuse for further issues.

Wars, with their resultant grabbing, or loss, of territory, are, of course, celebrated on stamps, as well as in the public streets and churches, and when the nation has no more anniversaries left to honour, it can turn to the history of its cities and underline, with special stamp issues, the redletter days in *their* story.

Stamps provide a very satisfactory and world-wide advertisement for those great international exhibitions which are now so often held and hardly one of these passes without its special issue.

There is one kind of commemoration which is most fittingly associated with postage stamps – the recording of events of importance in the postal history of a country. Anniversaries of such events as the establishment of the first postal service, entry into the Universal Postal Union, the issue of the earliest postage stamps, and the opening of new post offices, have been frequently commemorated by special stamps. Incidentally, in this group we find an example of how the 'commemorative habit' grows. Congresses of delegates from countries belonging to the Universal Postal Union are held at intervals of three or four years, each meeting being held in a different country. Because one country honoured the Congress by issuing special stamps when it met there, international courtesy has obliged the nation acting as host to each succeeding congress to follow the same example, and in 1929, Britain, in spite of official dislike for special stamp issues, had to follow suit.

The most prolific field for commemoration at the present day is found in the lives of famous individuals. Kings, presidents, and patriots, have now given way to saints, poets, engineers, authors, painters, scientists, aviators, explorers, and others whom the world delights to honour, and it is not surprising, in view of the importance now attached to sport, that a number of sporting sets have been issued, particularly in connexion with the Olympic Games.

In some countries, today, new postage stamps are as necessary an accompaniment of the opening of a railway, bridge, or public building, as are smiling ladies and pompous politicians. When there is no railway to be opened, a census will form the subject of special stamp issues, or perhaps a convenient earthquake or hurricane will provide an excuse. Even football matches are commemorated! In any case a search of old almanacs will disclose some individual of more or less importance, whose anniversary falls conveniently, though nowadays some countries do not even trouble about dates, but celebrate and commemorate just when they feel like it.

It is an interesting commentary on the commemorative stamps that, at first, apart from current events of real importance, most of the happenings commemorated had taken place at least a hundred years before. When the supply of centenaries and tercentenaries had been exhausted, the interval between event and commemoration lessened very rapidly, and some nations now think it necessary to wait only five or ten years before inflicting their independence commemoration on the long-suffering collector. Others prefer to delve further into the past, and millenary stamps are now coming into the picture.

Then there are the charity stamps – stamps which are sold to the public for a sum which is divided into two portions, one representing its postal value which carries a right to service, and the other being devoted to charitable objects. Here again, we have no right to criticize a state which offers its own nationals this easy method of contributing to charity, which implies, of course, as in the case of 'commemoratives', full distribution of supplies to all post offices and a willingness of the public to buy them. But what of the country which issues charity stamps which are not easily available to its own people, and the greater part of which go to collectors? Here the collector is being doubly taxed, for he is paying for postal service, which he does not require, and is also contributing to a charity in which he has no interest. It is not surprising, under these conditions, that unnecessary charity stamps are not popular, unless they have some special beauty to commend them, or when, by a cunning combination of commemorative interest with the charity appeal, the attention of collectors can be otherwise aroused.

A number of countries, particularly in Europe, now have their annual series of charity stamps, and vie with one another in making them as beautiful as possible. In most of these countries, by far the larger part of the quite respectable sums realized for charity in this way comes from the pockets of stamp collectors at home and abroad, and very little postal use is made of them by the general public. One notable exception is Switzerland, which for many years past has produced an annual set of charity stamps, the profit from which is devoted to child welfare work. At first these '*Pro Juventute*' stamps bore pictures of children in the picturesque dress of the various Swiss cantons. Later, the arms of the cantons formed the subject of the designs for many years, and more recently some really beautiful views of Swiss scenery have appeared on these 'children's stamps', followed by some pretty Swiss girls, Alpine flowers, and insects.

While large numbers of these stamps are sold to collectors each year, they also fulfil the proper purpose of a charity issue, for the Swiss take pride in using them for several weeks after they appear, in spite of their increased cost as compared with the ordinary postage stamps.

Purse-strings being looser and hearts softer at Christmas-tide, many of these annual charity issues appear in December, and the collector who, tempted by a pretty set, indulges in the purchase of stamps which he can hardly, on principle, regard with favour, can console himself with the thought that some of his money will be devoted to good works.

During the First World War enormous sums must have been raised by means of charity stamps for Red Cross and other work among the troops and on the Home front. After hostilities ceased, both in 1918 and 1945, the claims of widows and orphans, war-invalids and returned prisoners were urged by many stamps, while there were also frequent issues of anti-tuberculosis and similar stamps.

Child welfare work is always a popular draw, but the aged, the destitute, and sufferers from famine, earthquake, flood, and hurricane, have all, to some extent, been relieved from the pockets of stamp collectors.

Other groups of issues, besides Red Cross stamps, have been called into being by war. The term 'War stamp', as loosely used by collectors, applies to any stamp issued mainly as a result of wartime exigencies. Thus war charity issues, stamps overprinted for use in occupied territory (sometimes called 'occupation stamps'), stamps used by the armed forces, and various temporary issues due to local vicissitudes, all come within this wide definition, together with another class called 'war-tax' stamps.

'War-tax' stamps owe their existence to the necessity for new revenue which was paramount during the First World War. Many countries raised their rates of postage, but some, in order to mark the fact that the change was only a wartime measure, issued distinctive stamps for prepayment of the special war tax, or else issued stamps at a price which combined the tax with the normal postal rate. The idea was not new as Spain had issued similar stamps as far back as 1874, but now, in addition to the tax on correspondence, the various governments could rely on a big sale of the new stamps to collectors throughout the world, who thus made once more their contribution to good works.

After 1918 new groups of stamps came into existence. The stamps of the new nations of Europe, and of the older ones during the post-war reconstruction period, were then the centre of interest, under the title 'New Europe' (which, by some, was horribly abbreviated to 'Neurope'). Stamps issued in districts which decided their future nationality by popular plebiscite, bore witness to their temporary independence, while the Great Powers busied themselves with preparing permanent stamps for the ex-German colonies for which they received mandates, which took the place of the temporary 'occupation' stamps of the war period.

Similar events took place after the Second World War when, for example, Germany herself was divided into four zones of occupation – British, American, French, and Russian, while Berlin was placed under joint Allied control. Various stamps were issued by the joint Anglo-American, French, and Russian Zones until 1948–9 when political events and new governments created the three stamp-issuing entities which exist in Germany today – Berlin (Western Sectors), West Germany (German Federal Republic), and East Germany (German Democratic Republic). German stamps were used in Austria during the wartime occupation by the German Reich, and German-sponsored stamps were issued in Czechoslovakia (Bohemia and Moravia, and Slovakia) from mid-1939 until 1945.

Apart from war-tax stamps, other stamps have been issued, the use of which was made compulsory on certain dates, or for certain periods, in addition to the ordinary stamps. The taxes were for various purposes – to build a new post office, to help postal servants, or to raise funds for charity. It is a delicate question whether such stamps should be classed as postage stamps. They only paid a tax, but as correspondence could not be delivered unless they were affixed, they may be held to have served in some sense a postal function.

If, in connexion with commemorative and charity stamps, too much stress has been laid on the unnecessary issue aimed at the pocket of the collector, let me again emphasize that the unnecessary stamp forms only a small fraction of the issued total of stamps, that it is often distinctly attractive and interesting in itself, and that if any collector does not think that interest and attraction worth paying for, he can well draw his own line of demarcation, and collect only those stamps which he considers deserving of his attention.

This may particularly apply to that phenomenon of commemorative stamps, the so-called 'omnibus' issue. In 1935, forty-four Crown Colonies and eighteen other Commonwealth Territories issued stamps marking one theme: the Silver Jubilee of King George V. Subsequently other themes were the subject of comprehensive issues: 'Victory', in 1946; the Royal Silver Wedding, in 1948; the 75th anniversary of the U.P.U., 1949; and, more recently, the Commonwealth sets for Shakespeare and Sir Winston Churchill. Some omnibus issues, such as the Red Cross and I.T.U. centenaries and the Freedom from Hunger campaign, have world-wide participation, necessitating considerable expense for the acquisition of hundreds of stamps, if one aims at completeness.

Omnibus issues (and, indeed, commemorative issues of all kinds) occur with such frequency that the majority of collectors confine their interests to one country or a group of countries. The days of the truly comprehensive general collector are now virtually in the past – for all but millionaires!

Chapter Five

THE LIFE AND ANATOMY OF A
POSTAGE STAMP

THE use of the word 'philately' instead of the more familiar term 'stamp collecting' is often very slipshod, little distinction being made between them. The more erudite word, not too carefully coined from the Greek by some early collector, means roughly 'love of exemption from taxation' – a feeling which, in these days, is so widely shared as to have ensured the world-wide popularity of the hobby, if its title were truly descriptive. Actually the intended meaning of the word is 'love of that which exempts from taxation'.

We find in practice that the word 'philately' is sometimes used by collectors too snobbish to adopt the simpler term and by journalists (such as the present writer in other chapters of this book), in search of a synonym for stamp collecting. The use of the derived adjective 'philatelic' is almost inevitable as there is no equivalent to be drawn from 'stamp collecting'.

In its present sense, as used by serious collectors, a stamp collector is one who just collects, without any specific aim or purpose, while a philatelist is a student of what he collects, more particularly in the sense of the admirable definition given by the late A. J. Séfi in his book *An Introduction to Advanced Philately*:

Modern Philately may be said to comprise the study of stamps from every possible angle of historical and philatelic interest. It includes enquiries into the reasons and circumstances leading up to an issue, and researches as to the essays and proofs for the stamps thereof; studies of all the different processes and methods of production used, and of any resultant varieties on the stamps themselves and, finally, enquiries into all the uses or misuses to which the stamps, once issued, might be subject.

Within this definition is comprised the whole field of study which lies open to the collector who wishes to earn, in one way or another, the right to be called a serious philatelist. He need not attempt to cover it all, even in the case of one particular country or issue, but may deal with only one or two of the possible angles, as will be shown in the section of this volume which deals more particularly with collecting. For the moment we are more concerned with the production of postage stamps, and the interest which the various stages and processes have for the collector.

It is a curious thing that, even among the inner circle of advanced students of stamps, there is great ignorance of how stamps are produced, and a tendency to discuss the *effects* of productive methods, as seen in the stamps themselves, with no more than a very vague idea of the *causes* which have given rise to those effects. Among the majority of collectors, who have vaguely assimilated the idea that any variation in a stamp or its design is of importance, or at least may affect its value, ignorance of first causes is almost complete and the result has been the creation of a band of 'dot-and-dash hunters' who worry themselves and the editors of stamp magazines with infinitesimal variations, and bring our hobby into disrepute among those who do not know it at its best and sanest, and who can say, 'Jones must be mad to collect stamps. He keeps showing me spots and specks on his specimens, but when I ask him what they mean, he can't tell me.' Let us lay it down, here and now, that the only stamp variations which have any real importance are those which help us to build up the history of an issue, on the lines of Mr Séfi's definition, quoted above.

In order to place philatelic study clearly before the reader, let us follow a postage stamp rapidly through its life, regarding it, meanwhile, from every point of view from which it can be of interest to the student.

In writing the biography of an individual, the author usually tries to give us some idea of the home into which he was born, and of the family background which may have influenced his early upbringing. Similarly, the collector who wishes to appreciate fully the stamp which he is going to study, will first try to gain some idea of the postal system and earlier postal history of the country from which it comes. There is nothing which can take the place of such knowledge, as an imaginative background to a stamp collection.

I remember being present once when a famous American collector was displaying a very highly specialized collection of stamps issued by a certain British Colony in the pioneer days. A large and attentive audience was looking at the stamps as they were passed round, but while they noted the various details which were of technical interest, the owner's description of the collection took them, with early settlers, along the trail of the gold rush, or conjured up visions of the hardy mail carriers struggling through snow and ice, or by crazy coasting steamer, to the end of their route. So near did the speaker bring us to the life of which the stamps and envelopes in his collection had formed part, that he was even able to tell us something about one or two of the early settlers to whom they had been addressed, some seventy years before. A collection with a background like that will live in the memory of anyone with sufficient imagination to appreciate the romantic story which lies behind it.

Having got our background, we shall want to know the reason why the stamps we are studying were issued. If they were the earliest stamps of their country, the story may be full of interest, but for the appearance of more modern stamps there are a hundred-and-one prosaic reasons. There may be a change in postal rates, a monarch may die, territory may pass from one nation to another, or a temporary shortage of stamps may give rise to a provisional issue. The commemorative and charity stamps naturally owe their existence to the national celebration or the national need of the moment. At all events, there is a reason for the existence of every postage stamp, and the collector who 'wants to know' will have to find out that reason.

Now we come to the actual preparation of the stamps. Having decided on an issue, the authorities are faced with the problem of obtaining designs. The work of preparing them may be committed to an artist of repute, or an open competition may be held in the hope of discovering unexpected talent. Sometimes an official personage may make suggestions or a rough sketch, leaving these to be worked up by an artist, or by someone on the staff of the stamp printers. (*see page 100*)

The 'design' will consist of the pictorial part of the device on the stamp, together with any framework and ornamentation which may be necessary, but space must be left for the necessary 'inscriptions' such as the name of the country, the cost of the stamp, its purpose ('POSTAGE', 'REVENUE', 'EXPRESS', or whatever it may be), and perhaps a few words descriptive of the picture. The word 'design' is also often employed in a broader sense to signify the whole of the printed portion of the stamp.

Having a general idea in his mind, the artist may make a rough sketch or series of sketches, on a large scale. He has a difficult task, for even the largest postage stamp is a small affair, and while he tries to preserve artistic balance, he must make the essential inscriptions fairly prominent, for practical reasons, and he must not overcrowd his drawing with fine lines, or the printer will find it difficult to reproduce it. These artist's sketches do not often come the way of the collector, but are much prized when they do, as they give a very good idea of the evolution of the design in the artist's mind, and they often bear comments by officials, with suggestions for improvement, or notes by the artist to the engraver, pointing out essential details.

At this stage, also, the 'essay' has its birth. Large-scale sketches would hardly come under this definition, which implies an attempt to show what a stamp would actually look like, when printed. For example, an existing stamp may have its centre cut out and a photograph stuck in place of it, to show how a different portrait would look in the existing framework, or the artist may do some work with pen or brush, to indicate various ways in which a design might be improved upon. Many 'essays' are very similar to stamps, as the artist has often gone so far as to have his design engraved and printed, in order to show clearly what it would look like. The term 'essay' is, however, only applied to designs which are not finally adopted, or, at least, are not adopted in that particular form and without alteration.

From a consideration of sketches or essays, a design is finally chosen, and the engraver now takes up the task. His job is to engrave the 'die'. (I am running rapidly through the preparation of an engraved stamp by the most usual methods, variations in method being treated later.) Simply put, this is just the cutting of the lines of the design in metal, a very delicate task, and one which is likely to occasion some argument between the artist, the official, and the engraver, each of whom is trying to satisfy a particular need – the artist, his love of art for art's sake, the official, the needs of the postal clerks and of the public (clear figures, etc.), and the engraver, who has to see that the design is one that can be satisfactorily reproduced and printed.

The argument will be carried on by means of 'die proofs' – prints taken from the die, either in black or in colour. These, being submitted to the authorities concerned, will often be returned two or three times, with suggestions for alteration, before the die is finally passed as satisfactory. Die proofs, showing the successive stages in the evolution of the adopted design, are very interesting additions to a collection, when they can be obtained, but naturally the supply is limited. Proofs from the finished die are required for a variety of purposes, and are likely to be more plentiful.

When the printing plate or stone has been prepared, as will be described later, prints will be taken from this, which are called 'plate proofs'. If they are in colour, they will be termed 'colour trials', provided that the colours used are not those in which the stamps are finally issued. Proofs in the issued colours are called 'colour proofs'. (It should be noted that in all these descriptions, I am using the terms familiar to stamp collectors, who have adopted their own vocabulary, which quite frequently does not agree with that of the printer or other technicians employed in the manufacture of the stamp or its materials.)

A collection which starts with the essays for an issue, continues with the die proofs, in black and in colour, follows these by proofs from the plate, in black and in the issued colours, and adds a nice range of colour trials, really shows something of the history of the stamps, and it is a curious fact that the adopted design nearly always seems inferior to many of the essays and sketches, and that the adopted colours are often bettered in the series of colour trials. Possibly familiarity with the issued stamps has bred contempt for them in the mind of the collector.

The materials of which a postage stamp is composed are the paper, the ink (which gives us the colour and design), and the gum (if any).

Stamp collectors have not, so far, made any intensive study of the nature of the inks with which stamps are printed, so that we need not pay particular attention to this subject, which is highly technical. Metallic inks are occasionally used to give a striking effect as, for example, in some of the stamps of Greece and Persia, while silver ink has been used for overprinting certain stamps of Palestine and Transjordan, and in the production of many modern stamps.

The subject of ink as it appears to the collector's eye, i.e. as colour, will be dealt with in a separate chapter.

The majority of stamps issued at the present day are provided with gum on the back, in order that they may be easily stuck on correspondence. Quite a few early stamps, were, however, issued ungummed, while the same practice has been followed from time to time in hot moist climates, where the stamps are likely to stick together in the post office, and in such conditions it is usual for a pot of gum or paste to be provided on the post office counter, for public use. The modern issues of China and North Korea are sometimes without gum.

As the paper on which stamps are printed is often gummed before it is passed through the press, a type of mucilage is required which will not cause the paper to curl. The majority of sheets of stamps do curl, however, as the collector will find to his cost if he has to deal with them. The 'ripple' gum, adopted by Germany for her stamps at one period, employed the principle of breaking up the gum, to give a non-curling effect. Some countries use different gum for stamps issued in winter and in summer, in order that climatic conditions may be allowed for.

Generally speaking, the authorities responsible for the issue of stamps will want a gum that is fully adhesive, tasteless, and probably colourless. Suggestions have been made that the gum might be flavoured with vanilla or other pleasant seasoning in order that the task of stamp-licking may be rendered more enjoyable, but these need hardly be taken seriously.

From the collector's point of view, an examination of the gum is only important when the fact that it is yellow or white, shiny or dull, crackly or smooth, enables him to distinguish between stamps printed at one period and those produced later, or between genuine and forged stamps or originals and reprints. In the case of forgeries and reprints, the gum is often the most difficult thing to imitate correctly, and it thus provides a very useful test.

The subject of paper has been more scientifically studied by philatelists than gum or printing ink and, indeed, the processes of paper-making are of great interest. They need not, however, be described in detail here. From the point of view of the authorities, the paper provided for stamps must be suitable for the printer's purposes; it must not be too thick for convenient use by the public; and it should provide as much protection as possible against the work of forgers wishing to make imitations of the stamps or of anyone attempting to clean off the postmark, so that the stamps can be used again, with the intention of defrauding the post office.

Paper may be divided into two main classes, hand-made, which is produced sheet by sheet, and machine-made, which is turned out in continuous rolls by machinery. Hand-made paper was used for printing some of the earlier postage stamps of various countries. Its production being the result of manual skill, there is often variations in the thickness of a paper, even in the same sheet.

Of the kinds of paper which the collector will have to distinguish with the greatest frequency the most important are 'wove' and 'laid'. Wove paper has a plain even mesh, and is the normal paper employed for books, newspapers and similar work. Laid paper is watermarked with parallel lines, close together, so that, by transparency, a stamp printed on this paper shows light and dark lines in the paper alternately. When the lines run from top to bottom the paper is described as 'vertically laid' and when they run across the stamp as 'horizontally laid'. A distinction is drawn between laid paper, with its close lines, and *bâtonné*, which is watermarked with straight parallel lines some distance apart. The paper is described as wove *bâtonné*, or laid *bâtonné*, according as the spaces between these lines show the characteristics already described. Paper watermarked with *crossed* lines, making it appear to be covered with small squares, is called *quadrillé*.

'Granite' paper has coloured fibres in its texture, while ribbed paper has close parallel ridges on the surface of the paper, often not intentional, but arising out of some part of the process of manufacture or printing. Paper ruled with faint coloured lines has been used on occasion for printing postage stamps. Latvia provides an instance, and the stamps of that country also remind us of the various makeshift papers which were used for stamp-printing after the First World War. In addition to its ruled paper, Latvia employed the backs of German staff maps, cigarette paper and bank notes, while Lithuania used a greyish paper, formerly employed for making ration-coupons.

The thickness of paper is often taken into account in catalogues or books describing postage stamps, but as the terms used are usually the vague 'thick', 'thin', or 'medium' without any accurate basis, the collector is often puzzled. It is not necessary, however, in most cases, to draw any close distinctions, as only very marked differences in thickness have any serious importance. The thinnest paper used for stamp printing is the tissue paper employed for some Afghanistan stamps. This type of paper is sometimes erroneously called 'pelure', but in its correct philatelic application, pelure paper, though very thin, is hard and tough. At the other end of the scale we find 'carton' paper, a thick semi-card paper.

For the general collector there is no need to enter into a distinction between the papers made by different manu-facturers, where these occur in the same issue of postage stamps. Sometimes, as in the stamps of Norway, a distinc-tion can be made by the watermark, or, as in the Basted Mills, Cowan and Waterlow papers of New Zealand, by their texture and general character. It is only the advanced philatelist who need enter into such refinement of detail and, in actual fact, other collectors may disregard paper differences with little loss, when it is merely a matter of thickness or texture.

One special paper which is worth mentioning is the Dickinson 'silk-thread' paper, on which the Mulready envelopes and wrappers of Great Britain were printed. In this paper, a silk thread is embedded in its substance, during manufacture. The embossed 10*d*. and 1*s*. postage stamps of Great Britain were also printed on this paper, but the stamps most likely to come the way of the tyro are some of the earlier Swiss issues, for which a similar paper was used.

The Dickinson paper was the first of a long range of stamp papers intended to provide protection against frauds on the revenue. In the early days of the postage stamp, the authorities were in constant dread of the forger being able to imitate their postal labels as, if such imitations were turned out in large quantities, considerable loss would result. In point of fact, the early postage stamps of many countries were successfully imitated by rogues, but in later years the fraternity have found it more profitable to imitate the stamps for which collectors will pay good money, than to run counter to the powers-that-be, so that forgeries intended for postal use are not now very frequently produced. The use of special papers was one of the means adopted for defeating the forger, and many ingenious suggestions have been put forward from time to time for papers which it would be extremely difficult for the forger to procure or imitate, as also for papers which would render the cleaning off of postmarks or pen-cancellations impossible without detection.

The protective paper most frequently met with today is known to collectors as 'chalky' or 'chalk-surfaced'. 'Enamel' paper belongs to the same class of coated papers, all of which have a specially prepared surface which is supposed to show at once the effect of any attempt to clean off the cancellation. The unlucky collector, who immerses a chalky stamp in water, will find that the idea is quite effective as far as he is concerned, for the colours will run very rapidly, but the rogue who removes pen-marks or post-marks so that the stamps may be used again, or else sold to collectors as unused, has found means of doing his work and leaving very little trace behind, though, as we shall see later, science has come to the collector's aid, and traces which the eye cannot see are now easily revealed by the quartz-lamp.

As an example of ingenious protective papers which never came into general use, we may instance the 'double paper' of the United States. The face of this paper was thin and porous (another type had narrow slits cut in it), and it was backed by a layer of firmer paper. Attempt to remove the postmark and hey presto! the thin paper vanished, and with it the design of the stamp, which was thenceforth useless.

Supplies of these stamps were used experimentally, and the collector may occasionally come across one among the early issues of the U.S.A.

The colour of paper now remains to be considered. The vast majority of postage stamps are printed on paper approximately white, but where a long series of stamps has to be produced in the same design, coloured papers are sometimes used to give a wider range of colour distinction than can be given by varying the colour of the design alone. The issues of many British Colonies provide examples of this practice, yellow, green, blue, and red papers being employed for certain denominations. These British Colonial papers are usually coloured right through, but France, for some of her own stamps and for many of those of her Colonies, used surface-coloured paper, not dyed, but with the colour printed on the surface of the paper.

Many countries now use surface-tinted or -coloured paper in producing stamps by any of the various surface-printed methods, and, in some instances, the actual stamp designs are 'bled-off' onto the surrounding sheet margins.

In recent years British definitive stamps, and some Australian issues, have appeared on 'whiter-than-usual' paper, but these need concern only the student or specialist in these stamps.

The term 'blued paper', for which the French '*bleuté*' is sometimes substituted, is applied to paper that has unintentionally been turned a bluish colour by something used in its manufacture, or in making the ink with which the stamp is printed. The early stamps of Great Britain provide examples of very vivid blueing of the paper, while later stamps, such as the 1897 issue of Barbados, show a fainter blueing.

An apparently surface-coloured paper, which is a source of much trouble to inexperienced collectors, is often produced when stamps are being printed from engraved plates. These plates, as we shall see later, should be wiped thoroughly after they are inked, but if this is not carefully

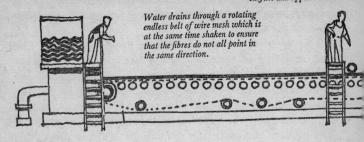

Water drains through a rotating endless belt of wire mesh which is at the same time shaken to ensure that the fibres do not all point in the same direction.

done, ink will remain on the flat portion of the plate and will be transferred to the surface of the paper, which will thus appear coloured. Such variations are of no importance to the collector; nor should attention be paid to stamps accidentally stained at some time after issue.

Another method of protecting stamps against imitation is to print on paper watermarked with a special device. To make special paper calls for larger resources than the forger can usually command, and with very careful checking of the quantity of paper handed over to the printer and actually used by him, any chance of the correct paper coming into wrong hands can be avoided.

Paper is made from pulp which, in the machine-made variety, is run, in its liquid state, on to an endless 'web', and at one stage in its progress, and before the paper is fully formed, it comes under the pressure of a revolving cylinder known as the 'dandy roll'. This cylinder is covered with wire cloth, and if the wire is interwoven like cloth, the result is a 'wove' paper, while a dandy roll whose wire is in parallel lines will give 'laid' paper.

To produce the watermark, which is really a thinning in the paper, devices made of wire, or cut out of brass, are attached to the dandy roll at the desired intervals and, being pressed into the wet paper as it passes, reproduce those devices as thinner portions in its texture, which can be seen by transparency when the paper is held up to the light.

FIRST PRESS SECOND PRESS THIRD PRESS

Most watermarks can be seen in this way, but where the thinning is less pronounced the watermark can be detected by placing the stamp face downwards on a black surface. If even this is not sufficient, a drop of benzine poured on to the stamp will usually emphasize the watermark, and black trays or tiles, recessed to hold the benzine, are sold by stamp dealers under the name of watermark detectors. In the case of watermarks which are very hard to see, a print through the stamp may be taken on ordinary photographic paper, and if it is carefully watched, the watermark will appear before anything else shows on the paper. Turn the back of the stamp to the light, or the colour may fade. In using benzine, due care must be exercised, as its vapour is very inflammable, and smoking, or using it near an open fire or naked light, is dangerous. WARNING. *Do not use benzine on modern stamps printed in photogravure. The ink runs.*

It must not be supposed that all stamps have watermarks, for many countries use unwatermarked paper for stamp printing. Where the watermark is present it may take one of several forms:

(1) A paper-maker's watermark, which is just the normal watermark indicating the maker and (perhaps) the class of paper which is used. It may be a name, a number, or a device, but it has no postal significance, and is often disregarded by collectors, though it will be appreciated that

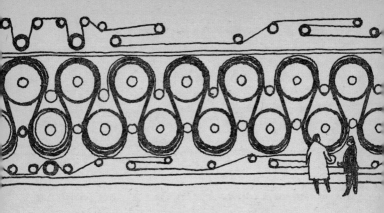

if two or more makers have been supplying paper for stamp printing, their distinctive watermarks may supply valuable data for deciding to which printing particular stamps belong. Many paper-makers' watermarks only occupy a very small proportion of the area of the paper so that most stamps printed on such paper are without watermarks, and for practical purposes the issue would be described in stamp catalogues as having no watermark.

(2) A single device, covering more or less of the surface of the paper, but in many cases leaving a proportion of the stamps in the sheet without watermark. The distinction between such devices, which are known to collectors as 'sheet watermarks', and the paper-makers' watermarks (apart from the fact that the latter may be repeated several times in the paper of a single sheet of stamps) is that the sheet watermarks are of postal origin, i.e. they represent the arms of the country, or some other device, which gives a definitely postal status and use to the paper. An example is the arms watermark of the 1854 issue of India.

(3) Single watermarks. Here small watermark devices are so arranged in the paper that, if properly printed, each stamp in the sheet will have its own watermark. The

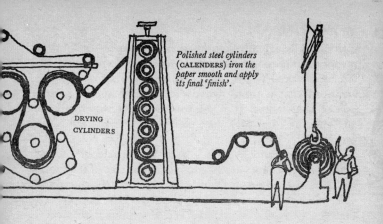

Polished steel cylinders (CALENDERS) iron the paper smooth and apply its final 'finish'.

DRYING CYLINDERS

'Crown over CC' and 'Crown over CA' watermarks of many British Colonies are examples. (*see page 203*)

(4) Multiple watermarks. Here the device is repeated at close intervals throughout the sheet of paper, so that each stamp may show a portion of several devices. A minor distinction may be drawn between a watermarked device and a watermarked inscription (such as some of the watermarks of modern Brazilian stamps), as the latter may be of such size that only one or two letters or portions of letters will be identifiable on each stamp, while the 'Multiple Crown over CA' watermarks of the British Colonies and other small devices are usually identifiable in their entirety from a single stamp, or at most one or two stamps, owing to their smaller size. (*see page 203*)

It is not always possible to secure properly watermarked paper for stamp printing, and in one or two instances a 'false' watermark has been printed faintly on the paper, to give the same protection which a real watermark would afford. An instance will be found in the 2c., 5c., and 20c. stamps issued by Argentina in 1922, during a temporary shortage of the normal paper.

Other methods of so-called watermarking have been adopted by Switzerland (for her 1862 issue), where the watermark is actually impressed in the paper – a kind of reversed embossing which can be easily seen – and by Czechoslovakia, which, in the anniversary series of 1923, arranged that a protective device should appear in the *gum* of the stamps. It is, of course, not a watermark at all, and does not look like one, but it serves the same purpose.

Another question which has to be considered by the authorities in connexion with paper, is the size of the sheets which are to be printed, and this is intimately connected with the size of the stamps, the space which is to be left between each row of stamps, and the number of stamps which have to be printed on each sheet of paper. (It may be noted here that the size of the 'printer's sheet' may be larger than that of the 'post office sheet', i.e. the sheet as sold over the post office counter, for printers often turn out two or more post office sheets on one piece of paper and these are cut up before being distributed for sale.)

The size of the stamps will, naturally, be determined at an early stage in the proceedings, and the number of stamps in the sheet will usually have some connexion with the currency of the country, e.g. countries with a decimal coinage usually have sheets made up of 100 stamps, or multiples of 100; many British Colonies base their sheets on multiples of 60, thus linking up with the sterling currency of 240 pence to the pound. Such arrangements facilitate post office accounts and sales to the public.

There are sheets which have a very small number of stamps in them, particularly at early periods in the history of stamp production, where a large stamp sheet would mean a good deal of extra work by way of engraving or otherwise reproducing the design. There are also modern souvenir sheets consisting of only one or a few stamps, usually issued in connexion with some special event. These are known as 'miniature sheets' and are often speculative.

The space between the stamps has to be calculated in relation to the question of the perforation, or means of separation of the stamps, with which we shall deal in a moment. The division of a sheet of stamps into smaller sections, by means of blank margins, will be considered in the chapter on sheets and booklets.

Having the design, his gummed paper, and his ink, and having decided on the general make-up of his sheets of stamps, the printer can now consider the actual printing, but this subject calls for a chapter to itself, so, before we follow his example, we will deal with what is really a later stage of the process of stamp production and consider the various means adopted for separating stamps from one another easily and expeditiously. (*see page 103*)

The earlier stamps, both of Great Britain and of many other countries, were 'imperforate', that is to say the paper was not weakened in any way between the rows of stamps, and the post office clerks and the public had to use scissors to separate them. This system was found so inconvenient that various methods of facilitating the separation of stamp from stamp were experimented with and some of them adopted by various countries, that which is known to collectors as 'perforation' being now the standard method. Stamps are now issued imperforate ('imperf.') only in an emergency, or to create extra varieties for sale to collectors, or to give a special character to a commemorative or charity stamp.

A system of separation which is now almost obsolete is that known as rouletting. This was done with a small wheel or series of wheels, with small points on their circumference, something like a spur. Where the cuts made by these points in the paper between the stamps are in short straight lines, the simple term 'rouletted' applies (or the French alternative *percé en lignes* is employed). Rouletted stamps, when separated, show a straight edge, corresponding with the length of the roulette cut, with a small projection between each cut.

In some cases curved cuts are made (arc roulette, or *percé en arc*) and when two stamps are torn apart, the edge of one will show a series of arched projections, nearly touching each other, while the other will show corresponding indentations. Another type has the slits cut in a zigzag fashion, and the edge of the stamp after separation looks like a saw (zigzag roulette, or *percé en scie*). Early stamps of Finland have a curious serpentine roulette which produces very long 'teeth' when the stamps are separated.

Rouletting in colour, such as is found in some of the stamps of Thurn and Taxis and elsewhere, which show each roulette slit coloured, is not true rouletting. The slits, in such cases, are produced during printing, by the use of thin strips of metal with sharp edges, which project higher than the blocks from which the stamp designs are printed and thus cut the paper and colour the edges of the cuts at the same time.

Rouletting is distinct from perforation, in that it does not remove any paper from the sheet, but merely pricks holes or slits in it, while a perforating machine punches circles of paper right out of the sheet. Sharp pins are sometimes used to produce a method of separation which while called pin-perforation, is really a roulette, as the pins do not remove any paper. Where proper perforating machines are not available, sewing machines have on occasion been used to produce a crude form of perforation.

Turning to perforation proper, with which the modern collector is more frequently concerned, this is done by rows of punches which remove circular pieces of paper from the sheet. (The lozenge perforation of some Bulgarian Postage Dues is an exception.) The simplest form of perforating machine has a single line of punches, which makes one row of holes at a time. The sheet has therefore to be moved as the space between each pair of rows of stamps is dealt with to produce the vertical lines of holes and then the sheet is turned round so that the horizontal rows of perforations can be made. A machine such as this is called a 'single-line' or 'guillotine' machine, and the perforation produced by it is known as 'single-line' or 'line' perforation.

A 'harrow' machine is so called from its resemblance to the agricultural implement of that name, for the lines of punches are so arranged that they perforate the vertical and horizontal intervals of a sheet of stamps at one blow. Such machines are not very much used at the present day.

The great difficulty which is met with in perforating stamps is that of ensuring that the lines of holes fall in their proper place between the stamps and do not cut into the stamp design. The spaces between the stamps are naturally small, as otherwise the stamps would have wide margins of paper around them and would look unsightly; and when millions of stamps are being printed the extra space would mean larger sheets, larger plates and more paper, all of which would involve waste of money and material. Time has also to be considered and it is obvious that, though the single-line perforator has its advantages, as giving more opportunities for accurate adjustment, it necessitates each sheet of stamps being put through the perforator twice, once for the horizontal rows of holes and once for the vertical, with a number of movements in each direction.

Another type of perforator has therefore come into use which is called a 'comb' machine. (*see page 104*) This has the punches so arranged that there is one long line equivalent to the length between two rows of stamps, and shorter lines projecting at right angles, at intervals equivalent to the width of the stamp. Such a machine, therefore, perforates the space between two rows of stamps and the spaces between the individual stamps of one row, at a single blow, and as the sheet moves along it thus completes both horizontal and vertical perforations without any necessity for turning the sheet round. In producing recent British stamps a 'multiple comb' perforator has been used, which perforates several rows entirely and three sides of the next row. In Britain and the U.S. a highly ingenious 'electronic-eye' device is employed, which automatically corrects the position of the sheet and thus ensures that the perforations fall accurately in the intervals between the rows of stamps.

In deciding as to the space between the punches in a perforating machine, consideration has to be given to the strength of the paper and its resistance to tearing. The perforation holes should be so spaced that, when an attempt is made to tear the stamps apart, the tear follows the line of holes and does not cut across the paper of the stamp. If the holes are close together, separation of the stamps will be easier than if they were more widely spaced, but the mesh of the paper, and the way it runs, may make it necessary to space the holes differently in the horizontal and vertical rows. To the collector, this spacing is not very important, unless it provides him with evidence that certain stamps were the work of a particular printer or period, but stamp catalogues differentiate between the various 'gauges' of perforation and in a later chapter we shall see how they are measured and described by collectors.

On *page 201* the reader will find illustrations showing the appearance of the holes at the intersection of vertical and horizontal rows of comb perforations and line perforations. In the case of a properly adjusted comb perforation the holes never overlap, whereas with a line perforator the holes frequently run into one another at the intersections.

The use of automatic machines for the sale of stamps has given rise to various special kinds of perforations, having as their object the holding of the stamps safely in the machine, or the prevention of the delivery of two stamps for one coin. Some of the experimental 'automatic-machine perforations' consist of large holes of various shapes, pierced for the pegs, etc., by which the machine grips them, but they also fulfil the ordinary function of perforations in making it possible to separate the stamps from those adjoining them. The best known of the regular 'automatic machine perfs.' are those used by the Netherlands in modern times. It was found that the stamps perforated in the ordinary way were not satisfactory for the machines, so special 'interrupted' perfs. were adopted, in which a couple of holes were omitted. These have been nick-named 'syncopated' perfs. (*see page 103*)

Chapter Six

STAMP PRINTING

THE methods by which stamps are printed are of very great interest to those who wish to know the causes of the variations which they observe in their stamps. The subject is far too technical to be treated fully here, and many collectors pay very little attention to it, but it has great fascination for men who like to try and work out the problems which are presented when certain characteristics are observed in stamps printed perhaps many years ago, and it is required to deduce the methods of stamp production which gave rise to those characteristics.

This may sound a little beyond the scope of the ordinary reader, but he is more concerned with the matter when it is looked at from another angle. He wants to know the various things that can happen to a stamp during the process of its manufacture and he is then able to say whether variations which he notices in his own stamps are of real importance, as throwing light on their birth and history, or whether they are merely casual.

There are three main processes of printing which the collector must have some idea of, but before we consider them in detail it will be advisable to summarize their main characteristics which are, indeed, very easy to remember. The names given to them are Line-engraving (or Intaglio or Recess-printing), Typography (printing from a raised surface), and Lithography (printing from a flat surface). A fourth method, photogravure, is a modern development of line-engraving.

In Line-engraving the design of the stamp is cut into

59

metal, the lines of the design being represented by miniature troughs. Before printing, the ink is forced into these troughs, but it is wiped off the flat surface of the remainder of the plate. The paper on which the design is to be printed, usually after being damped, though a dry process is now used by some printers, is forced against the engraved plate and into the cuts representing the design, which are full of ink. The ink is picked up by the paper, where it stands up in microscopic ridges, visible as such in many cases to the naked eye, when the stamp is held edgeways between the observer and the light, and often to be felt by the finger.

Surface-printing, or Typography, shows us the reverse of this method, for here the engraving is so done that the lines of the design stand up on the plate in ridges of metal, and the uncoloured parts of the stamp-to-be are represented by depressions on the plate. When the plate is inked only the ridges receive the ink, and from them it is transferred directly to the paper to form the design of the stamp. If too much pressure is used in printing, the ridges of the plate will be represented by corresponding ridges on the *back* of the stamp, but in good printing such ridges are often only present in a microscopic degree.

In the process named Lithography there is no engraving, the design being drawn, or otherwise produced, on a perfectly flat stone or plate of a special character, which is so treated that, when the inking roller is passed over it, only the actual lines of the design drawn on it will pick up any ink, the rest of its surface remaining free from ink. When the stone, with its inked lines, is printed from, there are no depressions or ridges on the paper, the print being quite flat.

The photogravure process entails the design image being laid on a copper plate or cylinder and etched. The resulting hollows on the plate are inked and the normal printing follows by what is called rotary photogravure or 'roto-gravure'.

To emphasize the characteristics of these four methods of printing, the reader may take a finely engraved seal, such as

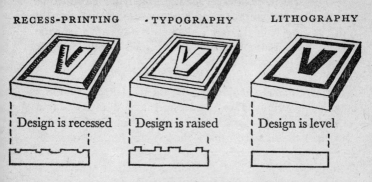

RECESS-PRINTING ·**TYPOGRAPHY** **LITHOGRAPHY**

Design is recessed | Design is raised | Design is level

Sectional view of stamp showing the effect of pressure on the paper

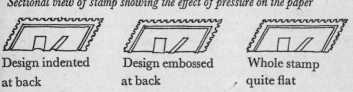

Design indented at back | Design embossed at back | Whole stamp quite flat

was once used for sealing letters, and thoroughly ink the lines of the monogram or device. When the surface of the seal is wiped, the ink will still remain in these lines. With a little ingenuity, a means can be found of forcing a piece of soft paper so hard against the surface of the seal that it is pressed into the recessed lines and picks up ink from them. The result is an extremely crude recess-printed design.

The ordinary rubber or metal hand-stamp, which is found in every office and home, provides a familiar example of the typographic or surface-printing method. When the hand-stamp is pressed on the ink-pad, only the raised portions of it receive the ink, and thence they are transferred to the paper by pressure.

To get an impression which will be in some degree comparable to that from a lithographic stone, draw with a pen a crude design on a piece of ink eraser. If the eraser is pressed on to a sheet of paper before the ink has time to dry, the design drawn on it will be transferred to the paper as a perfectly flat impression. The nearest approach to the dotted-screen background of photogravure-printed stamps is the coarse screening of newspaper half-tone blocks used in illustrations.

This is as far as the incurious reader need go in this chapter, but the majority will find in a description of the various stages of these processes many things which will help them to appreciate differences which they will notice in their stamps. In what follows, only the elements of a single method of printing by each of these processes are analysed, but numerous variations in method are employed by various firms and at various times.

In Line-engraving, the first stage is the engraving of the design in recessed lines on a small, flat plate of softened metal, which is the original, or 'mother die'. On this die, the design is in reverse, looking to the eye as the design of the stamp itself would look if viewed in a looking-glass.

After this die has been hardened, a soft steel roller is rocked backwards and forwards across it and receives a positive impression of the design, which, in its turn, is hardened. By a reversal of the process, i.e. the rocking of the roller, under pressure, on the surface of a softened steel plate, the design is transferred (as a negative impression, this time) to the plate. *(see page 101)* This process is repeated until the metal plate has received as many negative impressions of the design as the printed sheet of stamps is to contain, and when the plate has been hardened it is ready to print from, the impressions on the paper, from the negative designs on the plate, being, of course, positive.

It is obvious that everything that appears on the 'mother die' will be reproduced on each of the impressions of the design on the printing plate and also on the stamps, unless the engraver makes a deliberate alteration to the plate, which he can do by softening it, scraping off any lines he may wish to alter, and re-engraving them as he wishes. The scraping off of the surface metal naturally leaves a dent in the plate, and this is hammered up from behind until the whole surface is level. If the plate is damaged, so that some of the lines of the design are blurred or removed, similar work may be done, which is called 'retouching'. With all his skill, it is very difficult for the engraver to repeat the damaged lines exactly, and if one design on a plate has been retouched, it will probably differ slightly from the others, which are exact reproductions of the die. It is a great joy to the keen philatelist to hunt among his stamps for evidences of retouching, and such evidences he calls 're-touches'.

Another variation which sometimes arises during the making of plates by the process we are considering, is what is called a 're-entry'. When the roller-die is rocked over the plate under pressure, to transfer its impression of the design to the plate, it is obviously important that these impressions should be very accurately positioned. Between them, in the printed sheet, the perforation holes will come, and if they are too close together there will be no room for the holes.

It sometimes happens that, in entering an impression on the plate from the roller-die, the latter is rocked on the plate in a slightly wrong position – a little too high, or to one side. If the mistake is disregarded by the operative who is making the plate, the printed sheet will show one stamp similarly out of position, as is frequently seen among the earlier postage stamps of various countries. A careful worker will, however, note his error, scrape off the badly placed impression, and re-enter (that is to say, rock again) the roller on the plate in the correct position.

Suppose, however, that he does not erase very carefully every line of the first, incorrect impression, any lines that he leaves on the plate will take up the ink and reproduce themselves on the paper. They are lines similar to those of the correct impression, but as they are in the wrong position of the first impression, they will be found beside, above, or below the lines of the correct complete impression, and on the stamp it will appear as if portions of the design are doubled. This appearance, when resulting from the re-entering of the die, as described, is called by collectors a re-entry, but not every doubling of this kind seen in stamps is caused in this way. Re-entries are often detectable as a doubling of the frame-lines of a stamp, though sometimes an inner portion of the design will be doubled, and cases are known, as in the $1\frac{1}{2}d$. New Zealand, issued in commemoration of the South African War, where one stamp in the sheet has the greater part of the design doubled.

In preparing for the printing of stamps by the Typographic process, the engraving of the die is again the first stage, but in this case the design is engraved *en épargne*, that is to say, the lines of the design stand up as ridges of metal, instead of being minute troughs as in the line-engraved (or intaglio) plate. This is, of course, negative, and from it, in the process known as stereotyping, a mould is taken, in *papier mâché*, or other suitable material, and this mould is used for the casting of as many separate reproductions in metal (called clichés) as there are to be stamps in the printed sheet. When these are suitably locked together at the correct intervals, they form the equivalent of our engraved printing plate, but with the design in relief instead of in recess.

If electrotyping is employed to secure reproductions of the die, the latter is first used to make a wax mould. On this a thin shell of copper is deposited electrically, which, when removed, is found to reproduce faithfully the lines and ridges of the die. When as many of these reproductions as necessary have been made, they are suitably strengthened and can be locked or joined together to make our printing plate.

Coming to our third printing process, Lithography, you will remember that we have here, instead of a plate with the design in recess or in relief, a flat stone (or nowadays often a plate of zinc or other suitable metal) on which the design is drawn or transferred in flat lines on its surface. The surface of the stone or metal is prepared in such a way that only the lines of the design pick up the ink, and from them it is transferred to the paper.

An elementary example of the system of transferring the design to the stone is found in those coloured pictures (also called 'transfers') which, in our younger days, we were able, with the aid of water, to move from the sheet of paper on which we bought them, and where they appeared in reverse, to another sheet, where they became positive pictures. You will remember how easy it was to crease or damage this thin coloured film during the process of transfer, and the same thing happens sometimes when designs are being transferred to the lithographic stone. If the transfer is creased or damaged, and the stone is printed from without correction, the design will be distorted in the case of a fold, or its lines will be broken or absent in the case of a damaged transfer. It is, however, quite easy to wipe a faulty transfer off the stone, and then another transfer can be laid down.

The 'Offset' process of printing is a modern variant of Lithography, in which the design is not printed immediately on the paper, but is transferred from the plate to a rubber roller and thence to the paper.

The word 'offset' is also applied by collectors to an impression of the design which has found its way to the back or front of a sheet of stamps, either from some part of the printing machine which has accidentally received the impression from the inked plate, or from another sheet of stamps which has come in contact with it while still wet from the press. (*see page 74.*)

In recent times, photography has played its part in the production of postage stamps, the process mainly employed being known as rotary photogravure. The distinguishing characteristic of stamps printed by this method is that the design, under a magnifying glass, is seen to be broken up into a series of dots. Examples will be found among the modern stamps of Great Britain, Egypt, Mauritius, Seychelles, Singapore, Switzerland, and many others.

In rotary photogravure the design subject, usually a

combination of photograph and drawing permitting subtle gradations of colour, is photographed, the resulting negative being used to make what is termed a multipositive plate (the equivalent in size of a sheet of stamps). The multiple design is then printed down on to a specially prepared sheet of carbon tissue, the surface of which has been photographically superimposed with a fine grid or screen. It is this screen which breaks up the design into fine dots. The tissue, now containing positive impressions, is wrapped round the copper cylinder for etching. Subsequently, the cylinder is made ready for printing, the recessed design first contacting ink rollers, then paper, in the rotary printing press.

Embossing was used in earlier times for producing stamps and beautiful examples are provided by Gambia, Great Britain, Heligoland, Portugal, and other countries. The relief effect in embossing is achieved by the use of two dies, one engraved in relief and the other in recess, between which the paper is pressed. Various methods have been adopted to provide the coloured part of the design.

If a sheet of stamps is to be printed in two or more colours, a separate plate or stone will have to be prepared for printing that part of the design which is to appear in each colour. In the case of British Colonial stamps printed in standard designs, but not always in two colours, an economical system was adopted by which the same plates could be used for printing the portrait and other parts of the design which were common to the stamps of the various Colonies and to various values, while separate plates were provided for the part of the design which included the name of the Colony and the value-denomination of the stamp. The plates which printed the portrait are called the 'head plates', while the others are known as 'duty plates'.

Nowadays, the printing of multicoloured stamps is performed in a single operation by high-speed presses which have separate printing cylinders for each differently coloured part of the stamp design.

We need not discuss in detail the actual mechanism of

printing, which, in itself, calls for just as much skill and experience as the stages of the work already described. The important factors which the printers have to consider, and which may affect the appearance of the stamps, are the mixing of the ink to the correct shade and consistency and the use of it under the proper conditions of temperature and humidity; the proper 'registering' of the sheet as it passes through the press, so that the stamp designs fall in their proper position in relation to the edges of the paper (a particularly important matter when stamps are to be printed in two or more colours, as the sheet has to pass through the press as many times as there are colours, and if wrongly positioned on any one of these occasions, the colours will overlap or portions of the design will be out of place); the application of the correct quantity of ink to the plate (and, in the case of line-engraved and rotary photogravure plates, the proper wiping of the flat surface of the plate, leaving the ink only in the recessed lines of the design); and the passing of the sheet through the press in such a way that it receives the design evenly and with only the requisite amount of pressure over all its surface.

Spoilt sheets will result if the sheet goes crookedly through the press or if the paper gets creased or folded, or if the ink on the freshly printed sheet gets smudged. Such sheets, in a carefully supervised stamp printing works, will be carefully destroyed, but where supervision is slack, they may leak out and come into the hands of collectors, often in an unfinished condition. Such sheets are called 'printer's waste', and are of very little importance unless they tell us something about methods of production which we cannot learn from the finished stamps.

It must be mentioned, too, that many modern stamps, mainly those printed by photogravure (such as our own British low-value stamps) and photo-lithography, are printed 'in the web', or from long reels of paper, subsequently cut into normal sheets.

Another modern development, the 'facing' and sorting of

letters by electronic machines, has brought about the use of phosphor-coated paper for stamps. Letters bearing such stamps are faced and segregated by electronic scanning devices, considerably easing the manual task of facing and sorting. Britain pioneered these experiments with graphite-lined stamps in 1957 and now uses stamps bearing phosphor bands on the face of the stamps. Among the other countries now using phosphor-coated stamps are Denmark, Germany, Switzerland, Canada, and the United States.

When the ink on the newly printed sheets has dried, they are ready for perforating, as already described, and then they may be packed up ready for transfer to the postal authorities, through whom they eventually find their way to the post offices and the public.

Chapter Seven

ERRORS AND VARIETIES

(For illustrations to this chapter see pages 201 and 204.)

IT is a curious trait of the stamp collector that, while other people consider a commodity which has been defectively manufactured to be of less value than the perfect article, he insists on regarding a postage stamp which shows the results of some mistake as being, in most cases, of greater interest than a correctly printed specimen. Naturally, if proper care is exercised, incorrect stamps will be less plentiful than correct ones, and as they are regarded as collectable they often have a greater value. All kinds of mistakes can happen during the complicated process of stamp production, and it will be as well to review these in detail, especially in regard to the relative importance attached to each class by collectors, as there is no very consistent basis of appraisal. It is true that the terms 'error', 'major variety', and 'minor variety' are used to indicate very roughly certain grades of importance, but they are loosely employed.

Looking at the story of the postage stamp, as given in Chapters Five and Six, it will be seen that the first possibility of mistake arises when the artist is drawing his sketch. He may be wrong in some essential detail of his picture, as when he put one of the Union Jacks on the 2½d. Jamaica, of 1921, upside down, or he may go wrong in the lettering of the inscriptions, mis-spelling a word or making one letter look like another. If the engraver of the die follows the artist faithfully, he will copy his mistakes and these will appear on the plate and in the designs of the finished stamps. Mistakes of this kind hardly come within the collector's definition of the word 'error', for every stamp is alike, and he employs the word more often to signify a variation from the normal run of a particular stamp.

In the next stage of preparing a line-engraved plate, we have already seen how retouches and re-entries occur. The importance attached to these by collectors varies in proportion to their prominence, but a really clear retouch or re-entry will be keenly sought for. So also will be stamps which show evidence of serious damage to the plate, particularly if stamps printed at a later date prove that retouching has been resorted to to repair the damage.

A scratch on an engraved plate, or accidental damage to a typographic plate, may result in one particular stamp in the printed sheet having a word wrongly spelt, as for example, the first British 1½d. stamp with King George's portrait, where the words 'THREE-HALFPENCE' appeared on one stamp of a certain plate as 'THREE-HALFPENCF'. Mistakes of this kind, which have a certain appeal to the eye and to the imagination, are popular with collectors, and often attain considerable value though, logically, they are of no more importance than similar damage which does not alter a letter, or any essential of the pictorial design.

The use of the two dies to produce plates for printing a particular stamp is very likely to result in the issue of stamps differing slightly in detail, unless purely mechanical means of reproducing the one from the other are adopted. Sometimes, a second die is intentionally different from the original one, with the object of improving the general appearance or some particular detail, but often, with hand-engraved dies, the second die will not be an exact replica of the first, and there will be unintentional differences in the design of the resulting stamp. In the catalogues, stamps or issues resulting from the use of a noticeably different new die are said to be in a 'redrawn design'. Good examples of pairs of dies differing slightly in minor details are to be found in the

Queen Victoria portrait used by Cyprus, St Lucia, and other possessions in the 'eighties and the head-plate of the familiar King George V colonial 'tablet' type.

Differences caused by the use of varying dies are varieties of primary importance to serious collectors, though they are not, of course, varieties in the widest sense of the term, which would describe as 'different' stamps only those which would be recognized as such by a postal clerk.

It sometimes happens that one die is smaller than another which is otherwise similar, and the resulting stamps are consequently of two different sizes, but a variation in size does not always betoken the existence of a different die, as many collectors seem to think. One very frequent cause of varying stamp sizes is paper shrinkage.

In printing from line-engraved plates, the paper, as we have seen, is usually damped before the actual printing takes place. If the paper is always of exactly the same character, and the damping is done under the same conditions, the shrinkage of the paper when drying will be practically constant and all the stamps will be of equal size. If, however, the shrinking varies for any reason, the stamp designs will shrink more or less, as the case may be, and you will get stamps of different sizes. Varieties caused by paper shrinkage have no interest or importance for the collector.

Some printers now use a process in which the paper is not damped. When this dry process is employed for stamps previously printed by the wet process, a change of size is likely to occur and may then be of value as indicating the adoption of the new method.

In some cases it occurs from the method of manufacture that a number of 'types' differing only slightly in detail may be identified among the stamps in a sheet. For example, a design may be transferred to a lithographic stone by 'laying down' a certain number of reproductions at one operation, and repeating this operation until the number of reproductions required for printing a sheet of the desired size is obtained. If the unit of transfer to the stone is six reproductions of the design, each of these six will probably differ in some small detail, and the stamps will show the same differences, and thus, in the printed sheet, we shall find six 'types', which, to a specialist, are collectable.

Following out the lithographic process, it is possible that, after some sheets have been printed from the stone, one of the designs on it may receive a scratch or other damage, or, as already explained in the previous chapter, the transfer may be folded or creased when first laid down on the stone. The resulting damaged or folded transfer is interesting to the specialist. Let us suppose that, for purposes of reference, he calls the 'type' of which one of the transfers has become damaged, Type C, to distinguish it in his own mind from the other five types which he finds on the printed sheet. In later printings from the stone, he notes that the variation caused by the damaged transfer has disappeared, and that, in the position it previously occupied in the sheet, there is now a stamp of Type B. Here he has evidence of a 'substituted transfer', i.e. the replacement of one transfer by erasure from the stone and the laying down of another.

Again, the collector might notice that in some sheets his six types are arranged in rows of six, A B C D E F, repeated down the sheet. In other sheets, he finds that, though the same types are present, they appear in groups of six placed side by side, thus

> A B C A B C
> D E F D E F

Obviously, though the same types of transfer have been used, they have been laid down afresh on the stone, and the resultant re-arrangement of the types in the sheet is called a new 'setting', a term which is applied to any particular grouping of types in a sheet of stamps, whether they be of the stamps themselves or of a surcharge or overprint.

It sometimes happens that, in making a printing plate, or in laying down the designs on a stone, one stereo is inserted, or one design laid down, upside down in relation to its fellows. If the printed sheet of stamps showing the results of such a mistake were cut or torn up into units, every stamp would still look exactly the same, but if the inverted stamp is retained in a pair with one of its fellows we have that much-sought-for error a *tête-bêche* pair. Some classic examples of such errors are found among the early stamps of France.

There is another way in which *tête-bêche* pairs may be created, which has not the same importance. Large sheets of stamps may be printed from two or more plates, or a single plate may be used to print half the sheet at one operation, the blank half of the paper being then brought beneath the plate to receive the impression in its turn. If, in the first case, the two plates are printed from, so that all the impressions from one are upside down in relation to those printed from the other, it will be possible to get *tête-bêche* pairs consisting of one stamp from the inner row of each section of the sheet, usually with more unprinted paper between them than there would be between adjacent stamps in the same section of the sheet. In the other case, the same thing would happen if the sheet of paper were turned round before receiving the second impression from the plate.

Turning to the actual printing of the stamps, we find that several mistakes are possible in the actual passing of the sheet of paper through the press. If, through inadvertence, it goes through twice, the design will be doubled, and the greater the distance between the two impressions, the more highly will it be prized by collectors. A slight doubling of the design may also be caused by the slipping of the paper as it goes through the press, but such variation has not anything like the same importance.

If the sheet is put through the press twice, once face upward, and then face downward, it will have the design on both sides, and *both designs will be positive*. I have emphasized the last few words, as a true 'printed on both sides' variety is regarded as being a first-class error, while there is another rather similar, and much more plentiful kind of variety which is of little, if any, importance to collectors.

When the printing press is running, a sheet of paper should be fed through it at each revolution of its mechanism. If this is not done, the plate is inked and makes the movement which would normally bring it into contact with the paper, and the latter being absent, an inked impression of the plate is transferred to the roller or flat bed on which the paper would rest when receiving the impression from the plate. When the next sheet of paper is fed through the press, it receives a positive impression on its surface, in the ordinary way, but it also receives a *reversed* impression on the back, from the bed on which it is resting. Such impressions are called 'offsets' or 'blanket prints' according to the circumstances under which they occur, and, as stated above, are of very little interest or importance.

Another type of offset, still a reversed impression, is due to sheets being piled on one another while they are still wet, so that the back of one picks up the ink from the surface of the one below it. A similar happening, but with the face of one sheet coming in contact with the face of another, might produce the appearance of a double print, one print being reversed, but none of these variations are of philatelic importance.

So far we have been considering stamps printed in one colour, but when two or more colours are employed, the possibility of the creation of 'errors' is increased, for the sheet of paper.has to go through the press as many times as there are colours to be printed. Here correct 'registration' of the various colours is very important, that is to say, each time the sheet goes through the press, it has to occupy exactly the same position in relation to the printing plate, otherwise the parts of the design in the various colours will not dovetail accurately. Taking the simplest example, a stamp printed with the centre in one colour and the frame design in another, incorrect registration will give us the centre misplaced to right or left or up or down. Slight misplacements are not regarded as of any importance by collectors, but a striking difference of position would find a place in many albums as a curiosity, for the two colours will overlap to a very noticeable degree.

It is, however, a slight displacement which causes most trouble to the inexperienced collector, where there is normally practically no white space between the portions of the design in different colours. The slight difference of position, and the overlapping of the colours, which will make part of the design indistinct, or even invisible, causes many collectors, keen to make discoveries, to think that they have found evidences of the use of a new die, whereas they are only noting one of the most ordinary happenings as far as two-colour stamps are concerned.

The printers of the 'King as Admiral' stamps of Rhodesia in which King George V's head is printed in black or a colour and the frame in another colour, did not destroy sheets of stamps in which the registration was poor, but filled in the gap between centre and frame with a wash of colour applied by hand, which effectively concealed the slight defect. These stamps, though only curiosities, are keenly sought for by specialists in Rhodesian issues, but they can, of course, very easily be faked.

If a sheet of stamps with the frame already printed in one colour is passed through the press wrong end first when the centre is to be printed, the resulting sheet will consist of stamps with centre inverted, an extremely popular class of error, and one in which great rarities are found. When sorting or looking at stamps in two colours, always bear in mind the possibility of finding an uncatalogued error of this class, for it is one of the 'sporting chances' of philately. In recent years a New Zealand stamp, printed nearly thirty years before, turned up with inverted centre, to the benefit of the finder.

If the sheet of paper is passed through the press twice, when either colour is being printed, we get stamps with centre double, or frame double, as the case may be, while through forgetting the printing of one colour we obtain specimens with frame or centre omitted. It is possible, also, to have a sheet of stamps with the frame printed on one side of the paper and the centre printed on the other. Such varieties are so easily noticed, however, that stamps showing any of those described above, save inverted centres or centres slightly misplaced, are nearly always from 'printers' waste', i.e. spoiled sheets, which have leaked out of the printing works when they should have been destroyed. Such printers' waste has little importance, as the purist requires his errors and varieties to have been accidentally issued over a post office counter, though it is not always easy to ascertain whether 'errors' of any kind have been the result of a genuine accident, and have got into circulation in the ordinary way through an oversight on the part of the checkers, or if they have been deliberately created by collusion on the part of someone in the printing works, or allowed to leak out through lack of proper control.

Now let us look at the printing ink, and see what mistakes the printer can make in this connexion. The most serious is, of course, that he should use an entirely wrong colour for printing a sheet or sheets of stamps – producing a brown halfpenny stamp, for example, where the normal is green. Such 'errors of colour', where due to printing accidents, are as keenly sought for as inverted centres, but the collector must exercise some care in accepting discoveries, for as will be shown later, it is possible for colours to change through exposure to moisture or sunlight, even to fumes in the air. Stamps coming from a certain part of Persia were found to be in curious colours, and on enquiry it was discovered that the change was caused by the fumes from the oil wells which were a feature of the district. Then, too, we shall see that it is easy for unscrupulous persons to change the colours of stamps by the use of chemicals, so that, before paying any money for so-called errors of colour, it is advisable to see first whether they are catalogued, and even if they are it is best to consult an expert, as to whether the colour may have been changed, as a mere 'colour changeling', even if accidental, is of no interest whatever, save as a curiosity.

Variations in the mixing of the ink and in the temperature and humidity of the atmosphere during printing and drying, will result in variations in 'shade' or tone. Marked shades are attractive to collectors, because they 'hit the eye', but their importance from the research point of view is limited to those occasions when they indicate, or serve to identify, stamps from separate printings. Heavy or light inking of the plate or stone will also produce shades, and so will any variation in the amount of pressure. In stamps printed by primitive methods, or where proper care is not taken, it is possible to find several shades in one sheet of stamps, due to varying pressure on different parts during printing. Further details regarding colour variations will be found in Chapter Ten.

Sometimes blobs or lines of colour are found on stamps which do not form part of the normal design. These may be due to defects in the plate or on the stone, as already noted, but frequently they are the result of dirt or other extraneous matter getting on to the plate. If a sheet of paper is fed through the machine with another piece, perhaps quite small, adhering to its surface, the latter will pick up the ink from the plate and will receive part of the design. If, then, this piece of paper is detached later, it takes with it part of the design, leaving a blank space on the sheet, which may be a small portion of one stamp, or parts of several. None of the varieties mentioned in this paragraph, though often striking in appearance, are of philatelic importance. They are merely 'freaks', and should be treated as such, and relegated to a separate page in the album.

Inking varieties are prolific on photogravure-printed stamps. One common occurrence is the white or coloured hairline running across the surface of such stamps. In the course of photogravure printing, surface ink is removed from the face of the cylinder by a flexible steel blade known as the 'Doctor' knife. The lines on the stamps are caused when a particle of grit becomes wedged between the moving blade and the revolving cylinder. The 'missing colours' on some photogravure-printed stamps are due to the gradual slowing down of the multicolour press (for adjustment, etc.), when one colour (i.e. one inking roller) ceases to be applied before the others run down. Strictly, this also is printers' waste and should be rejected. Far more interesting on photogravure stamps is the evidence of weak impressions and subsequent retouching.

Errors and varieties connected with the paper on which the stamps are printed are not of many kinds, if we leave watermarks aside for a moment. The most important errors of paper are due to the use of a wrong kind (e.g. laid for wove) or of a wrong colour. It is not easy, in a properly run stamp-printery, to make a mistake of this kind, as the paper is carefully checked before it is used, and every sheet is accounted for; while the method of manufacture of the paper itself would tend to ensure that all the sheets in a batch were alike in at least their main characteristics.

As already stated, variations in the thickness of the paper are not of value to the specialist unless he can thereby identify stamps as belonging to different printings, or distinguish between originals and reprints, but specimens showing any very marked difference should be kept. Occasionally one finds a local thickening in a sheet of paper, due, perhaps, to a lump of some foreign substance getting into the pulp during manufacture, or to some slight defect in the making of the particular sheet. The actual effect, in the printed sheet, will be that the colour will be deeper in the design printed on the thicker part of the paper, as the thickening will cause heavier pressure at that spot.

Curious things happen when sheets are printed on paper which is folded or creased. If a concertina crease is opened up after the sheet has been printed, there will be a wide, white gap across the stamps affected by the crease. If a corner of the sheet is turned over during printing, part, or all, of the design of some of the stamps will be missing. Freaks of this kind, which only occur in a single sheet, and are never twice alike, must be classed with the other oddities mentioned in connexion with colour.

Errors and varieties of perforation are not very popular, but there are one or two groups which come in the 'major variety' class. The first of these consists of stamps intended to be issued perforated, but of which a sheet or sheets has not been perforated at all. Actually some of the sheets from which our 'imperf.' stamps come are probably proof or trial sheets which the printers did not trouble to perforate, and which have afterwards got into philatelic circulation.

The collector should exercise very special caution in regard to stamps offered to him as imperf. errors, or even as specimens of a normally imperforate issue, where the same stamp was also issued perforated. Some stamps are printed with very wide margins around them. This was particularly the case with many of the older stamps, and it is therefore quite an easy matter to create imperfs. with a pair of scissors. No stamp which exists perforated should be accepted as imperforate unless it has so much margin on each side that it is larger than the largest possible stamp that could be produced by trimming the perfs. off a perforated stamp. Even the presence of part of the design of the adjacent stamp, with an imperf. margin between, is not sufficient evidence, as a stamp with perforations so badly misplaced as to cut into the next design may have been trimmed. There are, of course, special indications such as colour or other details, which enable some imperforate stamps to be identified regardless of the extent of their margins, but expert knowledge is required in most cases, and naturally, in the case of imperf. 'errors' the characteristics of the perforated and unperforated stamps will be the same. Many collectors adopt 'safety first' tactics and collect imperf. stamps in pairs.

Next we come to the varieties caused when the sheet is fed through the machine but the perforating process is not completed. If a single-line perforator is being used, and it misses one stroke, there will be an unperforated space between two rows of stamps and the result will be pairs of stamps 'imperf. between', i.e. perforated all round their outer edges, but not at their line of junction. Though the cause, in each case, is only the omission of a single stroke of the perforator, stamps from the outer edge of the sheet with one side imperf. are not popular, while pairs imperf. between are now keenly sought for. Perhaps the lack of attention paid to stamps from a sheet with an outer edge accidentally imperf. is due to the fact that some countries, looking at perforating in a very practical light, have intentionally issued their stamp sheets with the outer edges not perforated. This means that the corner stamps of the sheet will have top (or bottom) *and* one side imperf. while the other outer stamps will have one of their four sides imperf. Many examples will be found among the stamps of Canada and the United States and the resulting partly perforated stamps are known as 'straight edges', and are denied access to most collections as being defective specimens, though in actual fact they are just as they were printed and issued, and are really scarcer – though owing to the lack of demand, less valuable – than the stamps perforated all round.

Stamps with these 'straight edges' must not be confused with stamps normally issued with two *opposite* sides imperf., such as are issued for use in coils by Canada and the United States.

When a comb machine misses a stroke, the effect is different, for it will be remembered that the comb perforates three sides of the stamps in a row at one blow. A mistake of this kind will therefore give us stamps imperf. on three sides, unless the stroke of the perforator is that in which the 'teeth' are engaged in perforating the marginal paper of the sheet, while the 'back' of the comb – the long line of pins – is perforating the outer margin of a row of stamps. In this case we shall get stamps with only one side imperf.

It is a curious example of the freakishness of philatelic taste that whereas double prints, double centres, and double overprints and surcharges are regarded as highly interesting, a double perforation receives little attention. Where the second blow of the perforator has descended alongside the first row of holes, the double perforation is quite obvious, but if the two rows of holes fall in the same line, and the holes do not quite coincide, the effect when the stamps are separated, may be to make them appear as if they had been finely rouletted, one set of holes having cut into the other so that the resulting perfs. seem quite small. Examples of this may be found in early British stamps.

If the pins of the perforator become blunt, the resulting holes will not be so sharply defined as those made by sharp pins. We thus get 'clean-cut' and 'rough' perforations, while in certain early British Colonial issues a further 'intermediate' subdivision has been made, but these refinements need not trouble the ordinary collector. In the instance mentioned, the variations serve to group stamps more or less in chronological order.

Where the pins are so blunt, or the strike of the perforator is so badly adjusted, that the holes are not punched out, we get a series of circular depressions instead of perforations, and these are called 'blind perforations'.

As we have seen in an earlier chapter, the differing 'gauges' of perforation are due to various spacings of the perforating pins, while perforations showing large or small holes naturally result from the use of pins of large or small section. Neither gauge nor size of holes is of any philatelic importance except when it enables us to distinguish between one printing and another, or between genuine, forged or reprinted stamps, but where a number of different perforating machines have been used for an issue, many collectors will try to secure specimens with every possible gauge of perforation. 'The catalogues list them, so we must have them' is the excuse for going so far in this direction. Every one to his taste, but I should be the last to urge the

reader to worry about perforations at all, if he has no leaning
that way.

It is not an easy matter to ensure that the lines of perforation holes always fall in the narrow spaces between the rows
of stamps. Even if the distances of the printing plate and
perforating machine exactly agree, it may happen that the
paper itself may shrink in one direction or another during
the process of printing (this frequently happens when
printing from line-engraved plates on paper which has been
damped) so that the intervals become not quite accurate.

Whether the cause be inaccurate placing of the sheet of
stamps in the perforating machine, inaccurate adjustment
of that machine, or paper shrinkage, the result will be
similar – instead of the line of perforation holes lying dead
in the centre of the space between two rows of stamps, it will
be nearer to one row or the other, and may even cut into the
design of the stamp. (*see page 201*) Extreme cases of this are
found in the old British 'Penny Reds' where one sometimes
comes across a stamp which is so freakishly perforated that
it is actually made up of the right half of one stamp design
and the left half of the adjacent design.

The usual result of inaccurate perforating is to make single
stamps, when severed from the sheet, appear 'badly
centred', i.e. the design of the stamp does not lie centrally
in the space bounded by the perforations. If the perforations
cut into the design of a stamp, it may well be refused a place
in the album, and even a specimen which looks particularly
lop-sided owing to bad centring may be eschewed, but I
would not go so far as some cranks do today and refuse a
place to every stamp whose design is not mathematically
in the centre of the perforations, for super-carefulness of this
kind is not far removed from madness.

Among the early surface-printed stamps of Great Britain
and some of her colonies will be found some which have the
marginal paper between the design and perforations on one
side very wide. This is due to the fact that the white 'gutter'
or margin between the panes only received one row of

perforation, so that the margin became part of the stamps. Such stamps (colloquially called 'flappers' or 'wing margins') are not popular because of their lop-sided appearance, though they are exactly as issued. For this reason, fakers are able to buy the stamps with wide margins cheaply, trim them down to normal, and provide them with faked perforations.

Misplaced perforations, however curious the results of them may appear, can only be allocated to the 'freak' section of a collection. The same applies to varieties, less frequently met with, where a sheet has been torn or damaged before perforating, patched with adhesive paper, and then put through the perforator, proof of this being afforded by the fact that the adhesive paper is perforated as well as the sheets of stamps. Creased or folded sheets give some very curious perforation effects when the folds are opened out, but these too can only be reckoned as freaks.

'Mixed' perforations, some of which are given catalogue rank among the pictorial issues of New Zealand, are found in sheets which were first perforated with a machine of a particular gauge, and then found to be inaccurately or incompletely perforated. The defect was remedied by patching them on the back with strips of paper, and the defective parts were then re-perforated with a machine of another gauge.

Errors and varieties of watermark must next claim our attention. Their causes are in most cases very similar to those we have noted in connexion with the printing of stamps in two colours, but here instead of two parts of the design, we have the watermark in the substance of the paper, and the design which is printed on it, and it is the relation of these which gives us our errors.

The normal position of a watermark (unless it is of so symmetrical a design that it cannot be said to have a 'right way up') is usually with its top and bottom at the top and bottom of the stamp design, respectively, and with the design or lettering *reversed when looked at from the back of the stamp*.

Catalogues usually show the watermark designs as they appear from the *front* of the stamp, but the collector normally looks at the back of the stamp (or through it when he holds it up to the light) in order to see the watermark, and in that case a normal watermark, say of words or letters, would read or appear backwards as in a looking-glass.

If, however, the printing is done on the wrong side of the sheet of paper, the watermark will read normally when looked at from the back of the stamp, which is then said to have the watermark reversed.

If the sheet is fed through the press wrong end first, the watermark will be inverted, i.e. its foot will be at the top of the stamp, and if the sheet goes through sideways, the watermark will be sideways. Some sideways watermarks are normal for their particular issues, however, sheets of paper having been printed on in a certain direction in order to accommodate the stamps of, perhaps, a different size from those for which the paper was originally intended.

A combination of printing on the back of the paper and with the sheet fed in the wrong end first will give us a watermark which is inverted and reversed, that is to say that the watermark lettering or design will appear positive (not looking-glass way) from the back of the stamp, and will also be upside down in relation to the design of the stamp.

Double watermarks may occasionally be found, but these are merely freaks, the second being a 'ghost' taken up by pressure from another sheet at some stage during manufacture or storage.

Readers may have noticed that, in the stamp booklets sold at British post offices, some of the stamps have inverted watermarks. This is not due to a mistake, but to the special arrangement of the plates used for printing booklet stamps. Fifty per cent of the booklet stamps have normal watermark while the other half have it inverted. There is thus obviously no extra value or interest attaching to these varieties. In the same way, exigencies of manufacture produce stamp rolls for certain automatic machines in which all the watermarks are sideways. Some collectors take them, and they sometimes have an extra value.

Few of the watermark variations referred to above are regarded as of sufficient importance to find a place in the stamp catalogues, and in certain issues, such as the middle issues of some of the Australian States, so little care was taken as to which end of the sheets went first through the press, that inverted watermarks are so common as to have hardly the interest of abnormality. A page or two may be kept for watermark varieties, even in a general collection, and most specialized collections would of course include them.

As far as major watermark errors are concerned, the principal of these is when a stamp is printed on paper which has the watermark allotted to another issue. A striking example of this is provided by the 1d., red, Transvaal, with portrait of King Edward, issued in 1905, which is found normally on paper with 'Multiple Crown CA' watermark, but which is also known on the Cape of Good Hope paper, with watermark anchor. It is always worth while looking out for this stamp, even in your own collection, as it occasionally turns up.

In the same way, it may happen that a sheet of unwatermarked paper is used for a stamp which should be printed on watermarked paper. As this has happened in the case of quite modern British stamps, the paper for which is most carefully checked in and out of the printing room, and has to be accounted for down to the last spoiled sheet, it is hard to find an explanation for unwatermarked paper getting into use, unless, as sometimes happens, experimental printings have been made, and the sheets either deliberately or inadvertently put into circulation. Another explanation put forward in the case of certain 'no watermark' errors, is that when the paper was being made, the dandy roll was badly adjusted so that the watermark design was not impressed in the pulp; but I am not able to say whether this is a likely cause.

Where whole sheets of stamps are issued without watermark when they should normally have one, the result is obviously an error of major importance, but there is another class of stamps which miss the watermark, which is of comparatively minor interest.

In many cases sheets of stamps, as printed, show blank, unprinted paper round their edges, and sometimes between the different subdivisions ('panes') of the sheet. This marginal paper may have the same watermark as the stamps (though this is not advisable, as it could then be used by the forger for his products); it may be watermarked with some appropriate inscription, 'POSTAGE' or 'POSTAGE – REVENUE', with the name of the country, for example – or it may have no watermark at all. Even if there are watermarked inscriptions on this marginal paper, there may be intervals which are unwatermarked.

Now it will be clear that, if the sheet of paper is put through the press rather too much to one side or the other, the impression printed from the plate will fall to a greater or less extent on this marginal paper, and thus we get stamps from the margins of the sheet which either have no watermark at all, or show portions of the letters of the marginal inscription as their watermark. There is no more prolific source of confusion to the ordinary collector than these letter watermarks, which are, of course, never mentioned in the stamp catalogues, as they are purely fortuitous varieties. They may be kept as curiosities but have no particular value. To distinguish stamps from a *sheet* with no watermark, from those (much less important) which have merely been printed on unwatermarked sheet margins, it is necessary to have so many stamps *se tenant* (i.e. joined together) as will serve to prove that they come from a sheet without watermark. Usually a block of four will suffice, and sometimes even a horizontal pair, as sheet margins are narrow and it is rarely possible to get more than a single stamp printed on the marginal paper in the horizontal sense (or, in the case of top or bottom margins, in the vertical sense).

One final variation may be looked for in watermarks.

This consists in omissions from the lettering or design of the watermark, due to damage to one of the metal devices on the dandy roll. Instances are met with among British stamps with the various 'GvR' monogram watermarks, but the most interesting modern example is connected with the Multiple Script CA Watermark used by the Crown Agents. Here the crown fell off two different dandy rolls and stamps are to be found with the watermark showing a blank space. In correcting one of these mistakes a completely different type of crown was put in instead, resulting in yet another interesting variety for the keen-eyed collector.

While the outsider may smile at the idea of collectors prizing so highly the results of mistakes in printing, the enthusiast knows that stamp collecting would not be nearly so enthralling if it were not for the chance it holds out at every turn of making finds of scarce errors among the less valuable normal stamps. It is, however, necessary to keep a sense of proportion and to concentrate mainly on the errors and varieties which have been indicated as being of major importance, otherwise the collection will come to be a hotch-potch of minor freaks and curiosities, which have little interest and still less value.

Chapter Eight

OVERPRINTS AND SURCHARGES

WHEN stamps came into general use, it often happened that some sudden alteration was required which did not allow the necessary time for the complicated processes of engraving a fresh die and making new plates, much less ordering supplies of the stamps from a source outside the country of issue – and many stamps for countries overseas were then printed in England, or the United States.

A way out of the difficulty was found by taking existing stamps and making the necessary alteration by printing it across them, the overprint being applied either from ordinary printer's type, from a stereotyped plate, or in some cases from a lithographic stone. Such an addition to the stamp is described by collectors as an overprint, when it does not affect the face value of the stamp, and as a surcharge when it confirms or alters the face value. (These two terms are however rather loosely used by philatelists and 'overprint' sometimes means 'surcharge' in such cases.)

The most frequent occasion for an emergency issue of stamps of this nature was a sudden demand for a stamp of a particular denomination – perhaps due to a change in the postal rates – which caused an unexpected shortage, or even a call for an entirely new denomination. Surcharging was then resorted to, and the resulting stamp, supposing a 6c. stamp had been surcharged with the words 'Five Cents', would be described by collectors as '5c. on 6c.' or 'the provisional 5c. on 6c.'.

Again it has sometimes been decided to issue stamps for a

particular country or colony, at a date by which it would be impossible to have distinctly designed stamps ready. In this event, overprinting might be resorted to, the name of the new recruit being printed across the stamps of the mother country, or, as in the case of Gibraltar, on the totally un-related issue of Bermuda.

Another function of the overprint is to convert a stamp from one use to another, as, for example, when postage stamps are overprinted in a special way, to convert them into postage due, or express, or air stamps, or whatever it may be.

Sometimes it may happen that a stock of stamps may be stolen from a post office or central store, and it becomes a matter of urgency to prevent those stamps being used for postal purposes in order to avoid grave loss to the revenue of the country concerned. In such cases, the practice is some-times adopted of overprinting a device or inscription on the remaining stocks of stamps, and forbidding the use of any stamps which are not so overprinted. Overprints of this kind are called 'control marks' or 'control overprints' (not 'controls', a word which is usually applied to the letters and figures on the margins of sheets of certain British stamps). Examples of such control marks will be found on some of the issues of Persia whose stamps have been fre-quently looted.

In quite modern times the stamps of the United States have been specially overprinted with the abbreviated names of the states of Kansas and Nebraska, owing to the number of 'hold-ups' of post offices in those districts. Stamps with the names of these states on them could not be used in any other state and thus the chance of the robbers being able to profit by their sale was minimized.

When political changes took place, such as a change of ruler or government, the application of an overprint to the existing stamps was often the quickest way of meeting the situation. Thus when the Fiji Islands were ceded to Britain, in October 1874, the stamps of the native King

Cakobau, which bore his initials 'C.R.', were quickly over-printed 'V.R.' and the world knew at once what had happened.

In Salvador, where presidents used to come and go with great and often painful rapidity, a certain General Ezeta ordered the usual annual set of stamps from the United States, but by the time they were ready the General was, at least politically if not actually, no more. A new supply of stamps was needed, so the Ezeta portrait issue was over-printed with the arms of the country, so effectively that only very faint traces of the portrait can be seen.

When Yugoslavia became a state, the only stamps avail-able in certain parts of the country were those of Hungary, but on them appeared the portrait of the Emperor Charles and the Iron Crown of Hungary, the wearer of which was *ipso facto* king of Hungary. In this case the crown, as the symbol of rule, was blotted out by an overprint, but the por-trait of the Emperor was allowed to remain visible.

On stamps of Peru, issued in 1894, a portrait overprint appears, the likeness of General Bérmudez being employed to blot out the national arms and devices.

At the present time there are few purposes for which stamps have been issued, which have not also their distinc-tive overprints or surcharges. We have war and occupation overprints as well as stamps, for it is naturally a great satisfaction to a conqueror to sprawl his mark across his opponents' stamps, pending the issue of a special victory series. Thus we find stamps of the German colonies over-printed with the inscriptions of the Allies who captured them from her in 1914–18, and stamps of the Allied powers overprinted for use by the German Armies of Occupation. There were many similar happenings during the Second World War.

Then there are a host of Charity, Commemorative, Jubilee, and Exhibition overprints, in connexion with events and anniversaries in all parts of the world. Overprinting is economical, as has been said, but it has not proved a paying proposition for those countries which have adopted a cheese-paring policy and yet have at the same time tried to entice money from the pockets of collectors, for most collectors, while they may be tempted by the pictorial designs of a commemorative series, do not find a commemorative *over-print* very attractive, and the demand is therefore much less than for distinctive issues of stamps of this nature.

Stamps overprinted 'SPECIMEN' (Spanish 'MUESTRA', Italian 'SAGGIO', German 'MUSTER') are sample stamps for official record purposes, or for distribution to the various postal authorities of the world through the International Bureau at Berne, Switzerland, for their official collections. The overprint is intended to prevent such sample stamps being used for postage. These stamps may be included in an advanced specialized collection. They are in most cases numerically rarer than those without the overprint, as only small quantities are overprinted, but their market value is usually only a small fraction of that of the normal stamp, except in the case of great rarities where many collectors will prefer to have a specimen stamp instead of a blank in their albums and the demand is therefore keen.

Looking at overprints and surcharges from the point of view of philatelic study, it will be obvious that, as these are printed by the methods already described when dealing with the production of postage stamps, they present similar problems. Thus, in the case of lithographed overprints, we may distinguish flaws, substituted transfers, and other typical varieties, while typographic overprints provide us with evidence of damaged plates and stereos.

When overprints are applied from printer's type, which consists of loose units 'locked up' in some kind of frame-work, there is an additional possibility – that the type may work loose and that letters may either become misplaced during the printing, or may fall out altogether and fail to print.

Major errors of overprint or surcharge are caused in the same way as are the errors we have considered in the case of stamps. A sheet which is put twice through the over-printing press will bear a 'double overprint' (or surcharge). If put in face downwards, it will be overprinted on the back, or it may, by some freak of fortune, be overprinted on the front and on the back. Fed into the press the wrong way round, the sheet will have an inverted overprint, and in the case of double overprints, if the second overprinting is done with the sheet the wrong way round, we shall have the overprint 'double, one inverted' as the stamp catalogues describe it. Triple and quadruple overprints are known, but when one reaches this stage suspicion of deliberate intent on the part of the printer begins to approach to certainty. Even the simpler errors are often the result of deliberate mistakes on the part of someone wanting to make money out of collectors, but there are naturally many instances of errors occurring through carelessness in printing and slack-ness in checking the printed sheets before issue.

Another important class of overprint or surcharge error is that in which the new inscription or device is applied to a sheet of the wrong stamp. This is a not infrequent happening nor is it a rare occurrence to find an overprint applied in ink of the wrong colour.

If a sheet of stamps is put through the press for over-printing, and care is not taken to 'register' it correctly in relation to the overprint plate or type, we get the kind of variety known as a 'misplaced overprint'.

If the misplacement is in the horizontal direction, we shall find the overprint falling either towards one side of the stamp instead of in the centre, or perhaps even on the junc-tion of two stamps, so that, instead of each stamp bearing a complete overprint, it is provided with two halves of an overprint. Such varieties, due to sideways misplacement, come in the 'freak' class, and rarely have any increased value; in fact in most cases collectors would prefer a normal overprint in the proper position on the stamp.

Similar misplacement in an upward or downward direc-tion, which results in the overprint being out of position, or partly on one stamp and partly on another, produces varieties of equal unimportance. If, however, we have a two-line overprint, reading, for example, 'WAR' in the upper line and 'TAX' in the lower, and this is misplaced vertically to a certain degree, we shall find that there are stamps in which the word 'TAX' is above the word 'WAR'. Such varieties receive rather more attention than the other misplacements already noted, but are still not of great importance.

If, however, the misplacement is such that one row of stamps misses the overprint altogether, we may obtain pairs of which one stamp has the overprint, and the other has not, and these are regarded as important, and often valuable, varieties. They may be caused either by vertical or by horizontal misplacement, and in such cases there will usually be an unwanted overprint on the marginal paper at the edge of the sheet opposite to that which has the row of unoverprinted stamps.

'Offsets' or 'blanket prints' of overprints are also found, and these sometimes produce the effect of a double overprint, but their character can usually be detected because of a lack of sharpness and detail in the offset overprint.

We must devote a few words to type-set surcharges or overprints, for comparatively few stamps have been printed from loose type, whereas quite a number of overprints and surcharges have been applied in this way. In setting up sufficient repetitions of an overprint or surcharge for a sheet of, say, one hundred stamps, it is likely that mistakes will occur. The order of letters may be transposed, a wrong letter or an extra letter may be inserted, or a wrong figure may be put in in the case of a date or surcharge. Such errors are worth looking for, and one is never quite sure what will turn up, for even if one has seen a complete sheet with a type-set overprint, and has been convinced that it contains no important errors or variations, it does not follow that there are not any errors in that particular overprint. The sheet inspected may have been one of the earliest of the printing.

At a later stage the type may have worked loose, and one or two letters have dropped out of some of the overprints, or stamps may be found with various letters of the overprint widely spaced. Later still, the printer notices the loosening of the type and, stopping the machine, he tries to put things right. The letters which have fallen out he can replace, but he may replace them by the wrong letter, or he may lock up without replacing them, giving rise to fresh errors or to new defective spacings. There is thus an infinity of variation possible in type-set overprints, and even where overprinting is done from a stereotyped plate, the stereotyping may have been done from handset type showing errors of various kinds which will, unless rectified on the plate, be repeated throughout the printing. Letters which are merely out of alignment are not regarded as important variations, nor are minor differences of spacing.

The point to bear in mind in regard to surcharge and overprint varieties is that letters showing damage or breakage are of no special importance or value, unless they conform to the freakish rule of collectors that by this breakage they are made to resemble closely some other letter, in which case they may be worth attention. The only other value of *small* defects in the lettering of surcharges and overprints is when they enable a setting to be 'plated' or divided into its types, with a view to ascertaining their original arrangement, or, more important still, when they enable us to distinguish between genuine overprints and forgeries, a matter in which the collector will also be assisted considerably by the colour and sheen of the ink used.

Another method of converting stamps to fresh uses consists in perforating them with lines of holes to form devices or letters. Thus the stamps of the Australian Commonwealth have been perforated 'o s' for official use, British stamps perforated 'b t' were used by the Board of Trade, and there are many other instances.

Not all initials of this kind are authorized, however, for many firms perforate their stamps with their own initials in order to prevent theft from their postage boxes. For the same reason, unofficial overprints have been applied to stamps, perhaps the most frequently met with being the word 'CAVE' on the stamps of Ceylon. These firms' overprints and initials have no philatelic interest and in fact often destroy the value of a stamp.

Chapter Nine

DESIGNS AND INSCRIPTIONS

A book could be written concerning the pictures and inscriptions which are to be found on stamps, and its scope would be nearly as wide as the story of the world. Stamp designs embrace every conceivable subject, from the king on his throne to the beggar by the roadside, and from the starry firmament to the depths of a coalmine, while the inscriptions are in a vast number of languages, and deal with as great a variety of subjects as do the pictorial designs.

In days when kings and princes were more plentiful than they are today, the normal subject for a stamp design in a monarchical state was the ruler's portrait. The lead given by Britain may have had something to do with this, but the practice was more probably based on the association of stamps with coins. A portrait had the added advantage that any alteration by way of forgery changed the expression of the face, and such a change was more likely to be detected than any other, as men and women are accustomed to noticing variations in human expression.

If the royal portrait was not used, the arms of the country or reigning house were often taken as a suitable symbol, though frequently they are incorrectly represented on the stamps. Armorial and portrait stamps are still plentiful today, but very few monarchs now figure on the world's issues, and the number is decreasing year by year. Most of the portraits, apart from rulers, are those of men and women to whom their country is giving the once high honour of representation on stamps.

The spread of various political and cultural ideas has

The 'Post Office'
Mauritius,
2d. blue

The 1d. and 2d. 'Post Office' Mauritius
used together on a letter

Mrs. Moses G. Ashton
271 County Street
New Bedford
Mass.

Frank

Personal Delivery

Official

Postage Due

Departmental

Telegraph

Special Delivery

Railway Parcels

Farmers' Parcels

Acknowledgment
of Receipt

Parcels

Late Fee

Military Post

Mourning

Marine Insurance

Plebiscite

Charity

Commemorative

War Tax

Mandated Territory

Special Fee

Occupation

Exiled Government

Savings Bank

Internal

Newspaper

Red Cross Due

Municipal

Air Post

The original sketch

Photograph supplied for details of motor and gear

Stamp-size design prepared for engraver

The finished stamp

Designing a stamp

By courtesy of Bradbury, Wilkinson & Co Ltd

Recess plate making — transferring the design

By courtesy of The De La Rue Co Ltd

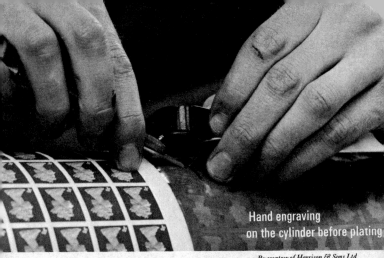

Hand engraving
on the cylinder before plating

By courtesy of Harrison & Sons Ltd

By courtesy of Harrison & Sons Ltd

102   Photogravure — delivery end of stamp printing machine

Zigzag roulette

Lozenge perforation

Arc roulette

Pin perforation

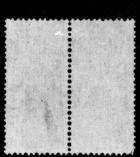

Roulette

Rouletted in colour

Interrupted perforation

Large and small holes

Larger holes in centre

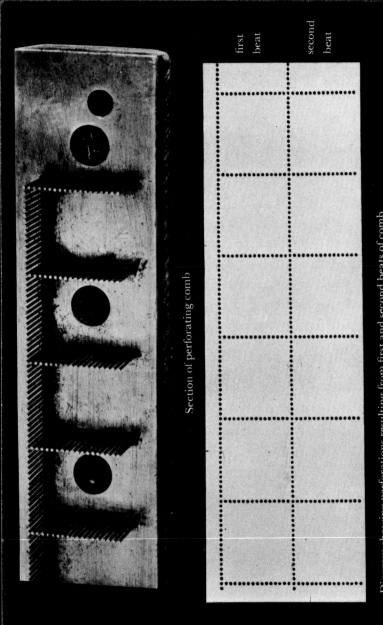

Section of perforating comb

first beat   second beat

Diagram showing perforations resulting from first and second beats of comb

also given rise to a host of allegorical and symbolical designs, while the advertising value of the postage stamp, and the interest shown by collectors in pictorial issues, has resulted in the production of large numbers of stamps bearing views of places, their inhabitants, industries, fauna, and flora. In the search for novelties to tickle the jaded palate of the collector, the whole field of history and a large proportion of the earth's surface have been drawn upon for subjects, until one wonders how countries can produce anything new – and still they do it.

Inscriptions on stamps cover such matters as the postal value of the stamp, its purpose, the country from which it comes, and sometimes the subject of its design, or the event in connexion with which it was issued. Overprints cover much the same field. The average collector is too often content to study the inscriptions only so far as they enable him to identify a particular stamp, but they are in many cases worthy of more than this superficial scrutiny.

Here is a stamp of Palestine, with lettering in English, Hebrew, and Arabic, typifying British rule holding the scales of justice evenly between Jew and Arab. On stamps of Russia inscriptions in Esperanto may be found, evidently intended to convey a message to a circle outside that country which could not be reached in the unfamiliar Russian characters. Other stamps of Russia, with inscriptions in three or four languages, indicate the wide area under Soviet rule.

Changes in stamp inscriptions are equally revealing. East India, of the Honourable East India Company, gives place to 'India' under the rule of the Queen-Empress. The Orange Free State changes its name after the Boer War to Orange River Colony. In Ceylon the adoption of Singhalese as the official language of that country in the face of violent Tamil opposition has been reflected in her stamp inscriptions. Where 'Ceylon' in English was formerly given greater prominence, the Singhalese version is now the most prominent, with the English and Tamil inscriptions in much smaller type. A recent innovation is the printing of stamps inscribed in Singhalese and Tamil alternately in the same sheet. The fateful word 'republic' appears on the issues of one country after another. So the story of the world is told.

Other changes are brought about by the granting of independence to British Commonwealth territories and the formation or dissolution of Federal alliances. Hence Gold Coast has become Ghana and the member countries of the former Rhodesia and Nyasaland Federation – Southern Rhodesia, Northern Rhodesia, and Nyasaland – have become respectively Rhodesia, Zambia, and Malawi. Tanganyika and Zanzibar have a political alliance as Tanzania, and North Borneo, a member of the Malaysia Federation, has become Sabah.

Sometimes mistakes occur in stamp inscriptions. Greece, on a stamp commemorating the Battle of Navarino, fell into the old trap, and described the British admiral as 'Sir Codrington', a mistake which was afterwards corrected. Stamps have appeared with a value figure denoting the singular, but with the word representing the coin, in the plural, e.g. '1 cents'. Spelling mistakes are not infrequent. (*see page 204*)

Thus there is no detail of the period of the printed portion of a stamp which may not tell the collector a story, even if he is not concerned with variations which have arisen in the course of printing. It is by learning to read such stories in the pages of his album that the owner of a collection extends his knowledge and keeps his enthusiasm alive.

Chapter Ten

STAMP COLOURS AND THEIR NAMES

THERE are several difficulties in connexion with the subject of stamp colours which the reader should appreciate before tackling the question in relation to his own collection, bearing in mind that the colour of a particular stamp may be of importance to him in the following ways:

(1) It may enable him to allot his specimen to a particular period or printing, thus fulfilling our first canon, that the stamps in a collection should tell us something of their own history, or else they really have no place there.

(2) It may be a guide or additional point of comparison when trying to decide whether a stamp is genuine, a forgery, or a reprint. It is also particularly helpful in the case of stamps which have been fraudulently cleaned.

(3) Though it may not have any importance historically, it may be one of those strikingly different shades to which collectors have come to give a special value, as compared with specimens of the same stamp in the more usual tones.

The difficulties in connexion with colours are these:

(1) There is no mechanism available to the average collector for measuring stamp colours scientifically. The majority of collectors have to rely on their eyes and appreciation of colour may vary, not only as between different individuals but even in a single person at different times, according to his state of health and the condition of his eyes.

(2) Even to a normal eye, the colour of a particular stamp will appear different according to the conditions under which it is viewed. It will appear one colour or shade in sunlight, another in a duller light, and perhaps something entirely different by various types of artificial light. (The 'daylight' lamp has gone far to overcome this last difficulty and the use of such a lamp is recommended to every stamp collector who wants to work on his albums by artificial light.)

Nor must the capacity of the eye for mixing colours be overlooked. After all, colour is only light, and light rays reaching the eye from various coloured surfaces, naturally mingle. Thus stamps should be compared under exactly the same conditions. Stamps printed in the same colour and shade will appear different if they are viewed against backgrounds of different colours. Similarly, in the case of stamps printed in two colours, you cannot accurately assess one colour without covering up the other, for your eye will mix them. Stamps with a heavy postmark appear darker in shade than unused or lightly postmarked stamps, for the eye mixes the black of the postmark with the colour of the stamp.

(3) Apart from distinct colours, the methods by which stamps are printed give rise in many cases to variations of tone which the collector calls 'shades'. Some of these variations arise during the course of a single printing, owing to inconsistency in the coloured ink which is used, or to unsuitable conditions of either temperature or humidity when the printed sheets are drying. Though the inks used are scientifically compounded, it may not be possible to get quite the same result with a second printing as was achieved on a former occasion. If the colour and shade of the first printing were consistent, then even a slight variation will enable stamps of the second printing to be identified, and here a variation in shade has a definite historical value which it does not possess when it occurs within a single printing.

Shades also occur through variations in the pressure with which the ink is applied to the sheet of paper during printing. The printer, before he finally starts his machine on its task, 'makes ready', as he calls it. This process, which in simple terms consists in making the printing surface of the plate or type meet the paper at a dead level all over, is achieved by placing packing, which may be only the thinnest of slips of paper, to give the desired even pressure.

If this is not done at all, or is done inaccurately, it is quite possible to have stamps of several shades (in this case depths of the same basic colour) in a single sheet, and though these may be sufficiently distinct to attract the eye, they have no historical importance.

Similarly, in the case of some of the earlier stamps, printed on hand-made paper, which varied in thickness even in a single sheet, these variations caused differences in shade.

(4) Apart from variations of colour or shade which occur in the course of manufacture, the collector has to be on his guard against changes which occur at later periods in the life of a stamp. These may be due to fading, caused by exposure to bright sunlight, or they may occur when stamps are kept in a hot, moist climate such as is found in the tropics.

Readers are familiar with the changes which occur in the colour of the paper of very old books, which often turns very yellow with age. Similar changes take place in the paper of some old stamps, with consequent alteration in their apparent colour, while the gum of many stamps also has its effect as time goes on.

There are possibilities of colour change through chemical action between the ink in which stamps are printed and the atmosphere. The early 'Penny Reds' of Great Britain may be found in an almost black colour on occasion, and other stamps printed in vermilion or other inks of a certain type also have this peculiarity of turning brown or black in course of time. Collectors apply the term 'oxidized' (probably inaccurately) to such stamps. They will revert to their original hues if brushed with peroxide of hydrogen, but do not let it touch the gum.

The action of water on stamp colours will be too familiar to the collector from painful experience, to need re-emphasizing here, though only a proportion of stamp colours are not 'fast' in water.

Then, too, there is the deliberate action of rogues who wish to defraud, either by changing the colour of a common stamp to that of a rarer one, or, particularly in modern times, by the creation of entirely new shades. This is done by the cunning use of chemicals and quite extraordinary results are obtained. It is always advisable to view with suspicion any hitherto unknown 'error of colour' that may be offered. Like prize animals for show purposes, they should have a pedigree before they can be regarded as valuable.

(5) Finally, the great drawback the collector will find in dealing with colours is that there is no recognized standard for naming them, so far as his hobby is concerned. Catalogues do not agree with each other, nor does one part of a catalogue agree with another, as they have probably been compiled by different persons at different periods and, without an absolute standard, discrepancies are inevitable. This applies to the Gibbons Catalogue, but Stanley Gibbons Ltd. have in recent years produced an excellent and popular Colour Guide, giving a basic 100 colours which they use wherever possible in describing at least modern issues.

The infinite range of shades would in any case render it impossible to find names for all possible tones and only some form of measurement by a scientific instrument, with its results expressed in numbers, could fully meet the case. There are such instruments, but they are beyond the reach of the ordinary collector.

The main practical difficulty in this connexion is met with when two shades are listed in a stamp catalogue, one being priced considerably higher than the other. There may, however, be intermediate shades, which the catalogue editor does not consider of sufficient importance to list. Without experience, or a definite standard of measurement, how is the collector to know that he is getting the rare shade and not an intermediate shade which has not the same value?

For practical purposes, and leaving aside the question of absolute identification, the reader may take the following description as a rough guide. Until stamp collectors get together, and produce a standard colour guide with agreed names for the colours shown in it, nothing more can be attempted. In reading what follows, however, it must be remembered that not every collector will be in agreement with what I suggest, and most certainly the colours given in catalogues and books on the hobby will differ in many instances from my descriptions.

If we regard the colour system as a circular railway, the main stations will, of course, be the primary colours, red, yellow, and blue. Midway between these we find colours produced by mixing equal quantities of two of them – orange midway between red and yellow, green between yellow and blue, and purple between blue and red. These colours are definite and should cause the reader no difficulty. Another writer adds to our list of definite colours olive, which is half orange and half green, slate, which is an equal blend of green and purple, and russet (a name not used by philatelists), which is half purple and half orange. Assuming the red, blue, and yellow colours in an ordinary paint-box to be truly compounded, some sort of elementary colour guide might be made by the reader, by laying down a wash of each, and of the necessary mixtures to show the secondary and tertiary colours so far described.

To return to our railway. Starting from the red station and going towards orange, we pass scarlet, a very bright pure red, vermilion, a red which is beginning to show traces of orange, orange-vermilion, and then we arrive at orange. As regards hyphenated names, such as the one just used, it must be remembered that in these the second is the predominant colour and the first the qualifying tendency. Thus orange-yellow is a yellow with something of orange in its composition, while yellow-orange is orange with a yellowish tone. The eye has to get accustomed to analysing colours to ascertain more or less accurately their proportions, if this system of colour naming is to be made use of.

These last-named colours are stages on our journey from orange towards yellow. On this section we also pass chrome, a very full, bright yellow, and lemon-yellow, which is yellow with some green in it, and thence we come to greenish yellow, yellow-green, and green. There is also a loop line from the yellows to the reds, which covers the brown group. At the yellow end of this loop we find bistre and yellow-brown, brown being the central station. Thence we find increasing amounts of red – a red-brown, chestnut (a very bright red-brown), and cinnamon, which is a duller red-brown, and then we find ourselves on the main line at red again.

From yellow-green we pass to grass-green, which may be taken as the standard green, and beyond this we begin to find traces of blue, in such shades as emerald and blue-green and turquoise, the latter being qualified as either turquoise-green or turquoise-blue according to the general tone.

There are side-tracks in the green section too, where the admixture of greys and browns gives us sage-green, olive-green, and olive, the latter being a brownish tone. Back towards blue again, we find that Prussian blue is a deepish blue, but one which shows traces of green, as compared with the pure 'Royal' blue. Colour names are rather lacking in this section, but we have cobalt, a greyish sky-blue, and ultramarine, which is used very erratically to describe shades from something approaching lilac, to a pure blue. In any case, however, ultramarine shows no green in its composition. Indigo is a very dark blue, which the paint-box will give by a liberal dosing of blue with black.

Going on from blue towards purple, we get violet-blue (with its deeper companion indigo-violet), blue-violet, and violet, all these showing more of a bluish character than reddish. Thence we come to lilac, and beyond it, in the direction of purple (i.e. with more red in its make-up), mauve, a very much misused name, which often covers any of the paler shades of purple. Proceeding we come to reddish-purple and purple, and thence we have a gradual decrease in the proportion of blue, in such shades as claret, lake, crimson-lake, crimson, and carmine, from which last we pass to carmine-red, and thence to our starting-point, pure red.

It is not, perhaps, so very difficult to see blue in the violets, or green in a lemon-yellow, but it sounds a contradiction in terms to say that we must train our eyes to look out for blue in the reds. If, however, you take a pure red, which is brick, and place beside it a stamp printed in carmine, your eye should be able to appreciate that in the latter there is a strain of blue.

There is another branch from the purples to the browns, which gives us brown-purple, purple-brown, plum, chocolate, and thence towards sepia.

I am afraid this railway journey of ours has done little more than give a general idea of the relations between the colours, and that not scientifically, but in the rough and ready way in which stamp collectors regard them. Until we establish some scientific basis for colour naming, collectors will have to do the best they can, remembering that colour-names are not of great importance, except to enable a distinction to be made between a common colour and a rare one, and even then, the names are so carelessly used by collectors that it is almost certain that experience, and not the name in the catalogue, will prove the best guide.

Chapter Eleven

STAMP SHEETS AND BOOKLETS

THE average stamp collector rarely sees a complete sheet of stamps, except perhaps for an occasional glimpse of one through the grille on the post office counter, but there are points of interest to be noted in connexion with these larger units.

As has already been said, stamps are printed in sheets containing a number of them which usually bears some relation to the coinage of the country of issue – a multiple of ten when the coinage is a decimal one, or of twelve when it is a question of shillings and pence, for example. For various reasons, these sheets are often subdivided into smaller sections, either by leaving blank, unprinted paper between each section, or by printing on the intervening paper some distinctive pattern or device. Such sub-divisions of a sheet of stamps are called 'panes', the intervening spaces 'gutters', and those round the outer edge of the sheet are known as margins.

Now the work of the stamp printer is a complex task, and he has found, in these margins, a very convenient place for making notes, while the postal authorities have also made use of the available space for various purposes. As the purposes of both printer and postal controller have to do with the printed sheet of stamps, each of them has had recourse to the method of making these 'notes' on the printing plate or stone, so that they are reproduced on each sheet of stamps that is printed. Thus the margins of sheets of early British stamps give particulars as to the cost of a single stamp or of a row of them, and remarks about the gum, which is described as 'cement'. The printer has added a 'plate number' on the marginal paper, this indicating the numerical order of the plate in the series made to print stamps of that particular denomination, while a 'current number' may also be found, which shows the position the plate holds in a general series which was not limited to stamps of one denomination, nor even to stamps of the mother country.

The plate number on the margin of the sheet must not be confused with the plate numbers for which collectors search, and which are incorporated in the design of each stamp of many of the earlier British issues. Modern Colonial stamps printed from standard key-plates also have plate-numbers in the margin, and it is thus possible to ascertain when a new plate has been brought into use for a particular stamp, when no detail of the stamps themselves is changed.

'Serial numbers', usually printed in black, run continuously through a printing, the first sheet being numbered '1' (or perhaps '0001'), succeeding sheets being numbered in sequence. These numbers are sometimes useful in determining a sequence of shades, but have no special value in themselves.

Numbers are not always used to indicate a different plate, for in some countries arbitrary signs are employed for this purpose, and in other cases dots or nicks are made in the 'jubilee lines' on the plate. These 'jubilee lines', so called because they were first noted by British collectors on the stamps of the Jubilee issue of 1887, are intended to take the shock of the inking rollers, and raise them to the level of the printing surface of the plate. Without such a protection, the edges of the stamp designs on the outer edge of the plate will have to do the lifting, and will wear away more quickly as a result. These lines appear on the sheet of stamps as lines of colour running parallel to the outer edges of the stamps. Where they run right round the sheet without a break, or with perhaps a small break at the corners of the sheet, they are termed 'continuous', but when they are broken into short lengths, equal to the length of the side of the adjacent stamp, they are called 'co-extensive'. On the typographic plate, the lines are, of course, ridges of metal, so that the printer can conveniently mark them with dots or scratches to convey to himself any message he likes concerning the plate and its history – a message which is often quite unintelligible to the collector.

When the Stamping Department at Somerset House took over some of the plates for printing the British King Edward VII stamps from Messrs. De La Rue & Co., the jubilee lines on the sheets printed by them showed mysterious markings which greatly intrigued collectors. These marks indicated approximate dates of printing, two cuts or dots under the last stamp of the bottom row of the sheet or pane representing 1912, while marks below the last stamp but one stood for 1911. In some cases there were also month cuts under the appropriate stamp.

Coloured dots are often printed on the margins of stamp sheets in order to facilitate registration of the paper in its correct position in relation to the plate. These dots are so placed that, when projections or pins on the machine pierce them, the sheet is known to be correctly placed.

The letters, or figures and letters, which appeared on the sheet margins of many modern British stamps until 1947, were known as 'control numbers' or more briefly 'controls'. These numbers were placed there for accountancy purposes, the figures having reference to the year and being prefixed by an index letter. Starting in 1884, only the $\frac{1}{2}d$. and 1d. of the Victorian and Edwardian issues have 'controls', but in the later reigns all values to the 1s. had them. They are collected either as single stamps with margin bearing the control attached, or in strips of three, or blocks of six, with bottom and side margin. The small figures on the margins of sheets of present-day British photogravure stamps indicate the cylinder (curved plate) from which the sheets were printed and are known as 'cylinder numbers'.

Some printers place their name below the design of each stamp in the sheet, and here also the name of the designer or engraver may sometimes be found. Other firms print their name on the sheet margin, when it is known as a 'printer's imprint'.

While the separation of a large sheet into panes facilitates the work of the post office clerk, enabling him to divide the sheet into quarters or halves, as required, many countries provide him with additional indications on the margins of the sheets. These may take the form of arrows or other marks, showing where the sheet has to be divided in order to obtain a desired fraction of it, or figures may be printed opposite each row of stamps, indicating the total cost of the stamps in the portion of the sheet if it is divided at that point. Blocks of U.S. stamps with marginal arrow are known as 'arrow blocks' while a block from the centre of a sheet, showing the intersection of vertical and horizontal dividing lines, is called a 'centre line block'.

If the number of stamps to be printed does not occupy the whole of the central surface of the sheet of paper used, it is customary to print on the blank portion some device which will prevent the paper being used by forgers, for their one desire is to obtain paper which will be sufficiently like that of the genuine stamps to pass muster, and unprinted paper as actually used would be a real windfall. The high values of the Russian arms types of the latest Tsarist and early revolutionary period have the intervals of the sheets printed with interlocking 'Vs'; Austria filled in gaps in her early sheets with a St Andrew's Cross, and these crosses, even unattached to the stamp, have a certain value in that country; while Britain, in the days when she charged a halfpenny for the privilege of buying stamps in booklets, omitted one stamp of that value from the book, and replaced it by a piece of paper of the same size, also printed with a cross – known as the 'kiss' stamp.

This mention of booklets brings us to another method of distributing stamps to the public. The great convenience of having stamps available in books containing a number of each of the denominations in most frequent use is now widely recognized, and many countries issue stamps in this way. Very often the booklet stamps are printed from special plates, arranged so that the resulting sheets may be cut up into 'pages' and bound mechanically, to give the desired number of stamps of each kind. In order to make up a booklet of the wished-for total, it is sometimes necessary to have an extra stamp of a particular denomination, and in Switzerland, Denmark, Germany, and other countries we find booklet pages from which we may detach a pair of stamps, one of which is in one colour and of one denomination and the other totally different.

Sometimes odd spaces are filled with advertisements or a printed device, as already mentioned. The special requirements of booklet printing often make it necessary that some of the stamps should be placed *tête-bêche*, in the special sheets, but usually booklet *têtes-bêches* are the result of the deliberate placing on sale of sheets printed for booklets, but not made up (as in the case of the first Union of South Africa 1½d. *têtes-bêches*), or of the leakage of booklet sheets from the printing works or stamp store (as happened with the British 1½d. King George V). It is this printing of sections of the booklet *sheets* (not pages) *tête-bêche* which give rise to the inverted watermarks in our British booklets, as mentioned in the chapter on errors and varieties.

Another way in which stamps are issued to the public is through the medium of automatic machines. Here the stamps have to be in coils or rolls, and at first these rolls were made up by joining together by hand strips of stamps taken from ordinary sheets. In early rolls, the overlapping joins may be noted, but nowadays the stamps for issue in rolls are printed in long strips and joining is not necessary. Where the rolls are sold at a post office, they are probably wrapped round with paper, attached to the stamp at the outer end, particulars of the contents and price of the roll being printed on this paper.

Complete sheets, particularly of the early issues of many countries, are of great interest, as they convey much information which cannot be gathered from a single stamp. Collecting in sheets is, however, a rich man's hobby, and the ordinary collector can only include such items when they come his way at a low cost.

In Germany during the inflation period of 1922–3, the margins of the stamp sheets were sold to business firms, who had the privilege of having their announcements printed on them – a novel form of publicity which gives such sheets a curious interest. A similar practice has been adopted in South Africa but there the announcements are usually of a national character. Advertisements also appear on the margins of the pages of French stamp booklets.

Chapter Twelve

THE OTHER SIDE OF THE STAMP

(For illustrations to this chapter see page 205)

We have already mentioned two characteristic features of a postage stamp, for which the collector has to examine its back – the gum and the watermark – while the paper is also best scrutinized from the unprinted side.

The back of the stamp is sometimes well worth attention, however, apart from any question of paper, gum, and watermark. Look at the back of any stamp of the St Anthony of Padua commemorative series, issued by Portugal in 1895, and you will find a Latin prayer printed on it – a feature which makes this issue unique. Fiume has also printed inscriptions or designs on the back of stamps, the word 'posta di fiume' on the back of the issue of May 1919, and the snake and stars badge of D'Annunzio's 'Arditi' on the back of the higher values of the 'Reggenza Italiana de Carnaro' series of 1920.   In such cases, the printing on the back of the stamps is probably an attempt to provide a substitute for a watermark, which would necessitate an additional operation by the forger before he could produce stamps which would pass muster.

Sometimes there is a definite attempt to imitate a watermark by a printed device, as in the case of certain New Zealand stamps of 1925. Experiments were being made with papers of various kinds and, in a temporary emergency, stamps normally printed on paper watermarked 'NZ and Star' were issued on paper with the same device faintly lithographed on the back.

Another purpose for which stamp backs have been employed is advertising. In Great Britain the idea never went beyond the experimental stage, but those who like curiosities may still find unused $\frac{1}{2}d$. and $1d$. Victorian stamps with the words 'PEARS' SOAP' printed on the back. In New Zealand stamp advertisements were actually permitted for some time and the Queen's portrait series of 1882–97 may be found with a variety of advertisements on the backs of its stamps, some of them even being illustrated.

Advertising has been brought into contact with stamps in other ways. In Italy a scheme was put into practice of issuing certain postage stamps to which was attached an advertisement, which may be said to have formed an integral part of the stamp as there was no perforation between stamp and announcement. The idea was soon dropped, as it met with the objection which has wrecked most of these postal advertising schemes, whether by stamp, or by postmark – that a manufacturer or business man might find his correspondence going out franked or postmarked with publicity for a rival firm.

Belgium has also experimented with stamps with advertisements attached, and in the British stamp booklets there have been small perforated squares of paper, of the size of a stamp, which bear an announcement of some kind.

Returning to the backs of our stamps, we find that, in times of stress and difficulty, materials quite out of the normal have been used to print stamps on. Thus, as already mentioned, the first stamps of Latvia were printed on the backs of a large stock of German military maps, owing to shortage of paper. Cigarette paper was also used for one issue and Bolshevik bank notes with inscriptions calling on the proletariat of the world to unite, but the stamps printed on wall-paper and on jam-jar labels are the result of an attempt to exploit the popularity of the war-map issue, and are not official productions.

In Lithuania, under similar conditions, the paper used during the war for ration tickets was employed for stamp printing, while in Oaxaca, Mexico, during a revolution, post office forms were printed on.

Perhaps the strangest case was that in which the back of a stamp became the front. From 1910 to about 1912, Nicaragua was hard put to it to maintain supplies of stamps. Presumably funds were not available to pay for printing a new issue in the United States or in Britain, whence previous definite issues had come, and for a time fiscal stamps were provided with surcharges which converted them into postage stamps. When supplies of these failed, the authorities turned out a stock of railway stamps and considered how they could convert these for postal use, the difficulty being that they already bore a surcharge converting them to fiscal use, on the front. But the Nicaraguan mind was by that time fertile in expedients, so a postal surcharge was added to the back of the stamp, which had thus been in turn a railway stamp, a fiscal, and a postage stamp.

Among the stamps of Russia listed in the catalogues under dates between 1915 and 1917 are some which are printed on card paper, and with an inscription on the back. These are actually paper coins, rather than stamps, for they were intended for use as small change, though the designs on the face of them are similar to those of the postage stamps in use at the time. A few have been found used on letters, but it is doubtful whether they have any right to be regarded as postage stamps. There was a similar use of stamps as coins in France and other countries during the 1914–18 war, but in these cases ordinary stamps were enclosed in small containers with transparent sides. Rhodesian stamps were also once used for money, in a time of emergency, being stuck on cards bearing the fiat of the local authorities that they should be accepted as change.

If the backs of stamps are always examined with the same care as is given to their faces, it will be found that there are other interesting points to be noted from time to time. A stamp whose back is of special interest may be hinged face downward to the album page, or enclosed in a small transparent envelope, so that both sides may be seen.

Chapter Thirteen

POSTMARKS AND OBLITERATIONS

THE official definition of a postmark is 'Any mark struck upon letters, etc., passing through the post. A special postmark employed for defacing stamps is more properly termed an *obliterating mark*.' The word 'obliteration' is an alternative term.

The term 'cancellation' is also frequently applied where 'obliterating mark' would be more correct, for though an obliteration is a cancellation, a cancellation need not necessarily be an obliteration, as the definition includes any kind of mark or defacement applied to a stamp, etc., to prevent its being used (or re-used) for its original purpose. Thus a fiscal penmark, the 'SPECIMEN' overprint, the 'cancelled to order' bars of Labuan and Borneo, and the bars printed across, or holes punched in the stamps of Spain, are equally cancellations while none of them are either postmarks or obliterations.

Postmarks of various kinds were in use long before the adhesive stamp was thought of, and there is quite a respectable number of collectors of what are termed 'prestamp covers' which are often quaint in appearance and of historical interest.

Postmarks may tell the place of origin and the destination of a letter; they may indicate the route or method by which a missive is to be carried; they may have reference to the weight of it, or to the amount chargeable for carrying it, or as a fine if a proper sum has not been prepaid and, most important of all to the stamp collector, they may tell the date on which the letter was dispatched.

Putting on one side the various marks which convey general information, let us consider for a moment the two essentials of the modern postmark and their value to the collector. These features are date and the place of origin of the letter, and if, in addition to the postmark of departure, there is an arrival postmark giving the destination and the date on which it was reached, the student can ask for little more in the way of valuable evidence as to the use of that individual stamp. An envelope with an arrival postmark on the back is said to be 'backstamped'.

The date is usually given quite clearly in the average postmark, sometimes with the hour of the particular mail in addition. Even where no date is given, however, the form or size of the particular mark employed may give an approximate dating, if research has proved that such a mark was not in use until a certain period.

The place of posting may be indicated clearly in words, or it may be shown by a code in which figures or letters stand for a particular office. Such were the early postmarks of Great Britain with their figures, or letters and figures, in a frame of bars. For a time some of these obliterations were assigned to British post offices in overseas colonies and in foreign countries and this has given rise to the study of British stamps 'used abroad', these being identified by the postmark. (*see page 202*) It should be noted that at a later period some of the obliterators which had been used abroad were re-allotted to offices at home, so that it is only when they are found on certain issues that their overseas use can be proved.

In some postmarks, the portion which obliterates the stamp contains the details of place and date, while in others, there are two sections, an obliteration (or 'killer'), either of bars or some other suitable pattern, and a portion, intended to fall on the envelope, and therefore to be more legible, which will give the place and date of posting. There are, however, many types of postmark which are solely obliterations.

There is an infinite range of variety in the patterns both of obliterations and place-and-date marks, and many collectors nowadays are paying more attention to the study of these than they do to the actual stamps. Where there is a series of numbered postmarks indicating the various post offices of a country, it is quite an interesting study to try to find out from old postal notices, etc., to which offices the various numbers were allotted, and then to try to complete the series of numbers on stamps or entire covers. If documentary evidence is not available, then the information must be acquired gradually from the envelopes and letters themselves.

There is also a fascination in studying the changes in postmarks, which frequently have an historical interest. An examination of the postmarks on the early stamps of Lombardy-Venetia (sometimes called Austrian Italy) will show the extent of Austrian domination in Italy prior to the creation of the Italian kingdom. During and after the war of 1914–18, many postmarks were altered, at first temporarily, and then by replacement, as German colonies came into other hands, or when a new state sprang from the ruins of an old one, and insisted on having even its postmarks in its own language and not in that of its former masters, and similar changes are occurring today.

Early cancellations are also collected for their quaint form, while there is a bias, even among stamp collectors, in favour of postmarks and cancellations in colours not normally used. Thus a collector will pay more for a red postmark of a type which was usually applied in black, though why the fact that a clerk happened to use the wrong ink pad should have any particular significance is not stated.

To the philatelist, who is studying *stamps*, or postal history, the postmark is valuable as evidence. If he does not know the date of issue of a stamp, he is always on the lookout for dated postmarks, and if he finds an 'early date' earlier than any yet known, he is correspondingly triumphant. Absolute reliance cannot be placed on a single dated copy, however, for the dates in most postmarks are composed of loose pieces of type inserted into the hand stamp used for cancelling, and it is quite easy for mistakes of transposition to occur. If there is a postmark of the place of arrival (and this is usually found on the back of the envelope) this will serve as a check on that of departure. It will also indicate the length of time taken on the voyage, while, if postmarks of intermediate places are also present, it is possible to work out the route followed by the particular mail. All this information is very helpful to a student who is trying to build up the history of a stamp issue, and to find out the conditions under which it was used. Postal markings giving information other than place and date of posting are also extremely helpful on occasion, and it is this informative value which was the chief cause of the modern cult for collecting entire covers, though, as in other directions, the zeal of the collector sometimes outruns discretion, and he includes with covers of real value others which tell him practically nothing.

A close study of postmarks is very helpful to the expert. Some rare errors were only used at a particular place so that all copies that are genuine must have the postmark of that place – a fact which the forger often does not know. On other occasions he ignores the fact that at the time when a certain stamp was in use, a particular type of postmark had not yet been introduced, so that he frequently produces fakes with a cancellation which immediately 'gives the game away' to the collector who has studied postmarks.

Another opportunity is provided for the stamp detective when the forger has tried to apply an overprint or surcharge to a used stamp – a frequent practice of the less skilful of these rogues. His overprinting will naturally lie over the postmark – not always an easy thing to see, but when seen, a definite proof of faking, as, in the life-story of any respectable stamp, overprinting always *precedes* postmarking!

Stamp collectors are creatures of prejudice, and in spite of all that can be written in the philatelic press, certain opinions persist from generation to generation. One of these is that a violet postmark or cancellation is necessarily a proof that a stamp has been used fiscally (i.e. on a bill, or other legal or commercial document, and not on correspondence). As a matter of fact, many countries, particularly in South and Central America, use violet ink regularly for postal cancellations and it must therefore be clearly understood that it is the form and not the colour of the postmark that matters, though violet ink is used so frequently for fiscal markings that its presence on a stamp may certainly afford a warning.

In the same way, the practice of writing across stamps used on receipts and similar documents has given rise to the belief that *all* stamps in any way penmarked are fiscally used. Here again, the collector is wrong, for in several countries there was a period when postmarking was done with pen and ink – on the early issues of Venezuela for example. (*see page 202*) Even now, in times of emergency, handwritten cancellations are resorted to, and these are naturally of special interest, and so the collector who at once spurns any penmarked stamp may be missing something of value.

It is necessary to be quite clear on this subject of fiscal versus postally used stamps. There is a good deal to be said for the point of view that a stamp of dual usage is collectable as a postage stamp only when it can clearly be seen to have been used postally (or in unused condition, in which state it is potentially a postage stamp), and it is this attitude which is responsible for the rejection of fiscally-used stamps by the majority of collectors. Against this, from the average collector's point of view, is the fact that many stamps, quite beyond his reach in unused or postally used condition, are easily obtainable with some form of fiscal cancellation. May he not take them as space-fillers? If I were a general collector, I certainly would take penmarked fiscally cancelled stamps when I knew that I could never get the right thing, rather than have a blank space in my album. Those who see my album will at least know what the missing stamp looks like, and an honest note, 'fiscally used', will save the owner from any charge of ignorance or intent to deceive. I would not, however, include common stamps, fiscally used, for these will come along, sooner or later, in the proper postal condition.

A word of warning is necessary to those who decide to take the rather unorthodox step suggested in the last paragraph. Stamps fiscally used are usually not worth anything like as much as postally used specimens, nor are they to be compared with unused stamps. If you fill spaces with fiscal specimens, they must be very cheap, or you are wasting money. We shall see how fiscally-used stamps are converted into unused, in our chapter on faking and forging.

There is a less reasonable prejudice in the minds of advanced collectors against stamps used telegraphically, i.e. which are stuck on telegraph forms or receipts for telegraphic fees instead of on a letter or parcel. Many of these bear the ordinary postmarks, and are indistinguishable from stamps which have paid for other postal services, but in some cases a distinction can be drawn, by means of the shape or wording of the cancellation. Frankly I cannot see why any prejudice should exist against stamps used on telegrams. A telegram is a message just as much as a letter, and its transmission is an entirely postal service. There is a story of the early days of the telegraph, about an old lady who wanted her son in a distant town to receive a pair of boots very urgently – so she hung them on the telegraph wires, and waited for them to move off! Presumably if telegram forms were hung on the wires, even if they refused to move, our pundits would allow that the stamps which franked them were collectable.

The group of stamps specially issued for use on telegrams by certain countries was jettisoned from our British stamp catalogues solely for reasons of space, but it still figures in some Continental catalogues and albums, and with good logical reason. Why then should we refuse to receive stamps whose postmarks show them to have paid telegraphic fees?

My advice to the collector is that he should try and know as far as possible when he is admitting telegraphically-used stamps into his collection, but, apart from being able to recognize them, he should give them house room on the same footing as postally used specimens.

There is another class of cancellation against which the collector may care to be on his guard, though here he will have only a mild prejudice to contend with if he decides that a space filled cheaply is better than a blank. Stamps 'cancelled to order' are those which have been postmarked or obliterated, not in the ordinary course of post, but in bulk, either because the purchaser of them wishes to have them in used condition, or in order to prevent them being used for postage.

It sometimes happens, though now, fortunately, less frequently than of old, that a government decides to sell its surplus stocks of stamps withdrawn from circulation. The natural outlet is the stamp collector – the natural channel the dealer. It may not be convenient for the postal authorities of the country concerned to demonetize (i.e. to forbid the postal use of) the supplies of these stamps held by the public, yet if they sell their stamp 'remainders' at less than their face value, while they are still available for postage, they are simply going to lose revenue, for the stamps will be used to pay postage instead of going comfortably out of the way into the albums of collectors. It is often the practice, therefore, to cancel the stamps in some way, usually with some form of postmark, before handing them over to the dealer who buys them.

Cancellations of this nature may be easily recognized as in the case of the later issues of Borneo and Labuan, where a cancellation of bars was used which, though employed as a proper obliterator in earlier times, was not in *general* use during the currency of the issues to whose remainders it was applied. On the other hand, when the authorities decided to sell remainders of certain issues of Rhodesia, they cancelled them with town postmarks such as were in use when the stamps were in current use, and arranged the dates of the postmarks to correspond.

Specimen sets of current stamps sold to collectors by the Australian postal authorities were lightly postmarked before sale and some stamps are commoner thus than when postally used.

It is nearly always possible to tell a cancelled-to-order stamp from one postally used in the ordinary course, for the latter has undergone vicissitudes which leave their mark upon it, while the pseudo-used stamp looks clean and fresh and its postmark is probably clear and neat – *and* in many cases, the stamp will have its gum.

Remaindering of issues is not now so frequent as it used to be. It is a sign that a country puts money before its national honour, for stamps, until demonetized, are, in effect, government securities – promises to perform certain services on presentation of the stamp as proof that payment has been made. Demonetization is only carried out after due warning, so that the public can exchange their stamps for others still available for use, and thus the man-in-the-street receives fair play. But what of the stamp collectors? Whether they will admit it or not, most governments (and certainly those which stoop to the practice of remaindering their issues) rely on stamp collectors to help them to balance their postal budgets. They charge the collector full value for stamps when they are issued and then, when they want to put out another set in order to draw more money from him, they have the effrontery to annul the value of what they have already sold him, by putting their surplus supplies on the market at a fraction of what he paid. Small wonder that such countries are not in high favour with collectors.

It must not, however, be assumed by the collector, when he buys a packet or set of stamps which contains cancelled-to-order stamps, that the vendor is trying to take advantage of him. Stamps of this kind are regarded as saleable and

collectable, and it must be remembered that cancelled remainders are nearly always cheaper than the same stamps
either unused, or postmarked in the course of post.

Attention must also be drawn to stamps which, while
apparently cancelled to order, owe this appearance to a
special feature of the postal service. The Netherlands had a
system by which, when correspondence was posted in bulk,
it was not necessary to put a stamp on each item, but the
total postage due on the whole lot was reckoned, and the
sender had only to hand in sheets of stamps to the total
value, for cancellation. Naturally he handed in stamps of
high face value, for he received them back after they had
been postmarked, and he was then able to sell them to
collectors. Here, there is no suggestion of double-dealing.
The stamps, even if they were not affixed to letters, have
been cancelled in the ordinary routine of the postal service,
and are as much genuinely postmarked as if they had
franked a letter from Holland to the East Indies. The result
of the system was that the collector got his high value
modern Dutch stamps in used condition much more cheaply
than he would otherwise have done, the man who posted
the batch of correspondence got part of his money back,
and everybody was happy.

Mention of this method of paying postage brings us to
another system, also used for saving time, when correspondence is posted in bulk. Postmarking the stamps on a
batch of thousands of circulars or letters occupies a great
deal of time and therefore someone thought of the 'pre-
cancel'. (*see page 202*) This is, in effect, a cancellation of
some kind *printed* on the stamp before it is sold to the public.
As the stamps are already cancelled before they are stuck
on the letters, the time of the postal clerks is saved and
economy achieved. Certain safeguards are necessary, however, for obviously there is always a possibility that pre-
cancelled stamps which have once been used, may be rescued
and used again – in fact frauds of this kind on a large scale
were detected in the United States at one time.

Another method of dealing with big lots of circulars and correspondence, all of which have to be franked at the same rate, is by an automatic franking machine. No stamp is necessary. The sender simply hands in his batches of letters, etc., to the post office, agrees with them the number, and the amount of postage payable on each, and pays down a lump sum in settlement. The whole batch is then run through a machine which prints a frank on the envelope which will bear some such legend as 'Paid 3*d*.' and the date, time and place of posting. (*see page 202*)

Postmark and stamp also meet together in the machines which are now supplied to large commercial firms in many countries. These take the form of a kind of postage-meter, which is set by the local post office to provide a given value of franking, and is then locked, and handed over to the firm using it. By working a lever it is possible to impress on correspondence a device indicating that postage of a given amount has been paid, together with the date of posting, and some index letter or number which shows which machine made the device. Correspondence thus franked causes no further trouble to the post office, save that the weight has to be checked to see that the correct postage has been indicated. When the meter runs down, i.e. when it has franked letters to the value for which it was set, it is taken to the post office for re-setting, when a further sum is paid for the franking it will do on its next run. Collectors apply the term 'meter-mail' to correspondence dealt with as described above.

Sometimes these office franking machines are so arranged that they will print an advertisement of the firm which uses them on the envelope or wrapper, in addition to the frank and postmark. This is only a development of the practice inaugurated by many governments, when using mechanical methods of postmarking, to incorporate in the machine some announcement or advertisement, which is thus printed on correspondence at the time of postmarking.

These advertising or 'slogan' postmarks cover a very wide

field. They are peculiarly appropriate for postal announcements, but they are also used for general government
propaganda on such subjects as voting at elections, keeping
Sunday, using the telephone, investing in loans, wise farm-
ing, careful driving, and a host of other matters. They are
employed too for announcements regarding the charms of
health resorts, the holding of exhibitions, fairs and fêtes,
appeals for charitable funds and notices of important forth-
coming events.

Postmark advertisements of commercial firms have been
tried and proved unpopular for the same reason as advertisements attached to stamps – the announcement of one firm
too frequently went out on the correspondence of a rival.

Another type of postmark deserving of attention is that
which indicates that no postage is payable, and which
therefore takes the place of a stamp. Many governments use
such franking postmarks in their various offices.

Some collectors make a point of securing an envelope
bearing a copy postmarked on the day of issue of every new
stamp of their pet country. This craze for 'first-day covers'
has nothing to recommend it, as the dates of issue of
modern stamps are usually recorded in the Press, so such
covers have no value as evidence for future generations.

Altogether the study of postmarks is very interesting, and
may well be taken up as a side-line, but to the stamp
collector who works on orthodox lines, postmarks will only
appeal in so far as they provide him with evidence of time,
place, or route, which cannot be obtained from the stamps
themselves.

Chapter Fourteen

FORGERIES, REPRINTS, AND FAKES

In case anyone should be deterred from taking up stamp collecting by knowledge of the existence of forgeries, let me say here what I am going to repeat again at the end of this chapter, that the inexperienced collector can collect on normal lines, and amass a collection of thousands of stamps, and never see a forgery. It is, of course, essential that, even in his 'cheap packet' days, he should not try to get something for nothing, or at least for half its market value, for it is this greed which exposes collectors of all classes to the wiles of the forger and faker. So long as they are content to pay a fair price to one of the many reliable firms, instead of playing into the hands of cheapjack advertisers, who either sell fakes deliberately, or else have not even the knowledge to distinguish forgeries, and therefore cannot protect their customers, they will be safe; but let them, lacking knowledge and experience, try to build up a collection on bargain-hunting lines, and their experience will be that of an old man (only one of thousands like him) who once offered me a collection, having spent hundreds of pounds on his 'bargains', which he thought were worth double what he paid for them. Actually he asked £250 for his treasures, and the market value, on the most liberal scale, was £15! If he had put the same energy into studying his stamps and finding out whom it was safe to buy from, as he had into rushing to rogues to hand them his hard-earned money, he would have had a collection of considerable value to show for his outlay.

Before going any further, let us clear the ground of one or

two excrescences, and then turn to consider the main classes of undesirable stamps.

There are many labels which creep into stamp collections which are not really postage stamps at all. Such is the Finnish 'mourning stamp', which shows brightly coloured arms of Finland on a black ground; such are the Sinn Fein labels of Ireland; while many are no better than matchbox labels.

More interesting are those labels which purport to be postage stamps but are not – 'bogus' stamps. In the early days of the hobby, when communications were not so well organized, and dealers had not their sources of information in every country, it was a fairly frequent occurrence for attempts to be made to market the stamps of a mythical kingdom, or at least of a place which was very unlikely to need postage stamps.

In *Phantom Philately*, by the late Fred. J. Melville, the collector will find details of many of these bogus stamps, and the story of some of them is most interesting. There is, for example, the series for Brunei, which you will find listed in no general stamp catalogue, simply because it was engineered by a European on the spot, who was quite willing to sell these stamps to dealers, without mentioning the fact that there was at the time no postal service for which they could possibly be used. Bogus issues were made for Clipperton Island, Sedang, and Trinidad (an island in the South Atlantic), for the two last-named by persons claiming to be kings of the respective territories. Needless to say, they had no more right to the title than their labels had to be called stamps.

Perhaps the most famous 'bogies' in the old days were the stamps of Moresnet, for they never existed. A certain leading dealer on the Continent, who published a very good stamp magazine, was extremely annoyed by the fact that other journals frequently lifted large slabs of his exclusive news about the latest stamps, and did not have the courtesy to make any acknowledgment of the source of their information. One month his magazine listed, described, and illustrated a new issue for the state of Moresnet. The details were most circumstantial, in spite of the fact that a little enquiry would have shown readers of the notes that, even if Moresnet existed at all, it was not likely to issue stamps, and so the next numbers of a dozen or so Continental stamp magazines all listed the new issue – and were promptly black-listed by the dealer as stealers of news. He added that they could not possibly have got their information from any other source than his magazine, for the stamps only existed in his own imagination!

On the fringe of the 'bogus' groups are the so-called 'Sun Gate' stamps of Bolivia. An archaeologist interested in the Inca ruins of Tiahuanaco planned a series of stamps which, when fitted together, would represent the famous 'Sun Gate' there. He came to Europe and had the stamps printed, flaming in bronze and gold, and very impressive they looked. Unfortunately he forgot to obtain the authority of the Bolivian Government and, still more unfortunately, he told his scheme to some people in the stamp trade and sold them some of his 'stamps'. The philatelic press at once denounced them as an unauthorized issue, and the Bolivian Government disowned them, but any collector who is able to obtain a set will have a very striking page in his album.

A forgery is an imitation of a stamp, surcharge, or overprint, made to deceive either the postal authorities or what is now more profitable, the collector. (*see page 208*) Forgery on a scale sufficient to make profits by deceiving the post office is now only occasionally practised, but in the early days of postage stamps it was quite frequent. It is a rather natural fashion to despise forgeries, but many stamp specialists now include all forgeries in their collections, for comparison with the genuine stamps, while forgeries of the older stamps, which have actually passed through the post, are in many cases very much more valuable than the genuine stamps they imitated.

A very interesting type of forgery is that made by the

secret service of a country at war, in order to frank letters or propaganda material posted in enemy territory. In the First World War stamps of Germany and Bavaria were forged by the British authorities; while in the more recent conflict the United States authorities are said to have imitated the German Hitler head stamps and the French resistance movement used forged stamps of France. It would come as no surprise to learn that the British also repeated their exploits of the 1914–18 period.

On the German side some very crude imitations of British stamps were made – not for postal use, but for sale to collectors in neutral countries. The Soviet 'hammer and sickle' device was cleverly worked into the designs, while some stamps were overprinted with the names of the air bases leased to the United States. The whole thing was so childish that it is difficult to imagine any sensible reason behind the effort.

A reprint is on rather a different footing from the forgery for it is printed from the original plate, block or stone from which the 'originals' were printed, but after the issue of them had ceased. (There are some exceptions, where an original die has been used to construct fresh lithographic stones from which posthumous printings have been made.)

In early times, it was not thought to be wrong to make fresh printings from the plates, after the stamps had gone out of use. Those mad stamp collectors want them, and there are no originals available. Let's make some more. And they did! Not many collectors appreciated the difference in those days, as can be seen from the collections which were formed at the time.

Sometimes the plates were sold to a dealer with the remaining stocks of a withdrawn issue ('remainders'), and then he went on gaily printing reprint after reprint as needed. The Seebeck reprints of the 1890s are notorious, but there are others among quite modern stamps. Compared with earlier times, however, the practice of reprinting is not general, as most countries look after their plates and stones, and would as soon permit anyone to make un-authorized printings of banknotes as of stamps.

Just as the growth of scientific stamp study has given a value to forgeries intended to deceive the post, so it has given a value to many reprints, and particularly those made by governments for official purposes. It sometimes happens that the postal authorities of a country are asked for complete sets of all their old stamps, perhaps for a museum or for some monarch who is visiting their own king or emperor. Search is made, but no stocks are to be found of many of them, but here are the plates. And so the plates are put to press again, and an official set of reprints comes into being. It will be appreciated that reprints are in many cases easier to obtain than the original stamps, and where they are printed from the original plates or stones, they provide valuable material for purposes of study, whether they are from official or unofficial printings. Most specialized collections worthy of the name, therefore, include all known reprints for comparison with the genuine stamps.

Under the heading of fakes may be classed all those attempts to deceive which have at least a part of a genuine stamp as their basis. The most popular methods of faking today are cleaning and repairing.

Cleaning is mainly directed to taking out pen or fiscal cancellations with chemicals, either leaving the stamp in the resulting (more or less) 'unused' condition, or else going a stage further and providing it with a forged postmark.

Repairing is carried out with the object of improving the condition of a stamp. The craze for wide margins on imperf. stamps renders it a profitable game to take a stamp with little or no margin, and to graft lovely wide margins on to it. The work is most delicately done, and is quite imperceptible in most cases until an expert sense is acquired. The early stamps of Ceylon in the octagonal shape are frequently provided with new corners in this way, as these were so often cut to shape in the old days in order to fit the spaces in stamp albums of the period.

If the stamp that is defective is a perforated one, margins will be added and perforated, though it is not easy to imitate a particular gauge and style of perforation satisfactorily.

If there is a thin spot in the paper of the stamp, or even a hole, your repairer will fill the deficiency, even to the extent of painting in the missing portion of the design on the paper with which he patches the hole.

There are numerous variations of the faker's art, which in some cases amount to partial forgery. Thus, in the standard key-type stamps of the British Colonies, one value may be very rare. A stamp of a similar colour, in the same type but perhaps of a different denomination, or from another colony, has the inscriptions removed, and the result is a genuine design, with blank spaces into which the rogue paints the inscriptions of the rare stamp. He has overcome the difficulty of imitating the genuine paper by using an actual stamp as his basis. In some cases the faker will bleach out the whole of the design of a stamp and will print a new one on the resulting piece of blank paper, which will itself be genuine, and have a genuine watermark and genuine perforations.

Faking of rare colours is not difficult in these days of chemical knowledge. A rare shade may be produced from a common one, or colours can be changed entirely, from violet to grey, red to brown, or even more strikingly. Therefore, beware of uncatalogued 'errors of colour' or of rare shades offered to you from a doubtful source, or at a very low price.

Watermarks can be faked when their presence is necessary, either to confirm the 'genuineness' of a forgery, or to add to the value of a stamp that is common without the watermark. Many forged watermarks are made by pressure, in which case they show clearly when the back of the stamp is looked at, but when it is looked *through*, the watermark is not transparent.

A faker who wants to make a really good job of it will

thin the paper down very carefully by scraping, thus producing the characteristics of a true watermark. The results of his work should be easily visible under a microscope, however, for the fibres of the paper will be broken.

Many postmarks are keenly sought for nowadays, and the forger has quite a profitable time imitating these, while overprints and surcharges have, of course, always been fair game to him.

It must not be thought, however, that the odds in favour of the forger and faker are at all heavy. He has no difficulty in producing his wares, in fact it is probably easier, with modern methods, to produce fairly good forgeries and fakes than it ever was in the past. On the other hand, the knowledge and equipment of the expert collectors and dealers is more complete than at any earlier period, and, after many years of reliance on experience supplemented by an intuition which was often the result of experience, the experts are turning to science for help, and are using instruments which have made the work of the forger very much more difficult to market. Apart from this, collectors are in much closer touch with sources of information as to new forgeries through the Philatelic Press and the societies.

The value of a good information service is, however, largely negatived by the ostrich-like attitude of some dealers and collector experts. The former think that if information about forgeries is given in their papers, collectors will be afraid to buy stamps, while the latter seem to be of the opinion that the enemy will be helped if details of his work are published. Personally, I consider both these standpoints mistaken. The collector who wanders in the dark without any information about forgeries is the one who is going to get scared, whereas if, from magazines or books, he can learn to identify forgeries, he will be much better able to protect himself, and will feel safer to that extent. As for the forger, it is true that if *all* the details wherein his work differs from the genuine article were published, he might be assisted to improve his next batch of fakes, but it is not necessary to publish all, and the skill of the experts is sufficient to enable them to identify each lot of forgeries as it comes on the market, and then a salient identification feature of each may be published, and the public properly protected.

With the intensive knowledge of specialist collectors and dealers, backed by the instruments now at their disposal, the forger is not beaten, but he is held, and if proper use is made of the organizations which carry on this expert work, the collector need have little to fear.

To detect a forgery of an entire stamp should not be difficult, provided that a genuine stamp is available for comparison. It is not hard to imitate the design of a stamp with fair accuracy, but apart from this, the paper, colour, and (in the case of unused stamps) gum, also have to be accurately reproduced, and this is not so easy. In forging used stamps, a postmark has to be applied, and we have already seen in the previous chapter how the forger is likely to go wrong in this direction.

Forged overprints and surcharges are not always easy to detect, for the basic stamp is usually genuine, and only the ink and the shape and spacing of the lettering are available for comparison. Measurements of the various parts of the overprint with a graduated rule, or screw-adjustment compass, will sometimes serve to identify a forgery, but you must, of course, first be certain that there is no variation in the genuine overprint. Examination of the colour and appearance of the ink is often helpful. The depth may vary, and the ink may be shiny instead of dull, or rough instead of smooth. All such differences will provide grounds for suspicion.

There is one instrument now much used by experts – the quartz lamp – which uses the ultra-violet rays to, as it were, analyse the materials which are placed under the lamp. Thus if two pieces of paper, similar in appearance but differing in actual composition, are placed side by side under the lamp, they will appear of different colours, and similarly if two stamps which appear to be printed in ink of exactly the same colour are placed under the lamp, and one of them is a forgery, it will show, under the rays, that its ink is made up of different ingredients from that in which the genuine stamp was printed.

Reprints, like forgeries, are distinguished by their colour, paper, and gum. Most reprints date back a considerable period, and their characteristics are well-known to the stamp expert, who can also familiarize himself with the details of the very few new reprints which are made, as they appear.

It is in detecting cleaned stamps that the quartz lamp has proved very effective, for penmarks which have been 'removed' by the use of chemicals, and are invisible to the naked eye, still show clearly under the lamp. Cleaning nearly always leaves some results on the paper or colour of the stamp, and the expert can often detect these changes without the use of the lamp, and even the inexperienced collector will gradually be able to train himself to notice differences that will put him on his guard.

A word of warning is necessary regarding the use of the quartz lamp. It has been found that marks caused quite innocently, will show up in the lamp, and give rise to suspicion. For example, a drop of water which has fallen on an unused stamp may appear as a blot when viewed under the rays.

Repairing can often be detected by the trained eye, or by the feel of a stamp, though it is frequently marvellously done, margins being grafted on with no visible sign of what has happened. If a stamp which has been repaired is dipped in benzine, the added portions will frequently stand out clearly with a different appearance. In the quartz lamp, where differences of material are so easily detected, the added paper is nearly always seen at once, but if a stamp has been 'backed', i.e. if the whole of the back of the stamp has been reinforced by added paper, neither this test nor that with benzine will work.

The reader will ask, 'How can I best protect myself against acquiring forgeries and fakes?' The best advice is, 'Buy only from dealers who will guarantee every stamp they sell, and see that the dealer concerned is likely to be in a position to honour his guarantee.' It is useless having a guarantee if the firm giving it is untraceable, or not in existence, when you want your money back for a fake you have bought. Actually, with the reputable firms who give guarantees, you have your best safeguard in their expert knowledge and experience. A guarantee would not be much good unless it were backed by such expert service. Every expert will make mistakes on occasion, but the best firms make very few, and you are therefore able to deal with them in confidence that you are getting what you are paying for.

If you decide to disregard this particular safeguard and go bargain-hunting, you are, of course, vastly increasing your risks. If you buy a scarce stamp cheaply, it will pay you to test the stamp and the vendor at the same time, by sending the stamp to one of the recognized Expert Committees. In England those of the Royal Philatelic Society and of the British Philatelic Association are available, while there are others in the United States and elsewhere. A fee proportionate to the value of the stamp is charged, and if the stamp is genuine, a certificate, with photograph, is provided, and such a certificate is a valuable asset if you ever wish to sell the stamp. *These committees do not, however, value or identify stamps.*

It may be possible, in some cases, to get the vendor to allow you to have a stamp expertised before you definitely take it, but if this is not possible, and the stamp turns out to be bad, a claim should be made against the dealer. If he does not meet it, you will know where you are when future business is in question and will very wisely leave his wares alone. If he takes back the stamp, and refunds your money, you may assume that he is an honest man – but do not neglect to test the next few stamps you buy from him by reference to your expert committee, for he may not be.

By using the services of recognized expert committees, even the inexperienced collector can safeguard himself, but most collectors seem to prefer to assume that every one of their precious bargains is genuine, and leave the time of disillusionment till they or their heirs come to sell the collection, when it is too late to learn wisdom, or to recover the money which has been paid out for rubbish.

There is little danger for the small general collector from either forgeries, reprints, or fakes, for the sums he spends are usually for the commoner stamps, which are not so frequently forged or faked as the earlier, or scarcer stamps. Even if an occasional fake creeps into his collection from packets, etc., he need not be perturbed, for he has paid so little for them that his loss is negligible. It should be noted however, that the reliable firms take just as much care to ensure that their cheap packets are free from forgeries as they do with their rarities, while there are firms whose packets are at least leavened with 'duds'. 'Buy the best' is sound advice in philately as in other directions.

PART TWO · THE COLLECTION

Chapter Fifteen

THE OUTFIT

THE majority of stamp collectors display a marked reluctance to spend money on either album or accessories, once the passion for acquiring stamps has fairly gripped them. They leave their stamps in dilapidated books, often purchased second-hand after use by someone else, and refuse to avail themselves of the assistance which might be given by all those little gadgets which experience has proved to be so useful.

I am not going to advocate the purchase of a very elaborate outfit by the beginner, but I do suggest that stamps, at any stage of their career, deserve the best possible album their owner can afford to give them, for properly housed they give him more pleasure to look at, and are also a source of greater interest to his friends. I also advise the purchase and use of suitable accessories according to the progress made by the collector in technical knowledge.

The most elementary form of outfit used to be (and still is occasionally today), a cheap exercise-book and a few pieces of stamp-edging. While an exercise book is distinctly better than no album at all, the stamp-edging should be banished at once from the mind of any reader of this book as a possible substitute for the stamp-hinge. *There are, and can be, no substitutes for the latter*, for every other kind of gummed paper is meant to stick permanently to whatever it is attached while proper stamp-hinges are doubly gummed so that, when dry, they may be detached easily from the back of the stamp or from the album page. Therefore, whatever else you decide to omit from your outfit, get a box of stamp-hinges, and do not exercise false economy in the matter – get them of good quality. Bad hinges do as much harm to your stamps (and to their eventual value) as bad needles do to your gramophone records.

Stamp albums are of two main types, those which have printed descriptions and squares of some kind, so that there is a definite allotment of space for stamps of a particular sort, and 'blank' albums, which have pages all of a standard pattern, these being either of quite plain paper (black leaves being now often used) or else with a *quadrillé* background, to facilitate the arrangement of stamps, and possibly with a border pattern as well.

For the general collector making his first steps in the hobby, an album with printed squares is advisable. If the number of stamps he is likely to possess in the near future is under a thousand or so, the first collection should be formed in one of those albums which have pages headed by the name of the country or countries whose stamps they are to contain, possibly supplemented by illustrations of stamps and by brief geographical and historical details of the countries concerned. In such an album, a small number of stamps shows to the best advantage, while they would be lost in the pages of a bigger book. Then, too, the collector using these simple books, learns to identify stamps as belonging to a particular country, without concerning himself too specifically about the order in which the stamps were issued. It cannot be too strongly emphasized that from the earliest stages of the hobby it should be the ambition of every collector to possess a stamp catalogue, an elementary one if it must be so, but as soon as possible a big, general catalogue, even if the latter seems complicated at first sight. It is in threading the maze and unravelling those complications that the collector will really begin to know his stamps. The elementary catalogues will show him what he can get, looking at stamps in the most unscientific way, but the advanced catalogue will show him that many of his stamps may be divided and sub-divided into groups and that what he thought were duplicates can, by the more advanced system of classification, be considered as different stamps – and thus knowledge increases and the collection grows with it.

The next type of printed album is one in which there are definite spaces for each stamp, indicated either by numbered references to a catalogue which appears on alternate pages of the album, or by indications in the squares in which the stamps are to be placed. Owing to the very large number of stamps now in existence, a number which is increasing every year, albums of this type have to be produced on very simple lines, and even then they are bulky volumes, but the finding of an actual definite space for each stamp makes collecting much more fascinating, and the collector begins to learn something of the order in which stamps were issued and of the relations between those of different countries. Quite large collections can be formed in this type of album, and many collectors are content to use them throughout their philatelic career. It is advisable, however, that they should be supplemented by the use of blank, loose-leaf albums, one or more of which will be required for new issues which appear after the period for which the printed album makes provision, while at least one other should be set aside to include anything interesting which comes along, and for which there is no space in the main album – for example, air covers, special postmarks, distinct shades, etc. It is in such a supplementary album that the collector will be able to express his growing knowledge and give rein to his individuality, for the printed album gives him no scope for growth.

To most collectors there comes a time when either the collection outgrows the printed album, or knowledge and enthusiasm are irked by the restraints which its hard and fast limitations impose. Then the collection may be transferred entirely to blank albums, whose loose leaves can be arranged in any order, or taken out entirely, just as the owner may wish. There is absolute freedom when collecting in blank albums, but there is also an entire responsibility for the arrangement of the stamps, for the collector has nothing to guide him. Here the catalogue is more essential than ever, but its lists should only be taken as a basis, and the collector should feel himself absolutely free to arrange his stamps in the way he considers best, for slavery to a catalogue is nearly as bad as slavery to a printed album.

When selecting a stamp album of any kind, and particularly when choosing loose-leaf albums, whose efficiency depends on the proper functioning of some kind of retaining mechanism (a spring-back in the simplest kind, or pegs, rings, or projections engaging in holes or slots, in the more elaborate albums), it is a mistake to be too economical.

We shall learn more about blank albums when considering the arrangement of a stamp collection, and the only advice that is necessary at this stage is to avoid cheapness and eschew complicated mechanical devices (such as are used for some types of loose-leaf ledgers), for holding the leaves, as these are quite unsuitable for stamp albums.

An album, a catalogue and some stamp-hinges are the three essentials of the outfit. To these may be added a subscription to a stamp magazine, which will supplement the catalogue by listing all the newest stamps, by giving additional information regarding stamps already in the catalogue, and by publishing helpful hints about collecting and articles telling what other people have found out in studying particular issues.

To turn to less essential parts of the outfit, I would put first a good magnifying glass. Some of the cheap ones are quite powerful, but the glass in them is rarely true, and thus the small details which you want to examine may be distorted, and the value of the magnifier negatived. A good glass of fairly small field of the type which folds so that it can be carried in the pocket, is recommended. A really good one will cost a guinea or two, but a useful magnifier should be obtainable at any price from about five shillings upwards, if you cannot afford the luxury article. Even the cheaper ones are much better than no glass at all, however. There are also several kinds of illuminated magnifiers which are powered by torch batteries and brightly illuminate the stamp under inspection.

Next in usefulness comes the duplicate book, in which you will keep your stamps until they can be transferred to the album pages, or where you will store duplicates awaiting exchange. These books are made in all sizes. The pages are not of the kind used in albums but are provided with strips of transparent material stuck to each page, which form pockets, into which the stamps can be slipped and from which they can be easily removed. A supply of transparent envelopes of various sizes will also be found useful for sorting and storing cheaper stamps.

When the early stages have been passed, there are several accessories which will help you to examine stamps from the more technical 'philatelic' point of view. For seeing watermarks a 'detector' is employed, which is nothing more than a polished black tile or other recessed surface. The stamp is placed face downwards on this, and benzine is poured on the back of it, when the watermark in most cases shows up very clearly. A bottle of the 'dropper' type, to hold the benzine, will only cost a few shillings, and will save its cost over and over again, by preventing evaporation of the volatile liquid. Do not use benzine on modern photogravure stamps as the colours often run.

For measuring perforations a special gauge is essential, but here again, the cost can be reckoned in pence or shillings. On this gauge will be found rows of dots, and against each row a number, which indicates the 'gauge', as given by the figures in the stamp catalogue. If you have a stamp, for which there are two alternative perforations, described in your catalogue as, say, 'perf. 14' and 'perf. 15', this means that the perforation holes on all four sides of your stamps must fit either the row of dots numbered 14 on the gauge, or that numbered 15. All you have to do is to lay your stamp flat on the gauge and see which row of dots will fit exactly into the perforation holes of any side of your stamp. (The best gauges have three sets of dots or lines, which make it possible to measure the perforations, not only of loose stamps as indicated above, but also of stamps hinged in the ordinary way, or even stuck down on an envelope or sheet of paper.)

If your catalogue tells you that the perforation of a stamp is 'perf. 11 × 12', this indicates that the perfs. at top and bottom of your stamp will fit the '11' gauge while those at the two sides will gauge 12. (The gauge of top and bottom is always given first.) This is a compound perforation. The description 'perf. compound of 11 and 12' would mean that measurement of the perfs. on all four sides of a stamp would reveal the fact that some gauge 11 and some gauge 12, but the opposite sides do not necessarily have the same gauge, i.e. there might be three sides gauging '11' and only one with gauge 12. (*see page 201*)

'Perf. 12½, 13' (note the comma) is the rather round-about way some catalogues have of describing a perforation which actually gauges between 12½, and 13, which might be described as 12¾. Some perforation gauges do not show quarters, but most gauges have a millimetre scale on them, or else a black tablet two centimetres in length, which is the standard space, the number of holes in which gives us the gauge. If the stamp is laid on this black tablet in such a way that the edge of it bisects one tooth of the perforation you want to measure, you can ascertain the gauge by counting the number of complete holes included in the two centimetres space. If the other edge of the black tablet bisects a tooth of the perforations, then you have an even gauge, 11, 12, or whatever it may be. If it exactly bisects a perforation hole, then you have a half-gauge, 11½, 12½, and so on. If, however, the line does not exactly bisect the perforation hole, your gauge will be represented by the figure given by counting the complete holes on the 2 cm. tablet and adding a quarter, or three-quarters, the result being indicated, either as above (the two adjacent gauges with a comma between), or, more clearly and simply by the use of the fraction, as 12¾. A new type of perforation gauge, the 'Instanta', which gives very accurate readings, is now on the market and has proved a great success. It gives decimal readings, as well as the normal fractions.

The description 'perf. 12½–13' or '12½ to 13' indicates that the pins were spaced irregularly in the perforating machine, with the result that the space between the perforation holes is erratic to the same degree. In this case you may get part of a line of perforations gauging 12½, and just beyond it a section which measures 13.

All this sounds a little complicated, but with stamps and a gauge before you, it is really quite simple. Nor is there any reason for you to trouble about perfs. at all, unless you have a keen interest in technicalities, though the difference between one gauge and another will often make a considerable difference to the value of a specimen.

There are times when direct measurement, either of the stamp itself, or of an overprint or surcharge, is necessary, to prove genuineness or otherwise, or to make a distinction between two issues. There are two kinds of instruments used by philatelists for this work, the first being a millimetre scale engraved on ivory, or other material, and the other a pair of small dividers, with screw adjustment, which can be set to the distance it is required to measure and then applied to the part of the stamp that is being examined.

I have not mentioned stamp tweezers before, because to some collectors, possessed of very delicate fingers and hands not given to perspiring, they are not necessary, but I would advise their use by most of those who read this book, and particularly by those whose hands get hot very quickly, for moist hands may do a great deal of damage to a delicate stamp, while dry hands may be quite dirty without harming it in the least. With a little practice it is possible to handle, hinge, and mount stamps in the album without touching them with the fingers at all. Tweezers are also very useful for removing stamps from the water, when 'floating' them, and for this reason they should be made of non-rusting metal. They can be had with points ridged (or 'milled') so that they grip the stamps better, or with plain points. The gripping portion is also in varying shapes – more or less pointed, or with a kind of 'spade' end. The important thing is that your tweezers should be non-rusting, and that there are no really sharp edges where the points meet, as these might damage your stamps. You can test any tweezers offered you by picking up with them a piece of plain paper, and seeing whether they leave any serious mark.

For heading the pages of a blank album, books of gummed labels, bearing the names of the various countries, can be bought. Gummed labels are also sold which give dates, perforations, watermarks and other details, so that a whole collection can be annotated. If you want headings for good class blank album leaves which involve placing the same name at the head of a large number of leaves, the best method is to have them die-stamped. Your stamp dealer can give you particulars as to cost, which is quite moderate for a quantity, and the leaves look very neat, particularly if the initial of the name of the country is in red and the remainder in black.

There are quite a number of luxuries which can be added to the collector's outfit. He may acquire a dozen different perforation gauges, and twenty different patterns of magnifiers, while nearly every year sees the production of some new gadget, often quite useless. The collector who chooses from among the accessories I have mentioned above as he advances along the road to philatelic knowledge, will, I think, be sufficiently equipped.

Chapter Sixteen

HOW TO GET STAMPS

APART from stealing, which is not recommended, there are three ways of getting together stamps for a collection – by gift, by exchange and by purchase. Most junior collections are started by a present from a relative, either of an old collection no longer wanted by its owner, or of a stamp packet. As other gifts of stamps are received, duplicates are acquired and these are used as 'swaps' for exchanging, and so the collection is built up, until, one day, when there is a little spare pocket-money in hand, a dealer's shop is visited, or he is asked to send an 'approval book', and then the serious stage is reached.

The adult collector is rather at a disadvantage in the matter of presents, but if there is anyone who remembers his birthday or Christmas in the appropriate way, there is nothing to prevent him dropping a hint that he prefers stamps to ties of the wrong colour or cigars of the wrong kind. The hint should, however, be accompanied by a written description of the stamps he wants, for there is nothing more helpless than the non-collector, especially of the female sex, who is attempting to buy stamps for a collector. He may be a general collector, or he may collect the stamps of one country only, as the dealer kindly points out, and the poor lady gets so bemused that in the end she leaves the stamp shop and buys the usual brand of pseudo-Havanas.

The business man has, of course, the opportunity of begging stamps from his friends who have correspondence with countries abroad, and even if he is not interested in these current stamps he should take them, either for the benefit of some younger collector or with a view to possible exchange for something he does want. I know collectors who have built up quite good general collections by the happy chance of being in a position to secure the stamps from a big world-wide business correspondence. One specimen of each stamp goes into their albums, and the rest are kept and either exchanged, or sold to a dealer in quantity, so that there is a continual flow of stamps, and of cash which can be turned into more stamps.

'Never miss anything' is the motto of the keen collector, and this is why even the man who collects the stamps of only one country should have some knowledge of those of the rest of the world. In any case he should never miss the chance of picking up stamps, especially when they are offered to him gratis. To sniff and say: 'Oh, thanks, but I don't collect that', is to miss the opportunity of securing specimens which can possibly be exchanged or sold. Unless funds are plentiful the stamps one does not want have got to help to pay for the stamps one needs.

Going back to the elementary stage, which all collectors have to pass through if they are to have the experience which general collecting of the stamps of the whole world can alone give, we find that when occasional gifts and the results of 'swapping' fail to satisfy the desire for a quickly expanding collection, the aid of the dealer must be enlisted. In the early days of one's collection, quantity appeals rather more strongly than quality, and this is where the stamp 'packet' comes in. The dealer who receives an order for a hundred different stamps, each of which has to be looked out separately by his clerk, is forced to charge for his labour, and those stamps are therefore much dearer when bought separately than they are when purchased in a packet, though of course, in a packet, you do not have any choice, beyond what is afforded by the grouping in the dealer's list, that is to say he may have, in addition to his whole world packets, packets containing British Commonwealth stamps only, or packets of pictorial stamps.

The best start for a collection is the biggest whole world packet you can afford to buy, for you want to avoid duplicates and if you start with a small packet, the larger packet will almost certainly contain the same stamps over again. Looking at a dealer's list we find the following typical series of general packets, which we may expect to contain the commonest stamps (though some dealers give much better value than others – it all depends on their stocks):

150 stamps, all different, cost				3s.
300	,,	,,	,,	,, 7s.
500	,,	,,	,,	,, 15s.
1000	,,	,,	,,	,, 27s. 6d.

The cost per stamp naturally increases as we reach the larger packets, which contain stamps which are harder to get, but it is still far less than the cost of the same stamps if bought separately, one by one.

Now if you buy the packet of 100 different and then later on decide to acquire the packet of 500 different, you are certain to find many of your original hundred in the second packet and you will have unwanted duplicates to that extent. Therefore, buy the 500 packet at once (or better still, the 1000, if funds will run to it), and you are sure of getting that number of stamps without duplication.

When the contents of the packets have been absorbed in the album, other packets may be brought, until it is clear that this method of purchase is bringing in too many duplicates. The latter are always useful for exchange purposes if one is in touch with other collectors, but it is better to get stamps one really wants if possible. When packets have helped as much as they can, it is time to turn to sets.

Strictly speaking, a set should consist of stamps of one particular kind or issue, but the term is applied nowadays to lots of stamps which might with equal accuracy be called packets. The distinction is not important, however, so long as we know as far as possible what we are going to get for our money.

A most useful type of set and one which is very popular today is the 'One-country' set. This, as its name implies, includes the stamps of one country only. There may be several different sets of a particular country in the dealer's list, 20 different, 50 different and 100 different, and it is well to realize that as in the case of the packets, the larger sets will include the stamps that are in the smaller ones of the same country, plus others. Therefore buy the largest, if you can, straightaway.

The advantage of these one-country sets is that they give the collector the chance of buying to fill his weaker countries. Glancing through the album, he finds that he has only three stamps of, say, Guatemala. Looking at the dealer's list he sees that he can get for a modest sum 25 different Guatemala. Even if the three stamps he already possesses are included in this set (and it is quite likely that they are not) he is sure of adding 22 stamps to his Guatemala page, none of which will be duplicates. In this way, many countries can be built up to a reasonable degree of strength, and only a very few duplicates will be acquired.

The third stage brings us to another type of set – the kind which only includes the stamps of a single issue. Here the dealer's list will give the date and a fairly detailed description of the contents of the set, so that it is possible to know exactly what one is getting. Comparing the description with one's collection, it is an easy matter to select sets which will contain very few duplicates. Do not, however, as some too clever collectors do, refuse to buy sets of which you already possess the commonest stamps. For these low values you are paying very little, and even if they are not reckoned at all, you will still be getting the better stamps in the set far cheaper than if you bought them separately.

In recent years there has been a tendency for collectors to insist on buying even the older issues in complete sets only. As there are usually one or two scarcer items in every set, the dealer has to hold up his stock of the commoner values until he can complete his sets with the scarcer ones and, in consequence, he charges a higher price for the complete series than for the individual stamps of which it is composed. The collector fills all his album squares at one blow, but misses one of the greatest pleasures which the hobby can afford – the hunt for elusive varieties and their eventual discovery.

As new sets are continually appearing, set buying may continue until the collection is in quite an advanced stage. It will leave many gaps, however, and these will have to be filled by buying stamps singly. This can be done in two ways.

The first method is for the collector to send to the dealer a 'want list' – a description of the stamps he wants, usually given by quoting the reference number of each stamp according to the dealer's catalogue, or any other recognized catalogue. (No keen dealer will mind you sending him a want list by a foreign catalogue, for example, though in the British Commonwealth he would naturally prefer to have the Stanley Gibbons numbers, and in the U.S.A. the Gibbons–Whitman or Scott Catalogue references, which are the ones by which he arranges his stock unless he publishes a catalogue himself.) Don't forget to give the name of the country as well as the reference number, and state also whether you want the stamps unused or used. The dealer will then send you what he can supply of the stamps you ask for, and usually these are sent on approval, so that if they are not exactly as you want them, they can be returned.

The second, and more popular method of buying stamps singly, is to ask the dealer for an approval selection. These selections are arranged on sheets or in books, each stamp being priced separately. The simplest form of selection will include the cheaper stamps of several countries, and most dealers have quite a good range of these approval sheets, which you can work through gradually, filling up gaps as you find on the sheets the stamps you want. For collectors who need a more advanced type of selection, books are available containing the stamps of only a single country, or perhaps of one issue only, and the dealer eager to please his customers will be quite willing to send any part of his stock in this way, so that, even if you live many miles away from his shop, or, in fact, at the other side of the world, you can still do business with him, through the medium of the post, and can see the stamps before you buy them.

If you are to take full advantage of such a service as this, it is essential that you should give the dealer full details of the stamps you are collecting. It is no good merely saying you want a selection of the stamps of, say, France, if you take nothing but French stamps with Colonial postmarks. The dealer will send you a general selection of France, in which there will probably be nothing for you. Tell him exactly what issues you are collecting, whether you want unused or used, if you collect pairs or blocks, and so on, and then he will be able to send you the sort of selection you really want to see. Give him some idea, also, of the class of stamps you take. It is no good him sending you stamps priced up to £5 each, when you never pay more than a shilling for a stamp. While his stamps are in the post and in your possession, they are not earning money for him, except in so far as he may be able to tempt you to buy them. For the same reason, he will not continue to send you stamps on approval unless you buy a reasonable amount. Some dealers are more lenient in this respect than others, hoping that if you do not buy today, you may be tempted later, but it is obvious that no business man can afford to waste time and energy on someone who is obviously not a buyer. If, however, you are prepared to spend a few shillings when a cheap approval sheet is sent you, or more when better books arrive, you will probably be very satisfied with the service the dealer will give you, and will be able to spend many happy hours comparing his stamps with yours and filling the gaps in your album. Play the game, and return his stamps within a reasonable time, however, for they are his stock, and he has many customers waiting to see them. The quicker he can get his stamps back, as a general rule, the less he has to allow on his expense account for stock lying idle, and the cheaper he can sell.

I shall have more to say on this question of buying, when dealing with the money side of the hobby in a later chapter, but it should be noted that even in the elementary packet and set stages, the cheapest offers are not always the best value.

Chapter Seventeen

THE QUESTION OF CONDITION

To the collectors of early days, even a fraction of a stamp appeared worthy of a place in their albums, but nowadays the stamp lover should exercise a certain discretion in the stamps which he admits to his collection, and here he will meet for the first time the magic word 'condition'.

The 'condition' of a stamp implies the relation which its completeness, freshness and general appearance bear to what may be imagined to be the ideal specimen of the particular stamp. An unused stamp in perfect condition must be as fresh as on the day when it came from the printing-press, with colour bright, paper clean and uncreased, and gum untouched. If it is of an imperforate issue, it must have margins on all four sides as wide as can possibly be obtained, and certainly the scissors which separated it from its brethren must not have touched even the outermost line of its design. In the case of used stamps, the freshness, the margins and the uncreased and entirely undamaged character of the stamp also apply, while the postmark must be light, and applied in such a way as not to obscure the more important part of the design.

As far as perforated stamps are concerned, perfect condition forbids any shortness of tooth, in the perforations, and good centring is a *sine qua non*. This means that the printed design must be at an even distance from the rows of perforations which bound it, at top and bottom and on right and left.

This search for stamps in perfect condition has become a craze with many collectors, and is carried to such an extent in some cases that it obscures their sober judgment, and even leads them to actions which, in any other connexion, would be regarded as mad. What can you think of an enthusiastic amateur who, shown a very rare and interesting item of whose rarity and interest, moreover, he is, in his heart, convinced, spurns it and regards it as of no account because it does not reach his standard of condition? Again, what are we to think of the man who would rather have a gap in an otherwise complete collection than take the finest known specimen of a stamp, because it does not measure up to his imaginary standard.

It is, of course, for each individual to decide what he will do, but it is utter foolishness for the ordinary collector to follow these 'super-conditionists' for not only does he debar many quite sound stamps from his albums, but he also makes the hobby much more expensive for himself and his fellows. If the dealer who buys a hundred stamps of a particular sort has to discard half of them, not because they are damaged, but because they do not quite come up to the standard of the faddists, then whoever buys the remaining stamps must pay double the price for them.

The collector who thinks solely of investment must certainly cultivate sound judgment as to condition, when buying the rarer stamps, and if he buys inferior copies he must see that he does not pay more than their value, which will only be a fraction of the top price of the fine specimens, but the average collector will be well advised not to worry too much about condition, but fill his spaces with any stamps that are not damaged, or unsightly by reason of too heavy postmarks, for damaged and heavily cancelled stamps are an eyesore on the album page.

The removal of these damaged and ugly stamps is therefore the first step to be taken by the collector who is preparing to mount his stamps. The next is to remove all superfluous paper from the remainder.

If you know that stamps are printed in fast colours, any which are on pieces of envelope may be placed in hot or cold water until the paper can be peeled off. Stamps printed in many of the modern inks and all stamps printed on 'chalky' paper, or in inks of a deliberately fugitive character, must be treated more carefully. They may either be floated face upwards on the surface of a tray of water, until the damp has penetrated the adherent paper sufficiently to enable it to be detached, but not enough to affect the colour of the stamp, or a wad of damp blotting paper in a shallow trough or tray can be used instead of the water. In each case it is essential that the water should not touch the surface of the stamp nor be allowed sufficient time to penetrate its back.

It is not always desirable to remove stamps either from whole envelopes, or from pieces. Many early stamps, whether 'on cover' (the whole envelope) or 'on piece', are worth much more than when detached, and in this connexion the advice of experienced collectors should be sought. Then too it is often necessary to retain part of the envelope, in order to show an interesting postmark or inscription. If it is not essential to preserve the whole envelope, the paper should be cut to a neat oblong, and not trimmed round the postmark to a fantastic shape.

'Cleaning' stamps in the ways employed by fakers is not, of course, permissible to the collector, but there are one or two things which the ethics of the hobby permit to be done by way of improving defective specimens.

Stamps whose colours have become 'oxydized', may be restored to their natural tones by a bath in peroxide of hydrogen. (This affects the gum of unused stamps, by the way, so to such specimens the peroxide should be applied very carefully, on the surface only, with a camel hair brush.)

Stamps printed in fast colours, which look as if they are dirty, may often be improved by a good hot bath. Creases may be removed or rendered less prominent, by the use of a hot iron and damp blotting paper, but only when the colours are fast. If there are grease spots on a stamp, they can be taken out by ironing the stamp with a hot iron through clean dry blotting paper, or by immersion in benzine.

Chapter Eighteen

HOW TO IDENTIFY STAMPS

IT is when he tries to identify his stamps and allot them to their particular countries that the collector finds the need for a catalogue, for many countries do not put their names on their stamps at all, while others do not call themselves by the name we are accustomed to use in English, and a third group use alphabets with which we are not familiar.

It is therefore very helpful if the collector, before starting to identify his stamps, will make a thorough study of his catalogue, paying particular attention to the illustrations and trying to memorize characteristics of the various countries and groups of colonies.

When undertaking the identification of a mixed lot of stamps, the beginner should put on one side at once all those which bear the name of the country in English, or which, for any reason, he can identify without difficulty. He will, of course, have no difficulty with names which differ very little from the English equivalents, such as Brazil, Chile, or the French Colonies which end in a final 'e' where the English name ends in 'a' such as 'Indo-Chine', 'Mauritanie', etc.

In attempting to identify stamps with quite unfamiliar names, it is sometimes helpful to remember the equivalent for the word 'post' (or 'posts') in various languages. Thus the French word is 'postes', the Spanish 'correos', the Portuguese 'correio' or 'correios', and so on. This does not take us far, however, as many countries have their stamp inscriptions in French, and most countries of South and Central America use Spanish or Portuguese on their stamps.

Perhaps the widest indications are given by the standard key-type designs used by the colonies of various European states. If the catalogue illustrations of the French, German, Portuguese, Dutch, and Spanish colonies are studied, it will soon be easy to recognize the standard types in each group, and after this, allotment to countries is easy.

The first word in a stamp inscription is not always the name of the country. It may mean 'Republic', 'Kingdom', 'Postage Stamp', 'Post', or many other things, but a little practice will enable you to pick out the name. In some cases the name of the country is in the overprint, stamps of another country having been converted for its use by this method.

In the following table, the reader will find a list of many stamp inscriptions in alphabetical order, which should help him to identify a large number of stamps.

TABLE OF STAMP INSCRIPTIONS

In this table the word 'on' followed by the name of a country or group of issues in brackets, implies that the inscription given in the first column is an overprint on the issues thus indicated.

Syllables given in brackets are sometimes shown on stamps and sometimes omitted, thus 'Ned(erl)(andsch) Indie' implies that stamps may be found inscribed 'Ned. Indie', 'Nederl. Indie', or 'Nederlandsch Indie'. If you do not find the inscription you are looking for listed under one of its words, look under the others.

If there are two sets of inscriptions on a stamp, probably only the most distinctive is listed here, so look up both.

It should be particularly noted that the list of inscriptions here given is based on the assumption that the collector has already sorted out all stamps on which the name of the country is identifiable. Some of these may have inscriptions similar to those given in the list, but may be identifiable as belonging to a different country by a name which appears upon them in addition.

Açores	*Azores*
Amtlicher Verkehr	*Wurtemburg*
À Payer – Te Betalen	*Belgium*
À Percevoir (value in centimes with crown above)	*Belgium*
À Percevoir (value in paras or milliemes)	*Egypt*
Avisporto	*Denmark*

B (on Straits Settlements)	*Bangkok*
Bani (on Austrian Military Stamps)	*Austrian Occupation of Roumania*
Bayern	*Bavaria*
Bayer. Posttaxe	*Bavaria*
Belgien (on German)	*German Occupation of Belgium*
Belgique, Belgie	*Belgium*
Bollo della Posta Napoletana	*Naples*
Braunschweig	*Brunswick*

Cabo Juby	*Cape Juby*
Cabo Verde	*Cape Verde Is.*
C.C.C.P.	*Russia (Soviet)*
C.E.F. (on India)	*China Expeditionary Force*
C.E.F. (on German Colonies)	*Cameroons (Br. Occupation)*
Centesimi (and figures) (on Austrian Military Stamps)	*Austrian Occupation of Italy*
Centimes (on Austrian)	*Austrian P.O.s in Crete*
Ceskoslovensko	*Czechoslovakia*
Chine	*French P.O.s in China*
Colombia (with map of Panama)	*Panama*
Colombia	*This name often appears on stamps of the various Colombian departments, in addition to the name of the department*
Comunicaciones	*Spain*
Confed. Granadina	*Colombia (Granada Confederation)*
Congo Belge	*Belgian Congo (Congo State)*
Correio (and value in reis)	*Portugal*
Correos (and woman's head)	*Spain, or Cuba and Porto Rico, or Philippine Is.*
Côte d'Ivoire	*Ivory Coast*
Côte Française des Somalis	*French Somali Coast*

Danmark	*Denmark*
Dansk Vestindien	*Danish West Indies*
Deutsche Reichspost Deutsches Reich	*Germany*

Deutsch Neu-Guinea	*German New Guinea*
Deutsch Ostafrika	*German East Africa*
Deutschösterreich	*Austria*
Deutsch Sudwestafrika	*German South West Africa*
Dienstmarke (and figure of value)	*Germany*
Diligencia	*Uruguay*
D J (on Obock)	*Djibouti*
Drzava S H S	*Yugoslavia*
E.E.F. Postage Paid	*Palestine*
Eesti (Post)	*Estonia*
Eire	*Ireland*
Emp (ire) Franç (ais)	*France*
Equateur	*Ecuador*
Esculeas	*Venezuela*
Espana	*Spain*
Estados Unidos (or EE. UU.) de Granada	*Colombia*
Estero (on Italy)	*Italian P.O.s Abroad*
Établissements de l'Inde	*Indian Settlements (French)*
Établissements de l'Océanie	*Oceanic Settlements (French)*
État Ind (ependant) du Congo	*Belgian Congo (Congo State)*
Ethiopie	*Ethiopia (Abyssinia)*
Filipinas, Pilipinas	*Philippine Is.*
Franc (on Austrian)	*Austrian P.O.s in Crete*
Francobollo di Stato	*Italy*
Franco Bollo Postale Italiano	*Italy*
Franco Marke (and key in arms)	*Bremen*
Franco Poste Bollo	*Neapolitan Provinces or Italy (first issue)*
Frimærke 4 Skilling	*Norway*
Frimärke Kgl. Post	*Denmark*
G. (on Cape of Good Hope)	*Griqualand West*
G. & (or et) D. (on French Colonial)	*Guadeloupe*
G. E. A. (on E. Africa and Uganda)	*German E. Africa (British Occupation) (usually listed under Tanganyika)*
Gen.-Gouv. Warschau (on German)	*German Occupation of Poland*
G. P. E. (on French Colonial)	*Guadeloupe*
G (ran)d Liban	*Lebanon*
G. R. I. (on German Colonial)	*New Guinea*
Guiné (with Portuguese designs)	*Portuguese Guinea*
Guinée (Française)	*French Guinea*
Gultig 9 Armee (on Roumania)	*German Occupation of Roumania*
Guyane Franç(aise)	*French Guiana*

Haute-Volta	*Upper Volta*
H(au)t Senegal-Niger	*Upper Senegal and Niger*
Helvetia	*Switzerland*
Hrvatska S.H.S.	*Yugoslavia*
Hrzgl. Post. Frm.	*Holstein*
I. E. F. 'D' (on Turkish fiscals)	*Mosul (British Occupation)*
Ile Rouad	*Rouad Island*
Imper. Reg. Posta. Austr.	*Austrian P.O.s in Turkey*
India Port(ugueza)	*Portuguese India*
Instruccion	*Venezuela*
Island	*Iceland*
Italia	*Italy*
Kaiserl(iche) Konigl(iche) Osterr (eichische) Post	
(With values in kreuzer, gulden, heller, or kronen)	*Austria*
(With values in paras or piasters)	*Austrian P.O.s in Turkey*
(With values in centimes or francs)	*Austrian P.O.s in Crete*
Kärnten Abstimmung	*Carinthia (Plebiscite)*
Karolinen	*Caroline Is.*
K. G. C. A. (on Jugoslavia)	*Carinthia (Plebiscite)*
Kgl. Post. Frm. (value in 's' or 'sk.')	*Denmark*
(value in cents)	*Danish W. Indies*
K. K. Post Stempel (value in kreuzer)	*Austria*
(value in centes)	*Austrian Italy*
Kongeligt Post Frimærke	*Denmark*
KPHTH	*Crete*
Kraljevina S.H.S.	*Yugoslavia*
Kraljevstvo Srba Hrvata i Slovenaca	*Yugoslavia*
Kreuzer (with arms in oval)	*Austria*
K. u. K. Feldpost (value in figures only, or in heller)	*Austrian Military Post*
(value in bani)	*Austrian Occupation of Roumania*
K. u. K. Militärpost	*Bosnia and Herzegovina*
K. Württ. Post	*Wurtemburg*
La Canea	*Italian P.O.s in Crete*
La Georgie	*Georgia*
Lattaquie	*Latakia (formerly Alaouites)*
Latvija (Latwija)	*Latvia (Lettland)*
Lei (on Austrian Military stamps)	*Austrian Occupation of Roumania*
Lietuva	*Lithuania*
Lietuvos Pastas	*Lithuania*
Litwa Srodkowa	*Central Lithuania*
Losen (and figure)	*Sweden*

Magyar (Kir.) Posta	*Hungary*
Magyarorszag	*Hungary*
Marianen	*Marianne Is.*
Maroc	*French P.O.s in Morocco*
Marshall-Inseln	*Marshall Is.*
Mejico	*Mexico*
Milit(är)post. Portomarke (or Eilmarke)	*Bosnia and Herzegovina*
Montevideo	*Uruguay*
Moyen Congo	*Middle Congo*
M.V.i.R. (on Germany or Roumania)	*German Occupation of Roumania*
N.C.E. (on French Colonials)	*New Caledonia*
Nederland	*Netherlands*
Ned(erlandse) Antillen	*Netherlands Antilles*
Ned(erl) (andsch) Indie	*Netherlands Indies*
Ned(erlands) Nieuw-Guinea	*Netherlands New Guinea*
N. F. (on Nyasaland)	*Nyasaland Force in German East Africa*
Norddeutscher Postbezirk	*North German Confederation*
Norge	*Norway*
N(ouve)lle Caledonie	*New Caledonia*
Nouvelles Hebrides	*New Hebrides*
N. S. B. (on French Colonials)	*Nossi Bé*
Öltre Giuba	*Jubaland (Italian)*
Ortspost (with Swiss cross)	*Switzerland*
Österreich	*Austria*
Pacchi Postale	*Italy*
Para (with figures of value) (on Italy)	*Italian P.O.s in Turkey*
P.C.C.P.	*Russia (Soviet)*
Pesa (and figures of value) (on German)	*German P.O.s in Turkey*
P.G.S. (on Straits Settlements)	*Perak*
Piaster (and figures of value) (on German)	*German P.O.s in Turkey*
Poczta Polska	*Poland*
Pohjois Inkeri	*Ingermanland*
Polska Poczta	*Poland*
Porte Franco un dinero (or una peseta)	*Peru*
Porto (with eagle and figure)	*Austria*
ditto (with piastre)	*Austrian P.O.s in Turkey*
Porto-Pflichtige Dienst-Sache	*Wurtemburg*

Posta Cesko-Slovenska	*Czechoslovakia*
Postage Due (value in milliemes)	*Egypt*
Posta Romana	*Roumania*
Postas le Nioc	*Ireland*
Poste Estensi	*Modena*
Poste Italiane	*Italy*
Poste Locale (and Swiss Cross)	*Switzerland*
Postes (with portrait or heraldic lion)	*Belgium*
ditto (with value in centimes)	*Belgium*
Postes Dix Centimes (and portrait)	*Luxembourg*
Postes Ethiopiennes	*Ethiopia (Abyssinia)*
Postes Persanes	*Persia (Iran)*
Poste Vaticane	*Vatican City*
Postgebeit Ob. Ost. (on German)	*German Eastern Army*
Postzegel	*Netherlands*
Preussen	*Prussia*
Provincie Modonesi	*Modena*
Rayon (and Swiss Cross)	*Switzerland*
Regno d'Italia Venezia Giulia	*Italy (Trieste)*
Reichspost	*Germany*
Republica Dominicana	*Dominican Republic*
Republica Oriental (del Uruguay)	*Uruguay*
Repub(lique) Franç(aise)	*France or French Colonies (general issues)*
Republique Georgienne	*Georgia*
Republique Libanaise	*Lebanon*
Rialtar Sealadac na Heireann 1922 (on British) (Irish characters)	*Ireland*
Rümanien (on German)	*German Occupation of Roumania*
Russisch-Polen (on German)	*German Occupation of Poland*
Saargebiet	*Saar District*
Sachsen	*Saxony*
Saorstat eireann, 1922 (on British) (in Irish characters)	*Ireland*
Segnatasse	*Italy*
Serbien (on Bosnia)	*Austrian Occupation of Serbia*
Shqipenia (or Shqypnis or Shqyptare)	*Albania*
Sld. (with portrait or arms)	*Austrian Italy*
Slesvig	*Schleswig*
S. O. 1920 (on Czecho-Slovakian or Polish)	*Upper Silesia (Plebiscite)*
Soldi (with portrait or arms)	*Austrian Italy*
Somalia Italiana	*Italian Somaliland*
S.P.M. (on French Colonial)	*St Pierre and Miquelon*

S. Thomé e Principe	*St Thomas and Prince Is.*
St Pierre M——on (on French Colonial)	*St Pierre and Miquelon*
Suomi	*Finland*
Sverige	*Sweden*
S. W. A. (on S. African)	*South West Africa*
Te Betalen Port	*Netherlands, Netherlands Antilles (Curaçao), Netherlands Indies or Surinam*
Tjenste post frimærke	*Danish West Indies*
Toga	*Tonga*
Tunisie	*Tunisia*
Ultramar	*Cuba and Porto Rico*
Van Diemen's Land	*Tasmania*
Venezia Giulia (on Italy)	*Italy (Trieste)*
Venezia Tridentina (on Italy)	*Italy (Trentino)*
Von Empfänger Einzuziehen	*Danzig*
Z. Afr. Republiek	*S. African Republic (Transvaal)*

STAMPS WITH INSCRIPTIONS IN UNFAMILIAR ALPHABETS

(For illustrations see pages 206–7)

It is impossible to give any complete guide to the identification of stamps whose inscriptions are in alphabets other than that to which we are accustomed, but the stamp collector should make himself acquainted with the general characteristics of the Arabic, Greek, Russian, Chinese, Japanese, and the various Indian alphabets. The following table will then enable him to turn to the likely countries in catalogue or album and identify his stamps with reference to the illustrations.

(Alphabets not mentioned above are grouped under the heading of 'other Alphabets'.)

ARABIC INSCRIPTIONS.

Egypt.
Hejaz-Nejd (Saudi Arabia).
Iraq.
Syria (Arab Kingdom and Republic).
Trucial States (Ajman, etc.).
Turkey.
Yemen.
Arabic surcharges or overprints on some stamps of Hejaz or Palestine – Trans-Jordan.

Note. Persian inscriptions are not unlike Arabic.

GREEK INSCRIPTIONS.

Crete.
British P.O.s in Crete.
Ionian Is. (with Queen Victoria's head).
Greece and Greek Islands and Districts.

CHINESE AND JAPANESE INSCRIPTIONS.

China.
Corea, or Korea.
Japan.
Japanese Occupation of Burma, Malaya, Indonesia, etc. (Stamps and overprints.)
Manchuria (Manchukuo).
Overprints on Chinese stamps – Chinese Turkestan (Sin Kiang) Kirin and Heilungchang, or Yunnan.
Overprints on Chinese stamps with value in annas or rupees – Chinese P.O.s in Tibet.
Overprints on Japanese stamps – Japanese P.O.s in China or Corea.

RUSSIAN INSCRIPTIONS.

Azerbaijan.
Batoum.
Bulgaria.
Far Eastern Republic.
Finland (some designs very similar to those of Russia).
Moldavia (Roumania).
Montenegro.
Poland (first issue).
Russia, Russian Armies, Districts, Russian Levant, etc.
Serbia.
Trans-Caucasian Federation.
Ukraine.

Inscriptions in other Alphabets.

Abyssinia (Ethiopia).
Afghanistan. (Do not confuse the circular stamps with rather similar
    designs of Jammu and Kashmir.)
Armenia.
Georgia.
Mongolia.
Northern Mongolia (Tannou-Touva).
Persia (Iran).
Thailand (Siam).
Tibet.
Indian Native States (several different alphabets).
Overprint on Indian stamps – Gwalior State.

Chapter Nineteen

ARRANGING THE COLLECTION

IT is the easiest thing in the world to *collect* stamps, but, judging by what one sees, it must be the hardest of tasks to keep a collection properly mounted and arranged. Many collections, quite important so far as their extent and the value of the stamps they contain are concerned, are kept in dilapidated albums, cardboard boot boxes, old exercise books, and, possibly, a tin trunk, the latter usually containing envelopes from which the owner has been too lazy to float the stamps.

There are several reasons why a stamp collection should be properly arranged. First, you get a lot of pleasure out of the hobby and it is only fair to treat your stamps decently in return. In the second place, you rather like people to think well of you, and if you show your friends a dirty, ill-arranged lot of stamps, they will not say 'What rotten stamps!' but 'What a slack fellow!' Thirdly, you can give people a lot of pleasure by showing them a collection which is arranged with care and method, and can thus add to your own pleasure and possibly make new recruits for the hobby. Fourthly, stamps properly kept are less likely to get damaged or soiled and lose their value, while a neatly classified collection is of more value if you ever wish to sell – not because a dealer will pay anything for pretty writing-up, but because it is easier for him to see what you have got.

The collector who is using the elementary type of printed album, described in Chapter Fifteen, will have no difficulty in placing his stamps, for there is no specific square for each, and he has only to find the correct page. I have seen young collectors try to arrange their stamps in catalogue order in such an album, changing their places every time a fresh specimen came their way, but this, I think, is not advisable. The continual removals damage the album, and as there is not enough space for all the stamps of each country, and the collector does not know which ones he is going to get, any attempt to leave room for stamps still to come is doomed to failure.

In all types of printed album, the essentials are to put in no stamps on paper, to admit no damaged or heavily post-marked specimens, and to see that you get the stamps in level. Lack of attention to the last factor frequently spoils the appearance of a collection, but as printed albums always have ruled squares or lines, there is no excuse for getting stamps in crooked.

The choice of a blank, loose-leaf album has already been mentioned in Chapter Fifteen, where it was suggested that cheapness was the one thing to avoid. I do not mean that low-priced blank albums may not be quite good value for the money. It is the cheap albums which *look* as if they are worth a lot more which should be avoided, for there is usually some lack of wearing quality, either in the cover or in the all-important loose-leaf mechanism.

There are two main types of leaves in blank albums, those which are in one piece, with ridged (or 'fluted') edges, which are gripped by the springs of the cover, and those provided with a double linen hinge where they are gripped by the cover. The latter lie quite flat when the album is open and this is so great an advantage that it is advisable to pay a little more for an album in order to secure it. When working for any length of time on your collection, you will, of course, take the leaves out of the cover, and work on a single leaf, but there are times when you only want to add a single stamp or a brief note, and then the flat-opening, linen-hinged-leaf album shows its advantages.

Another point to be noted is the paper of which the leaves

are made. A shiny paper looks attractive, but it is not easy to write on, and even the most peelable hinges are apt to mark its surface. The best leaf to select is one with a good writing surface, free from spots and lumps, and of as high a quality as you can afford.

The *quadrillé* ruling, which forms the background of your page, and which is to serve as a guide to you in placing your stamps, should not stand out too boldly to the eye, but should be sufficiently visible for you to be able to distinguish each individual line without eyestrain by natural or artificial light.

Black leaves are popular as they show up the colours of the stamps so effectively. There are several good makes on the market. The ruling on these is in white. It is, however, most important that black-leaf albums should always be kept in a cool, dry place (they are not recommended for use in tropical, humid climates) and that the leaves themselves are always used in conjunction with transparent interleaving.

The three main types of gripping mechanism are the spring-back, which needs no description, the type in which the leaves are threaded on pegs, and those in which a projection of some kind engages with slots in the top and bottom of the hinges of the leaves. The peg system, having no sliding parts, is less likely to cause trouble than the slot system, but a properly made album with slotted leaves enables individual leaves to be taken out more quickly as there is no time wasted in unthreading them from the pegs. There is also the 'multi-ring' binding which also has the advantage that the leaves lie flat when the album is opened.

In any type of album, it is advisable to protect the stamps as far as possible.

The solution is the use of albums interleaved with thin, unprinted paper. It is possible to get all types of album with this provision and though it adds to their bulk and cost, it is an economy to have them, because the stamps are kept in proper condition.

Whatever album you decide on, make up your mind to treat it properly. Do not overfill a spring-back album, or the spring will eventually break. Do not use leaves of one type in a binder for which they were not intended. Keep the album in its box, if one is provided by the makers, and do not put a lot of heavy volumes one on top of the other; in fact it is advisable to keep albums standing upright on shelves, if possible.

The importance of using properly gummed hinges for affixing stamps in the album has already been insisted upon. A peelable hinge is the cheapest item in the collector's expense account, so there is no excuse for false economy. The use of the hinges in the proper way is also important. It should be noted that hinges are only peelable when the gum is quite dry. If a stamp is mounted, and then found to be in its wrong place on the page, it should be left for an hour or so before any attempt is made to remove it to its proper position. Detaching a hinge which is still damp is almost sure to damage the album page.

To hinge a stamp properly, a hinge should be selected which is not quite as wide as the stamp to be mounted. Hold the hinge with the gummed side downward, and fold back about a third of it with your tweezers, pressing the crease down with your thumb. The stamp is then placed face downward on the table with the top edge uppermost, and the turned back (smaller) portion of the hinge is lightly moistened with the tongue, and attached to the stamp within a fraction of an inch of the top edge and midway between the sides. The hinge must be clear of the top perforations or it will show when the stamp is mounted on the page. You now have your stamp with one-third of the gummed side of your hinge attached to it, and with two-thirds lying free. Pull the free end away from the stamp, so that your tongue will not touch the stamp, and then lightly lick *the lower part* of the free end. *Do not lick the free two-thirds all over*. The stamp can then be carefully placed in position on the page, by means of the hinge, and when it is in place

Fold over ¼ inch
and moisten here

Moisten here
slightly

*Method of hinging a stamp so that it may be
turned over for examination of the back without
damage or difficulty*

it will be found that this method of hinging permits of the
stamp being turned right back, for examination of the
watermark, etc., without any damage being done to the
perforations. This would be impossible if (*a*) the hinge had
not been placed right at the top of the stamp, or (*b*) the
free part of the hinge had been licked all over.

Some collectors like to hinge blocks of four stamps in the
same way, i.e. with the hinge right at the top of the upper
pair, but I have seen so many blocks get creased through
this method that I prefer to hinge blocks by placing the
hinge on the lower part of the two upper stamps. The block
cannot be turned back, but neither can it turn back
accidentally and get damaged or creased. In the case of
pairs, the hinge can be placed at the top of the stamps.

Some prefer to place the hinge on only one stamp, but this causes just as much damage as hinging blocks insecurely, and the hinge is best placed centrally at the top of the pair.

In arranging stamps on a blank page, it is advisable to do some planning before the actual mounting begins. First of all, there is your heading, which in the majority of cases will be the name of a country. If you distrust your powers of writing or printing neatly, you can get books of names, printed on gummed paper, which will do very well, while there are similar books of what are called 'Writing-up Labels' which give you all the dates, watermarks, perforations, printers, and other details which you will need for the headings of the different issues in a British Commonwealth collection. Even if you are going to write your own notes on the page, the appearance of your collection will be much improved if you have the name of the country die-stamped at the head of each page.

On the rest of the page, you have to place your stamps and whatever descriptive notes you are going to give. It is advisable to give *some* notes, otherwise your collection will mean very little to anyone who looks at it.

If the collection is an ordinary general display of the stamps of a country or group, you will only need a heading for each issue, giving the date, reason for issue (if a Jubilee, commemorative, or similar set), watermark, and perforation (if your collection takes note of these varieties), and perhaps the names of the designer, engraver, and printers, if known. (They can be found in many cases in the Stanley Gibbons Stamp Catalogue.) Apart from such headings, all that will be needed is an occasional brief note to indicate some special variety. Where the position of a flaw, or other detail you want to show, is not easy to describe in writing, you can use paper arrows which can be bought quite cheaply and which have one end gummed to the album page, with the loose end overlapping the stamp and pointing to the spot you want to indicate. Some collectors like to draw a red frame line round any particularly rare stamp.

If any special methods of this kind are used, it should be in moderation. Even the paper arrows should be used sparingly, or your collection will look like the Battle of Hastings!

In a highly specialized collection, it is often necessary to give very full notes, but even here the writing should be kept down to a minimum. A lot of description can be avoided by the use of enlarged sketches of details, which you can do yourself if you are clever with a pen, or small photographic enlargements of parts of the stamps can be mounted in the collection.

In a 'Thematic collection', i.e. one in which you are concerned mainly with the designs of the stamps, it will be necessary to have a brief note below almost every stamp. Very great care is necessary here, or once again you will find your pages full of writing and with very few stamps on them. For example, if you are describing a stamp bearing a portrait of a famous author, you cannot give his whole life story in your album. His name, the date of his birth and death, and one or perhaps two of his principal works, might be mentioned, but there will be space for little else – not that you have not got plenty of space in your album if you like to use it, but it is necessary to maintain some kind of balance between stamps and writing, otherwise you will have a treatise illustrated by a few stamps instead of a stamp collection 'illustrated' by your notes.

Before mounting a page of stamps, therefore, you must decide (1) What style of writing you will employ; (2) how much you are going to write about the particular stamp or issue you are dealing with; and (3) bearing these facts in mind, how many stamps you are going to be able to get on the page.

If your album pages have a *quadrillé* background, you will very likely find that the central point of the page is marked by a thickening of two *quadrillé* lines at their junction, and the central horizontal and vertical lines of the background will be indicated at the edges of the sheet by being prolonged very slightly. As far as possible, the stamps on your finished page should balance evenly about the central point. You will naturally mount your stamps so that, in each row, there is the same number of stamps each side of the central vertical axis of your page – if there is an odd number of stamps in the row, the centre stamp will of course be placed on the centre line and the others spaced off from it at even distances on each side.

As regards the vertical arrangement, though you will get more stamps onto a page by putting the maximum number of stamps into each horizontal row, the result will be very ugly. It is better to vary the number, alternating between long and short rows, according to the number of stamps you have to get on the page you are dealing with.

In a general collection, the unit of arrangement will be a set or issue. You will have sets of varying length, some of which will go on a page and fill it comfortably, while others will probably go two to a page, or, if you collect both un-used and used, a set can go on a page in both conditions. It is essential that the pages should not be overcrowded, even though your stamps call for more albums and leaves when spaced out neatly.

It is a good plan to lay out your page before you do any hinging at all. Pencil dots may be used to indicate how much space will be occupied by your notes – experience will soon teach you how much space a note will take in your adopted style of writing – and then the stamps can be laid on the page and moved about until the most attractive arrangement is arrived at. Do not, however, adopt any fantastic arrangements, laying out your stamps in crosses, circles, or other mathematical figures. Such arrangements detract from the appearance of the stamps, and over-elaborate borders and scrolls, with which some artistically minded collectors adorn their albums, should also be eschewed. You want anyone looking at your collection to concentrate on the stamps. 'The stamp's the thing', and everything else – notes, indicators, and whatever may be added to emphasize special items – must be subordinated to the stamps.

There are many points which crop up when arranging a collection which cannot be dealt with in detail in the limited space available here. Readers requiring further information are referred to *How to Arrange and Write-up a Stamp Collection* by the author and Mr C. P. Rang (published by Stanley Gibbons Ltd), which gives full details on all aspects of the subject.

Chapter Twenty

THE SPECIALIST

EVERY collector comes, sooner or later, to a period when he feels that general collecting – attempting painfully to acquire the stamps of the whole world – is too big a task for him to tackle, and that a lifetime's progress will not, as far as he can see in the pessimistic mood of the moment, make much impression on those numerous gaps in his albums. He then looks round for some means of limiting his field, and thus intensifying his effort, and the result is usually a decision to take the stamps of a single geographical group, country or issue. He may, on the other hand, decide to take up a 'subject' or 'freak' collection, like those described later in this book. (Chapters Twenty-one and Twenty-two.)

Before starting to specialize in the stamps of a country or group, the collector should have some idea of what specialism really means. Many call themselves specialists from the moment they have taken the fateful decision to abandon their general collection, but no mere limitation of field can earn the title. Your true specialist must study his stamps and try to add something to the sum of philatelic knowledge.

Here let me add that even when it is decided to collect only the stamps of a small section, it is very unwise to give up your general collection, at any rate to the extent of disposing of it. Keep it by you, and as you learn more about your pet issues, you will also find you are learning more about stamps in general, and will look at your old collection with a new interest and affection. It will be a bond of union between you and your fellow specialists when you visit the meetings of your philatelic society, and it will provide a nucleus for your further experiments in specializing, when you have exhausted the delights of the country first chosen. Too many specialists tend to become narrow in their views and interests, and the possession and occasional examination of a general collection act as a safeguard against carrying narrowness too far.

The reader who will turn again to the definition of modern philately quoted in Chapter Five will have at the same time a description of the scope of a modern specialized collection and, as I said there, only one or two corners of a particular field need be dealt with. Thus there may be several collectors, all specialists in the stamps of a certain country and all trying to make discoveries. One may be delving in the official archives to find out the history of the posts and postage stamps; another may be more interested in the production of the stamps themselves and in working out the 'settings' of certain issues or overprints; while the third is passionately interested in the postmarks and other miscellanea connected with the use of the stamps. If a group of friends can work in this way, each taking a section of the field and pooling information, much can be done, but even the lone student may do a great deal.

The preliminary to specialist study of stamps is to know what has already been learned by others. It is not very amusing to spend years elucidating problems by one's own unaided efforts and then to come proudly into the open with the results, only to find that someone had already made the same discoveries before one's own collection had even been begun.

While some collectors are too selfish, or never have the time or the ability, to put their discoveries on paper, most of the more important research work in connexion with stamps has been recorded either in books, or in the pages of the Philatelic Press. A great deal of information has been summarized in a German serial publication, the *Kohl Handbuch*, parts of which have been translated in the *Collector's Club Philatelist* of New York, while there are smaller specialized catalogues of many countries which provide a groundwork of information on which to base one's own researches. It is absolutely essential to start with a sound knowledge of what has been done before going on to independent study.

Another aid to the budding specialist is the examination of other collections. Many of the finest collections are displayed each year at one or other of the philatelic societies, and if you are able to find out where the country you want to see is being shown, it should not be difficult to get an invitation, even if you are not a member of the particular society, as most of them keep open house for visitors, and are only too pleased to welcome them. In this way, it may be possible to make the acquaintance of the leaders in your chosen field, as nothing brings collectors together like a common interest.

Having gained as much knowledge as possible, and perhaps been a little disheartened by the vision of other people's treasures, you can decide how far your own collection is to take you. It is certainly best to work by stages, concentrating on one issue or problem, and going as far as the available material allows before proceeding to the next group.

Let us see what the scope of a fully specialized display might be, under the late A. J. Séfi's definition of Modern Philately.

'*Enquiries into the reasons and circumstances leading up to an issue.*' A study of the postal archives of the country concerned and of the records of the printers, should yield much information, which might be supplemented by notes culled from the local Press, where the issue was the result of a popular agitation or of a public competition for designs. Government gazettes giving the particulars of the competition and its result, and similar notices concerning the issue of the stamp should be sought for. It is quite in order to include cuttings and official notices in a modern collection, but where these are not available, their contents should be recorded in a notebook or file, and perhaps summarized in the notes in your album.

If you are dealing with the first stamps of a country, the earlier postal history will be a necessary background of knowledge, and covers and wrappers illustrating the scope and methods of the postal service in pre-stamp days may well form an introduction to the collection proper.

Human curiosity is served by some knowledge of the life and non-philatelic achievements of those concerned in the production of the stamp and its design – the Postmaster-General who authorized it, the local Governor or Governor-General who approved it, the artist who designed it and the engraver who produced the die. Examples of other stamps produced by the two latter might be included, where these serve to throw light on the stamps to be studied, or provide an effective contrast to them.

'*Researches as to the essays and proofs for the stamps thereof.*' Our earlier chapters have shown what interesting material there is to search for under this heading which may at its widest include artists' sketches and designs in the prize competition if one were held, sketches by the staff of the printers elaborating or improving the artist's designs, essays in quite different designs, proofs from the original die in its various stages of manufacture and proofs from secondary dies and from the plate or plates, with colour trials which may be from die or plate.

These proofs will help us with our next task, '*Study of all the different processes and methods of production used,*' as they help to illustrate and elucidate the preliminary stages of production. The technicalities of this phase of philatelic study are out of place in a general work such as this, but the reader who has an inquiring or scientific mind can rest assured that the most fascinating problems are presented.

When access to the archives of the post office and the files and records of the printer is possible, the student can begin his work at the right end. He knows the method of production, with the exception of minor details peculiar to the particular printing works, and has only to connect printing causes with the results as he sees them in the stamps. But matters are very different, when he has no means of getting direct contemporary information as to methods of production, but has to take his stamps and laboriously deduce what these methods were – the number of dies, plates, or stones, their arrangement as regards the types and variations which he sees in his stamps, the number of printings from them, the dates of those printings, and a host of other minutiae.

It is not surprising that the cry of specialists of this type is always for fresh material. A promising line of research may have to be abandoned for years, simply because no large accumulations of the necessary stamps turn up to throw fresh light on the problems in hand. Some problems never will be solved. The solution of others is reached after infinite labour, and then, by chance, the original archives come to light, and results can be checked and proved to be sound or to have been build on sand – the shifting sand of unscientific premises.

Philatelic research at its highest and best is truly scientific. The collector will accept nothing as fact until it is proved, checked and re-checked. Adding fact to fact, his results must necessarily be sound, but like the scientist he must, on occasion, build a temporary bridge of theory, ready to abandon it and rush back to the firm ground of truth if it will not bear the weight of his further discoveries. The true philatelist is thus easily recognized by his reluctance to lay down the law, and by his readiness to modify his opinions in the light of new facts – but true philatelists are few and far between.

Space will not permit of a detailed summary of the scope of philatelic research under this section of our definition – of 'plating' – reconstruction from small sections, or even from single stamps, the sheets in their original arrangements or settings; studying every variation in the stamps in order to trace its cause and period, re-entries, flaws, retouches, damaged transfers, and other varieties already described – 'and resultant varieties on the stamps themselves' as our definition has it. There is something for every type of mind in this section, technical though it may seem, and no one need undertake to cover the whole field, even in the case of a single issue.

Finally we have the study of '*All the uses or misuses to which the stamps, once issued, might be subject.*' This does not merely imply finding out whether a stamp was occasionally or regularly employed for fiscal as well as postal purposes, but very much more. We have to trace it from the printing works to the central postal store and thence to the post offices, picking up as we go such official notices as will tell us when, and for what purpose, and by whose authority it was issued. We want to know what particular postal rate it was intended to pay and we want to see it, on covers, paying that rate of postage to various destinations. If it exists in various printings, identifiable in any way, we shall want dated covers showing at what periods and from what places or districts the stamps of each printing were used. The contemporary postal history and records of the country must be studied in order to find out as much information as possible, but theories may have to be built up and tested in order to arrive at many facts.

We shall have to study the types of postmark and cancellation employed in connexion with the stamps, and must not overlook any overprints or surcharges which may have been applied to them after issue.

When our stamps have been used for other than their normal purposes, we try to find out whether this was authorized or not, as for example when a stamp is cut in half and used for half its normal franking value. Under misuses may perhaps be included abuses – the making of forgeries, reprinting and faking. A fully representative study collection should include a section for these, as it will help both the owner and others to be on their guard against them.

The reader can learn for himself from the earlier chapters dealing with the printing and use of postage stamps how widely he may fill his net, and he will notice from what has been said, that not only stamps, but knowledge, must be acquired, in fact very good work can be done in the direction of *historical* research, with a minimum number of stamps, though technical research calls for as many stamps as it is possible to get, provided that they serve to add to the student's knowledge.

This brings us to the two essentials of a specialized collection. The first has already been mentioned, but cannot be re-emphasized too often. It is that the collector who claims the name of philatelist must *study* his stamps, even if it be but a single small problem in connexion with them, and, to go even further, it is a duty to his fellow-philatelists to publish his results when he is satisfied that they are correct, instead of selfishly keeping them secret, either through laziness or for private gain, as so many do.

The second essential is that a study collection should contain only such specimens as serve to elucidate the problem with which it is concerned, or others whose place in the scheme of things has not been fully ascertained and which are, therefore, in suspense. To fill a collection with repetitions of the same stamp, in the same state, which tell the student nothing, may be satisfactory to those who like their collections to illustrate the power of the purse as well as the interest of their subject, but it is not philately. It is merely accumulating, and accumulating which selfishly prevents others from having their share of the fun.

It is certain that every reader of this book can find some stamp problem within his means and the scope of his powers to study, and those who have brought to a satisfactory conclusion even the smallest bit of philatelic research will testify to the mental recreation and satisfaction which this branch of the hobby offers to all.

Chapter Twenty-one

THEMATIC COLLECTING

THE collecting of the stamps of a country, in chronological order of issue, is the earliest, and most conventional form of the hobby, which has developed, in the case of some collectors, into intensified specialized study of the stamps of a certain country or issue.

The development of the pictorial and commemorative stamp, and the tendency of our modern world to be more interested in life than in things, has given rise to a kind of horizontal collecting (as opposed to the vertical, or one-country method), which disregards geographical and political boundaries, and groups stamps in relation to their designs, inscriptions and associations. Not everyone is thrilled by collecting for collecting's sake, and the pleasures of spacefilling of the old kind have been known to pall, but there is hardly a man or woman who can fail to find some subject illustrated by stamps, in which to interest themselves. Hence the great popularity of what is now known as Thematic collecting.

From the historical point of view, stamps may be grouped to show political changes resulting from war or other causes. The stamps of the provinces or states of Canada, Australia and South Africa give place to unified issues for the federated dominions. The petty states of Germany and Italy become the German Reich and the modern Republic. The colonies of Germany become territories administered, under mandate, by the Allies of 1914–18. The map of Europe and Africa is remade and postage stamps illustrate the process. These and many other historic alterations can be shown by changes in stamp designs and inscriptions.

When actual portraits and pictures on postage stamps are considered, many gaps in the world's story can be filled in. Modern countries recall their ancient history – Rome reminds us of Romulus and Remus, Julius Caesar, and Augustus; Egypt of Rameses, Cleopatra, and the builders of her ancient pyramids and temples; Persia of Darius, and Ethiopia of Solomon and the Queen of Sheba.

Not many of the events and personages of modern history are now outside the ken of the stamp collector, for the demand for commemorative stamps has sometimes outrun the supply of important happenings and anniversaries, and in consequence comparatively unimportant persons and events have suddenly been elevated to the publicity of the postage stamp.

The collector who sets out to form an historical collection of any kind will need to have a certain knowledge of his subject, based on a reading of something more than reference books. The necessary link between reading and postage stamps is supplied by the Stanley Gibbons Catalogues (both Simplified and Complete), for these give, in most cases, the subjects of the stamp designs, without which the collector would be very much at sea.

Let me add that, in mentioning history, geography, and other branches of knowledge in this chapter, I am not one of those who go about telling fond parents, 'Oh, Mrs Jones, you really should let little Willie collect stamps. It will help him so splendidly with his history and geography.'

Not that the educational advantages of stamp collecting are neglected, for in most schools it is now fostered instead of being frowned upon, as it was for so many years. In some schools it now forms part of the curriculum, while in many it is used as an aid to instruction in other subjects and it has the approval and even the recommendation of many of the present-day inspectors of schools. The numerous school stamp clubs are also doing good work.

The geographical side of the postage stamp is one which is stressed by many of the albums provided for the collector.

There are pages for each country, and these are grouped in
continents and the colonies or dependencies of each country
are grouped together. So far as the former colonial empires
are concerned, their connexion is often emphasized by the
use of stamps of a standard type for a period. Such are the
numerous De La Rue keyplate types of the British Colonies,
the Commerce and Navigation type of the French possessions, and the 'Ceres' and other designs which have been
used by so many of Portugal's Colonies. Breaking away
from the purely geographical limitation of country or continent many collectors have produced most attractive and
striking displays by grouping the stamps which depict places
in various countries so that they illustrate a world tour.
Such a stamp tour may be made extraordinarily interesting,
if a proper sequence is observed, and the stamps themselves
are accompanied by brief notes about the places depicted
on them.

These stamp views are not confined to famous buildings,
statues, and memorials, but include some of the world's
most magnificent scenery – mountains, glaciers, waterfalls,
rivers, lakes, and seascapes – views beautiful in the miniature
form in which they appear to the unaided eye, but often
still more charming when seen under the magnifying glass.

Once we are started on this world tour, there is no limit
to the stamps which may be included, even though we do
not keep within the covers of the geography book. Many
countries of the world have used their stamps to show us
something of the races which people them, and of their life
and work. In undeveloped countries the natives are seen
doing crude tasks by hand, while on the stamps of modern
commercial states huge factories and mills are pictured.

From the races of the world it is only a step to the birds
and beasts, and a zoological collection is probably the most
popular of the 'thematic' groups. The fauna of the world
have been so freely illustrated on stamps that a wonderful
array can be got together, which will include many out of
the way species.

The botanist, too, is liberally catered for. Even where the central design of a stamp does not show a tree, plant, or flower, the artist will often use a spray or a flower as a fill-up for side or corner, so that a hawk-like eye is needed if the full range of stamp-botany is to be covered.

When making his world tour, the collector will not be altogether unprovided with maps and charts, as were so many of the early explorers in whose tracks he must follow, for there are quite a few miniature maps on stamps. As for means of transport, he will find in the stamp album a range of vehicles sufficient to give him, in themselves, the subject for a collection. If he wishes to voyage on water, he has the choice of every type of vessel, from canoe and coracle, through sailing ships of all types, to the modern ocean greyhound. On land, he may go afoot, on horse- or mule-back, in a litter, in wagons and carriages of all kinds, on motorbike or in a motor-car, or by rail. In the air, there are 'planes of all kinds awaiting him, and balloons and airships differing from one another as widely as did the first dirigible gasbag of Santos Dumont from the *Graf Zeppelin*.

Our sections here overlap, for many stamps which find a place in a 'transport' collection can also properly be included in an engineering collection. Stamp pictures include views of many famous canals, bridges, harbours, railways, and aqueducts, while if we add the work of the builder to that of the engineer, there are cathedrals, government buildings, post offices, lighthouses, wireless stations and other erections. (It is quite an interesting study to take a cross-section of the world's stamps to show the various types of architecture, the modern buildings being contrasted with the ancient, and the civilized with the native huts and kraals which are also depicted on stamps.)

The engineering section may also include a few stamp portraits of famous engineers, such as General Goethals, who was finally responsible for the completion of the Panama Canal; and this mention of portrait stamps brings us to a wider subject – the men and women of the stamp album.

In the early days of the postage stamp, the portrait of the monarch or other ruler was regarded as the natural subject for stamp designs. This was probably due to the association of stamps with coinage in the minds of those who produced them. Here and there a country made a self-denying ordinance, and forbade the appearance of its living rulers on its stamps. Chile, for example, would, for many years, have no portrait but that of Columbus on her stamps, while to this day only *dead* Presidents may be portrayed on the stamps of the United States. It was a natural vanity which made a President of some small republic (whose term of office, as he well knew, might be a very short one) wish to go down to posterity on the stamps of his country, and it was with an equally natural feeling of pleasure that the successors of some of these Presidents blotted out the stamp portraits of their predecessors.

A modern example is afforded by the order of the late Shah Pahlavi of Persia, on his accession, which instructed that the stamps then in use, which bore the portrait of his predecessor, should not pass through the post unless the likeness was thoroughly obliterated, with the result that adhesive paper, burnt cork, and other materials were employed to hide the ex-Shah, the zeal of the postal employee being apparently measured by the completeness with which he blotted out the offending visage. The Japanese also blotted out the stamp portraits of Queen Wilhelmina of the Netherlands when they occupied the Dutch possessions in the East Indies.

With the coming of the commemorative stamp, it was natural that the honour of portrayal on stamps should be extended to famous figures of the past and, in some special cases, to living men, and it is thus possible to form collections of stamp portraits illustrating various human activities, these being supplemented, in many cases, by pictorial stamps connected with their work.

Apart from the world's rulers, whose stamp portraits provide material for a collection, there are a number of

persons whose activities have been mainly political –
dictators, liberators, and lesser fry, the latter in many cases
so unimportant that it is extremely difficult to find out any
details of their life-story.

More interesting than these are the explorers, whose
portraits might well find a place in a geographical collection, though they form an equally suitable subject for a
special display. Most popular of these, with the stamp
designer, is Christopher Columbus, whose life and adventures
have been the subject of numerous stamp issues from countries on both sides of the Atlantic. There is hardly an important incident in the life of the great discoverer which has
not formed the subject of a stamp design. Captain Cook is
another popular figure, while the names of Pizarro, Balboa,
Magellan, Cabot, La Perouse, and others give the album its
flavour of adventure, which may be continued and ex-
panded if the collector adds to his explorers the generals and
admirals of the stamp world, and the many views of battles
by land and sea, which are found on stamps. Most of the
generals seem to be shown on stamps in a political capacity
– Grant, for example, as a President of the United States –
but the admirals include Nelson (though only as a statue),
Cochrane, who fought for Greece and Chile, after falling
foul of the British Admiralty, Sir Edward Codrington, who
commanded the Allied fleets which destroyed the Turkish
navy at Navarino, Farragut, the first admiral of the U.S.
Navy, and others.

Apart from these 'official' warriors, the stamp portrait
gallery shows us a host of patriots of many nations who have
fought for their countries' independence; in fact 'the story
of liberty' would make a good subject for a stamp collection
planned with a little imagination and knowledge, for there
are not only the portrait stamps, but others which show
declarations of independence, street fighting, formal battles,
councils, meetings of conspirators, and all the usual para-
phernalia of revolt. Two 'fighters for freedom' who have
earned their places on the various stamps which have been

issued in their memory are President Kennedy of the United States and Sir Winston Churchill.

There are also several 'subject collections' which may be formed in connexion with more peaceful pursuits. Literature, for example, is well represented by interesting commemorative stamps with which various countries have delighted to honour their famous sons. A case in point is Britain's celebrated writer and dramatist, William Shakespeare, whose 400th anniversary of birth in 1964 was the occasion for stamp commemoratives by Britain and some of the Commonwealth territories as well as other countries in the world.

King Solomon is not commemorated on stamps as a writer, but his throne appears on some of the issues of Ethiopia. (In making a subject collection, one must be ready to strain a point and bring in even indirect connexions with persons or places which cannot be immediately associated with the subject in hand.) Julius Caesar appears on stamps of Italy, Dante and Manzoni also, not to mention saints and apostles, who are portrayed for other reasons than that of authorship. St Paul, too, will be found on the stamps of Malta. France gives us Ronsard, Anatole France, Victor Hugo, and others and also a picture of Daudet's mill; Germany honours Goethe, Schiller, and Kant; Spain Cervantes; Hungary Petofi and Maurus Jokai; Norway Ibsen and Björnson, Denmark Hans Andersen; Fiume D'Annunzio; Portugal Camoens and Branco; Poland Sienkiewicz of *Quo Vadis* fame; Russia, Karl Marx, Gorky, and Tolstoy, as well as Dickens, Fielding, and G. B. Shaw; Samoa Robert Louis Stevenson and Austria a whole series of authors, poets, and playwrights, not very well known outside that country.

Nor are some of the countries content with honouring the man alone, for the whole diverting story of Don Quixote and Sancho Panza is pictured for us on the Cervantes issue of Spain; Portugal illustrates characters from the works of Branco and incidents from the life of Camoëns; while

Manzoni's *I Promessi Sposi* and the tales of the Bulgarian Vazoff also have stamp illustrations.

There are, too, a number of authors who have appeared on stamps in other capacities – King James I and Francis Bacon on the Cabot series of Newfoundland, 'Carmen Sylva' of Roumania and Queen Marie, and quite a number of others. A literary collection might also be extended to include stamps depicting scenes and events which have been mentioned in famous works of fiction, though this is, perhaps, going rather far.

The whole contents of the stamp album come within the realm of Art, for there are few stamps in the production of which some artist, however humble, has not collaborated. Quite a few stamp designs – particularly those devoted to historic scenes – and many portraits, are reproduced from paintings, and there are a number of stamp reproductions of really famous works of art. As examples, frescoes by Michelangelo are shown on stamps of Italy and Libya, paintings by Dyckmans and Raphael have found a place on stamps of the Saar, Rembrandt and some of his masterpieces appear on Dutch issues. Belgium has perpetuated designs by the famous war cartoonist Raemaekers, while France has reproduced a delicate Fragonard. Collectors interested in art have made a considerable study of the story of the artists and engravers responsible for stamp designs and the subject is a fascinating one.

Sculpture, good and bad, is plentiful in the pages of a stamp album. On the stamps of Greece there are beautiful reproductions of statues by Praxiteles, Peonias, and other masters, and from them we can turn to conventional representations of modern warriors and politicians, or to the crude images of native ju-jus and idols.

Music is very well represented on stamps. The stamp orchestra must be culled from many countries, and will be a varied one. Many of the instruments only appear on stamps incidentally and will take some searching for, often with a magnifying glass.

When we think of composers, we naturally turn to the Austrian charity stamps of 1922, a wonderfully engraved series of portraits, which includes Haydn, Mozart, Beethoven, Schubert, Bruckner, Strauss, and Hugo Wolf. Germany adds Bach, Handel, and Wagner stamps. Poland has given us portraits of Paderewski and Chopin – the former in his political capacity – while Czechoslovakia has honoured Dvorak and Smetana. From France come stamps in memory of Berlioz and Debussy, and the U.S.A. has a Sousa stamp.

The scientists and inventors might almost be grouped with our engineering section, already referred to above. Here we should find the astronomer Copernicus (Poland), the radio pioneer Popov (Russia), Volta (after whom the volt is named), and Galvani on stamps of Italy, Pasteur, Berthelot, Ampère, and Daguerre (France) and many others.

Perhaps the most dramatic of modern scientific themes concerns space research, the hitherto undreamed of achievements of getting man into space and of landing rockets on the Moon. Astronauts, rockets, satellites, and spaceships – all have appeared on stamps during the past few years.

The religions of the world form the subject of an interesting side-line collection. The gods and goddesses of Greece and Rome will be found on numerous stamps, while Egypt has not altogether forgotten her deities when designing her stamps. Some of the Eastern religions are recalled by stamps of the Indian Native States, Japan, and other countries, though sometimes the only reminder is a picture of a temple or shrine. Mythology, too, is the occasional subject of stamp designs, and legendary birds and beasts add variety to the album pages.

Christianity has its representatives mainly in the pictured lives of the saints, St Francis, St Anthony, St Benedict, and others having been honoured with special series. Italy has given us stamps illustrating the ceremonies of the 'Holy Year', and there are a number of churches and cathedrals on stamps. The Maltese stamps showing the shipwreck of St Paul have already been mentioned, and the stamp portrait of his host on that occasion, St Publius, afterwards first Bishop of Malta, should not be overlooked on the later 1s. 6d. stamps of the island. Of equal interest is the $2\frac{1}{2}$ piastre stamp of the 1928 Jubilee issue of Cyprus, which reproduces a quaint old picture which shows the finding of the body of St Barnabas.

A number of scenes of biblical history may be found on stamps of Syria and the Lebanon, not to mention the few views of the Holy Land which adorn the stamps of Jordan and Palestine.

Students of heraldry will find it possible to form an extensive collection of stamps bearing arms, badges and devices often more attractive to the eye than accurate to an extent which would satisfy the College of Heralds, but none the less interesting on that account.

Some coins are reproduced on stamps, but hardly sufficient for it to be possible to claim that a serious collection can be formed.

One collection which must not be overlooked is that of sports stamps. The craze for commemorating every event of importance has naturally been extended to include the various international Olympic meetings, and Greece, Holland, Belgium, Hungary, France, Bulgaria, Costa Rica, Cuba, Germany, U.S.A., and others have issued sets showing either the old Olympic Games of ancient Greece, or modern sportsmen of various kinds. Czechoslovakia overprinted stamps to signalize an international Olympic Congress and also a congress of the 'Sokols' or national athletic associations, while there are Scout stamps from various countries.

Field sports are pictured on many stamps. The Cabot issue of Newfoundland describes three of its values as illustrative of sports which might be enjoyed in the (then) colony – caribou hunting, ptarmigan shooting, and salmon fishing – and other countries have, directly or indirectly, added to the 'sporting print' section of the stamp album.

It is a tribute to the breadth of our hobby that there are very few branches of human interest and knowledge which cannot be in some way illuminated by postage stamps. By design, by association, by contrast, and by inscription, every stamp or group of stamps has its story to tell, and the collector who gets most fun out of the hobby is he, or she, who has the fullest appreciation of what lies behind the stamp and who does not merely treat it as just one more specimen to be added to a numerical score.

In connexion with this subject of stamp designs, the absolute necessity of possessing either the big Stanley Gibbons Stamp Catalogue or the Simplified Edition must be stressed if the reader is even to begin the study of stamp designs. It is quite obvious that no one can investigate the story of an event or person depicted on a stamp unless he knows what or who that event or person is; and though it is true that a number of stamps carry their own descriptions, these are often in foreign languages, while many have no descriptive wording at all. Once the subject of the design has been learned from the catalogue, works of reference and other literature can be searched for further details, and such details will then be incorporated very briefly in the pages of the album, the full story, if a good one, being noted mentally for the delectation of friends to whom the collection is shown.

It is undoubtedly to the pictorial side of stamp collecting, of which this chapter mainly treats, that the hobby owes so much of its popularity in our days. The cinema and television has accustomed millions of men, women, and children to think in pictures, and in the stamp album they find pictures which, though 'still', are yet alive with interest, while the new issues of the world, as they come out from day to day, provide an international illustrated newspaper which cannot be beaten for scope and variety.

Chapter Twenty-two

SIDELINE COLLECTIONS

In the last chapter we considered methods of collecting based, for the most part, on a consideration of the designs and associations of postage stamps, but there are several other methods of collecting, some of which aim at establishing a simplified basis for a collection, while others are the result of a search for novelty.

If the general collector sets out to obtain the stamps of the whole world, reckoning as varieties only those which the issuing post office would consider to be different issues, and disregarding all varieties of watermark, perforation and colour, he still has an enormous, and in fact an impossible task before him. That does not prevent it from being a very interesting one, and as completeness is obviously unattainable from the start, the inevitable gaps in his album need not trouble him.

There are, however, one or two methods of collecting, for which an even simpler basis has been adopted; and while it still remains impossible to reach completeness, owing to the presence of great rarities in every possible grouping, there is a marked reduction in the field to be covered.

The 'type' collection, to which these remarks refer, in its fullest form includes only the stamps of each country which differ in basic design; i.e., if there is a set of eleven values, all in one design, and with only the denomination altered, only one stamp would be needed for the collection. The saving is obvious. Alterations of inscriptions other than the value may be regarded or not, according to the taste of the collector. For example, if there are two sets of similar basic

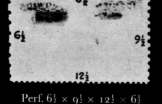

Perf. 12½ × 10   Perf. 6½ × 9½ × 12½ × 6½   Imperf. × Perf. 8

COMPOUND PERFORATIONS

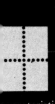

Characteristic intersection of 'Comb' perforation

Characteristic intersection of 'Line' perforation

Double perforation

Results of accurate and inaccurate perforation

Pen cancellation
(postal)

Afghanistan used to cancel
stamps by tearing them

Bar cancellation

Punched hole
(telegraphic use)

Pre-cancels

Travelling Post Office

Exhibition postmark

Army postmark

Canadian Duplex postmark

British 'Used Abroad' postmark

A machine frank

Crown CA single   Crown CA multiple   Script CA multiple   St. Edward's Crown CA

STANDARD BRITISH EMPIRE WATERMARKS

Star   Numerals   Spray

Umbrella   Mesh   Lozenges   Elephants

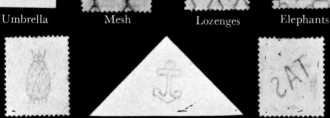

Pine   Anchor   'TAS'

Ant-eater without tail · · · · · · · · · · · Canoe without helmsman

Front · · · · · · · · Back

Walter lily

Head printed on back

'Sir Codrington'

Wrong yacht

Frame inscription inverted

Before telescopes were invented

5st. stamp in sheet of 3st.

Backs of Latvian stamps printed on German war maps and Soviet banknotes

Advertisement on back of New Zealand stamp

Stamp with Latin prayer on back

Nicaraguan back-to-front stamp

Spanish stamp with sheet number

Italian and Belgian stamps with advertisements attached

Russia

Serbia

Montenegro

Bulgaria

Japan

Saudi Arabia

Afghanistan

Turkey

Persia

China

Thailand

Georgia

Kashmir

Nepal

Tibet

Ethiopia

Morocco

Cambodia

Korea

Ceylon

Burma

Syria

Japan

Israel

Ryukyu Is.

Mongolia

Greece

Travancore

Armenia

Poonch

Crude forgeries found in old collections

Forgery   Genuin

design, one of which is inscribed 'POSTAGE' and the other 'POSTAGE AND REVENUE', it is for him to decide whether the scope of his collection is to include one stamp from each series, or one stamp to represent both.

Carrying simplification a stage further, the stamps of the world may be looked at as a whole, and where a basic design recurs in several lands, with the name of the country alone altered, one stamp can be taken to represent the whole group.

Going even further, such things as differing frame designs may be regarded as of no account, and the collection may be so arranged as to include only stamps which depict different events, things, places, or persons. In the case of much-portrayed persons such as our British sovereigns, a big reduction may be made by this method, though a little latitude may be allowed for the inclusion of portraits taken at different ages and in different costumes. This is about as far as reduction can go, if there is to be any representative character about the stamp display.

Another type of collection, suitable for people of limited means, finds a place for one stamp only from each country. Here a nice judgment is required in selecting stamps which will most fully typify the country of issue.

Perhaps even better, as it allows more scope, is a 'typical' collection in which each country is represented by a few stamps which are typical of the style and range of all its issues.

Sometimes a purely arbitrary characteristic is considered in order to qualify stamps for admission to a collection. Thus there are collectors who take nothing but black stamps and others who prefer stamps of another colour. Admitting that black, at least, shows up the design of a stamp clearly, these one-colour collections tend to become monotonous and methods which admit of more variety are to be preferred.

Collections of stamps of a distinctive shape are sometimes made, and the most popular consists of those of triangular design. There is a wide range of these, covering some very attractive issues, and the resulting display is something quite out of the ordinary.

A novel collection, which will provide a lot of fun for the owner and his friends, is one in which stamps are chosen bearing designs illustrating as many as possible of the words in the dictionary beginning with one particular letter. Ingenuity and a sense of humour will find full play here.

A collection which I have always warmly advocated, owing to the fact that it is an effective counterblast to those who are always telling their fellow collectors – particularly the younger ones – what they may or may not collect, may be described as a go-as-you-please collection. It *must* be formed in a loose-leaf album, and this is the only time the word 'must' need be used in connexion with it, for the rule of the go-as-you-please collection is that you take just the stamps that interest you. It may be that you like the designs of some stamps. Well, put them in. Others may interest you by reasons of some story attached to them, or because of their shape, colour, or some other peculiarity. Then, in they go! If a collection of this kind is arranged on some plan, so that the various stamps on a page are linked together by a common quality, and descriptive notes are added, to emphasize the interest which they have for the owner of the collection, he will find stamp-collecting a remarkable vehicle for the expression of his personality, in a way which filling the pages of a printed album will never permit him to do.

Chapter Twenty-three

AIR STAMPS AND COVERS

The collecting of airmail stamps and covers has enjoyed a considerable vogue for many years. If it has fallen off this is because now the great mass of overseas mail is carried by air and there is little 'pioneering' except perhaps in the introduction of new routes and the use of newer and faster jet aircraft. And while stamps are still issued inscribed 'Airmail' (or in the foreign equivalents), these are often part of a country's definitive issue and do not depict any particular aspect of aviation or the airmail services as the earlier issues did. Nevertheless many enthusiasts are still attracted to aero-philately, and this chapter is an acknowledgment of the fascination and romance of this branch of the hobby.

The air stamp is a fairly modern thing, for until mails were carried by air there was obviously no need for special stamps to frank them. On some of the pioneer balloon flights it was the practice to carry postcards of some special design, which were either posted on the arrival of the balloon at its destination, or were tossed overboard to be entrusted to the tender mercies of whoever picked them up. When the aeroplane began to be developed, aviation meetings and cross-country flights were organized, and on such occasions correspondence of a souvenir nature was often carried in the machines. Such correspondence might consist of special postcards or envelopes with distinctive designs, or ordinary letters and cards with a special postmark or handstamped design or inscription, the latter being described by collectors of air covers as 'cachets'. At some meetings special labels, looking as much like postage stamps as possible, were sold, and used to frank the cards, in fact some of these were postage stamps in a restricted sense, though they had only very limited franking power and rarely had any government authority behind them.

It was not until 1917 that the first official government air stamps were issued, when Italy applied special overprints to two of her 'express' stamps for use on correspondence carried on experimental flights between Rome and Turin and Naples and Palermo. Thenceforward, many of the important trial flights had their special stamps, issued under government auspices, and as regular air mail lines were established, some countries issued a series of special stamps for use in connexion with these services. The advantage of using distinctive stamps, in order that mail destined to be handled in a special way may be quickly identified, has already been noted.

At the present time a complete collection of the world's air stamps (including only those which rank on a par with government postage stamps for other purposes) would include many thousands even if minor variations are not taken into account.

The occasions for issuing them range from some of the great historic trans-Atlantic flights such as those of Hawker, de Pinedo, and Alcock, to the flights of modern jet planes. Their designs are as varied as the reasons for their existence. On some, the aerial character is indicated merely by an overprint, which may consist of words, or a device, such as an aeroplane propeller, or the machine itself. Of distinctive air mail designs, aeroplanes of all types, from the first Wright machine to the latest giant mail-carrier, are shown, sometimes 'in the blue' and on other stamps in flight over a particular town or stretch of country.

For the rest, artists have vied with one another in an attempt to symbolize the speed of flight. Birds, winged beings, a winged post-horn, and a flight of arrows are typical designs. The faces of famous pioneers of flight, or pilots of the day, look out at us from the album page, and on some stamps there are maps of historic flights, one of the most interesting being Newfoundland's map of the North Atlantic showing the routes followed by those who had flown, or nearly flown that ocean at the time. There are also stamps commemorating record stratosphere flights.

There are one or two countries, notably in South America, where the government has handed over the air services to a private company to develop and exploit, and where such companies have the right to issue air stamps backed by government authority. Such stamps are of almost as much importance as those issued by the national post offices and may well be collected. The 'S.C.A.D.T.A.' stamps of Colombia are examples, while Canada has permitted the issue of special stamps by companies carrying mail by air to outlying goldfields, etc.

The collector who wishes to start an air collection will be well advised to begin by acquiring as many of the government air stamps as he can, supplementing them, if he wishes, by the stamps of authorized companies, such as those described above. Apart from the fact that this group of stamps is the most interesting, it has the added advantage that it is collected not only by the numerous company of those who take air stamps only, but also by collectors of stamps generally – and where the demand is, there also is the ultimate rise in value.

If he likes, he can continue further, and include the often very quaint labels and quasi-stamps of the early aviation meetings, and other things of a similar kind. Many of these, though interesting as souvenirs of the early days of flying, were produced mainly with the object of making a profit out of collectors, and the reader will have to decide for himself whether he will collect from the historical aspect, in which case he need not concern himself with the intent with which the labels were issued, or whether he will try to import into air stamp collecting the same strict discrimination which he would apply to ordinary issues.

The same remark applies to air 'covers' – a term which in

its widest sense may be held to include any correspondence borne by air. In this section we have the various items carried on the early flights and at the early meetings already referred to. These may have been franked by special stamps, either governmental or private, or they may simply be distinguished by a pictorial device, by inscriptions descriptive of the occasion, or by hand-stamped 'cachets' which also may be either inscriptions or of a pictorial nature. Then there are covers carried on the great historic flights – trans-Atlantic, round the world, and so on. All of these have a great souvenir interest, but the most valuable will always be those of flights for which special government stamps were issued, for quantities of such stamps would naturally be small in most cases and the dual demand makes every air stamp printed in small quantities a potential rarity, in fact several of the air stamps issued in connexion with big flights rival many older stamps of equal scarcity, in value.

It must be frankly admitted that there are a great number of air covers which would have had no reason for their existence, if there had been no collectors. The craze for 'first flight' covers, i.e. covers carried on the first flight over a new air route, at one time bade fair to swamp the hobby, for the most flimsy excuses were used as a pretext for a flight, and every speculator tried to get exclusive batches of covers carried, with an eye to personal profit.

Finally there are the covers carried in the ordinary way of business on the established air mail routes. These have not the historic appeal of the world-famous flights, but they show the air mails doing their job, and there is no taint of the speculative about them.

The best test by which to decide whether an air cover should find a place in the album or not, is to ask, 'Was the flight on which it was carried of historic interest?' or 'Was the cover carried by air in the ordinary course of post?' If covers which satisfy neither of these conditions are included, it must only be because of the personal fancy of the owner of the collection.

The aero-philatelist who is really bitten by the hobby does not stop short at stamps and covers. He studies the various types of 'cachet' employed both on experimental flights, and on temporary and permanent air mail routes, and collects covers showing every variation in colour or detail. He has a collection of the adhesive labels ('etiquettes') supplied at the post offices of various countries for affixing to envelopes to indicate that they are to be carried by air. If there are official types of air-post envelopes, airgraphs, or air letter forms, he will want all these; while official notices and other documents in connexion with flights of all kinds will not come amiss to him. If a collection of this scope is formed on a definite historical plan, it can be made very interesting and instructive.

For the ordinary collector, I recommend a collection, as complete as possible, of the government air stamps of the world, with as many interesting covers as fancy dictates or the state of the purse will permit. Beyond this, a background composed of souvenirs of some of the early meetings may be added 'to taste'.

There are signs, however, that the postal rocket, hurtling through the stratosphere, may be the ultimate mail-carrier. Many experiments have taken place, sometimes successfully, sometimes with the destruction of the mail or damage to the experimenter, but our experiences during and since the Second World War have shown the distances they can cover and it will obviously not be long before their flight and point of arrival can be accurately controlled.

I do not recommend the collection of so-called rocket-post 'stamps' or covers. The rocket-post experiments were usually of a genuine character, but the experimenters, in order to raise funds, too often allowed themselves to be exploited by people interested in the stamp trade, who provided the 'stamps' and afterwards sold them and the rocket covers at a good profit.

Chapter Twenty-four

THE MONEY SIDE OF STAMP
COLLECTING

IN the early days of the hobby, the collector who paid a few pence for a postage stamp was considered a lunatic by his friends. Even to collect stamps at all was considered, if not insane, then at least not quite respectable, and even today something of this atmosphere hangs about Philately, and gentlemen with no other crimes on their conscience will hide from their friends the fact that they collect stamps, as if it were an unforgivable sin.

Nowadays there is such a general demand for stamps that every stamp has a cash value, and this value, generally speaking, has proved more stable in modern times than those of stocks and shares or even of national currencies. It is true that some very common stamps are worth so small a fraction of a penny that you have to have some thousands of them before you have got a shilling's worth, but at the other end of the scale there are stamps worth £500, £1,000, and even more.

Though stamp values as a whole are very stable, the value of an individual stamp will fluctuate, according to the conditions under which it has to be disposed of. A dealer who has a large stock of a stamp will not pay the same price for extra supplies as he might if he were short of it. A collector who is specially interested in the stamps of a country will perhaps pay more for a particular variety than one who is less keen. The issues of a country or group will be more in demand in one part of the world than in another, and will consequently fetch higher prices there.

Unfortunately, in stamps, there is no chain of central 'stock exchanges' which can give numerical expression to the world demand (or lack of it) for a particular stamp.

The chief cities of the stamp world, London, Paris, Berlin, and New York, are loosely linked together, and the leading dealers are more or less in touch, but not sufficiently closely for there to be any automatic system by which prices can find their own level through fluctuations of supply and demand.

The best guides to comparative values are the prices in the leading stamp catalogues, but these prices do not represent what his stamps are worth to the collector. They are the selling prices of the dealer who publishes the catalogue, and represent his own ideas, based on a wide experience, and on the facility or difficulty with which he sells or is able to buy stamps on the basis of his prices.

Even the prices given in the stamp catalogue may not be fixed. The dealer may secure a temporary supply of a stamp cheaply. He knows the supply will not last long, so there is no object in lowering the catalogue price. He therefore makes an offer of the stamp at a reduced price, for a short period. He probably also allows a discount off his catalogue prices to regular customers, and this rate may vary according to the popularity of particular stamps at a particular period, for certain stamps have their fashionable periods, and their periods of neglect.

The method by which stamps are sold also affects their price to the collector, for the sum charged includes not only the original cost of the stamp to the dealer, but the cost of stocking and selling the stamp (rent, salaries, taxes, advertising, etc.) plus a small profit. In other words, the collector is paying for service as well as for the stamp.

Now if stamps are ordered singly from the catalogue, the dealer's assistant has to take the order, and go from book to book, or from box to box, picking out each of the stamps one by one, putting them in a book, pricing them, adding up the value, and so on – quite a lot of work which, when the stamps are very cheap ones, it does not in fact pay the dealer to do. If, however, the dealer can pick, say, one hundred cheap stamps of which he has plenty of stock, and make them up into packets of '100 different', the work involved is much less, and those stamps will cost the collector proportionately less. To take an example, a packet of 500 stamps will cost you less than £1. The same stamps ordered one by one at even a penny each would involve an outlay of over £2.

In the case of rarer stamps, the purchaser is getting more stamp value and less service value, and is therefore getting more for his money. This is obvious, for directly he has bought a stamp, the part of its cost which represents dealer service and profit disappears so far as he is concerned, and he can get for it only its value as a stamp, i.e. what he is able to re-sell it for.

How can the would-be vendor of stamps (the private owner) find out their value, then? The catalogue will tell him whether he has any rare items, but the inexperienced must be careful that they are reading the catalogue aright, for slight differences may make a variation of pounds in the value, and the human tendency is to take the highest price as the correct one whereas the odds are naturally in favour of the stamp being the commoner, cheaper one. Then, too, allowance has to be made for stamps not in fine condition, which often have only the merest fraction of the value of perfect specimens. Your catalogue may give some indication of the range of value in this connexion. Finally, in old collections particularly, many of the stamps which seem to be rare and valuable are actually forgeries so that the owner is greatly misled as to the value of the collection as a whole.

The only way a collector can find out the value of his stamps is to have them valued by a reliable stamp valuer. Certain of the big firms are licensed valuers, and will carry out the work for a moderate fee. In the case of small collections even such a fee is often more than the collection is worth, so if you are sure of your dealer, and he realizes that you really do not know the value of your stamps, he may be willing to make you an offer for them, and if the firm is a reliable one, the offer will be a fair one. Do not, however, think that you can get a figure from him, and then go somewhere else and see if you can get more. He is not going to allow his offer to be made a basis for his competitors to bid on, and you will be politely told that you must take it or leave it, but that the offer is withdrawn directly the stamps leave his premises.

Therefore, if you want to sell stamps, find a dealer whose reputation stands high, and put yourself in his hands. You will find that in this way you will get a fair price, or, if your stamps do not interest the firm you have selected, you may get some helpful advice as to the best means of disposing of them elsewhere.

A good deal has already been said in previous chapters about the need for care in buying stamps, and emphasis has been laid on the fact that stamps which look the cheapest are often very dear. You want for your money genuine stamps with a guarantee behind them, and stamps in the right condition for the price you are paying. It is poor satisfaction to get stamps at say a sixth of catalogue price if they are in such condition that they are not worth a tenth.

It is also necessary to consider the service you are receiving from the particular dealer from whom you are buying, for you have to pay for this as well as the stamps.

This is best judged, in stamp business, by the quality and scope of the approval selections sent out by a particular firm, and by the proportion of your 'wants' that can be supplied at any given time. A firm which is able to let you have extensive and valuable selections of stamps to look at will naturally have to keep more capital locked up than one which can only send out small selections, and capital costs money in interest. On your part, the bigger selections give you a better chance of making a purchase of satisfactory specimens, while you gain valuable experience from seeing so many stamps, even if you are not able to buy them all.

It is an obvious convenience to you to be able to get a large proportion of your want list filled from one firm and at one time, but here again such service calls for the locking up of a large stock.

Now to the vexed question of making money from stamps – not as a dealer but as a collector. Many collectors seem to think that it is only necessary to spend a sum of money on stamps in order to be able to sell them at a profit in a comparatively short period. There could be no greater fallacy.

It is definitely possible to make money by stamp collecting (though the phrase reads rather horribly when we consider that we are discussing what is primarily an amateur hobby), but it can only be made by investing money in stamps *with knowledge and sound judgment*, or by luck, or by spending a considerable sum spread over a wide field, and leaving time and the general upward tendency of stamp values, to produce an ultimate profit.

There is much to be learned by looking at the values of stamps issued in the early days. It will be seen that many which were common seventy or eighty years ago, are still common today. It is obvious, then, that many low value new issues of today, which are printed in much larger quantities than those of earlier days, will be likely to remain common till long after the readers of this volume are dead. They will get scarcer and scarcer, owing to loss and wastage, but this increased scarcity will not show itself materially in the value of the individual common stamp, but only in wholesale prices. We can therefore rule out common stamps as a likely source of profit.

In stamps of medium price, there will be some that will almost certainly rise fairly rapidly in value, but who is to say which they are? Long experience or intensive study may enable a collector to say that certain moderately priced stamps are much scarcer than they appear, and he may be able to secure some of them and make an eventual profit, but this is not collecting. The man who tries to 'find the winners' by buying all the medium-priced stamps of a certain group will find that his gains on those that rise will be negatived by the loss on those that stand still – for obviously one cannot sell a stamp back to a dealer for what one gave for it, unless *his* selling price has risen in the meantime.

Except for an occasional speculation in a stamp which one thinks will rise rapidly in value, there is no great fortune to be made out of medium-priced stamps, though a collection of these will show a better return than one of common stamps, if a really long period is allowed to elapse between purchase and sale – say twenty years or so. Even then it is doubtful if a real profit will be shown, if the compound interest value of the capital invested be reckoned.

Speculation in stamps – usually in new issues which happen to be printed in limited quantities – is a favourite pursuit with some folk, but even those who know most of the game rarely make a profit when their transactions are regarded as a whole, the gain on one deal being swallowed up by the losses on others. It is just as hard to pick winners in stamps as it is on the Turf or the Stock Exchange. Dealers in stamps should know what they are about and those who have been most successful were not the ones who bought stamps and held them for a rise, but *those who never refused a profit*, however small.

Ruling out the common and medium stamps, we are left with rarities. Here there is a more promising field for investment. For most rare stamps the demand is greater than the supply and, generally speaking, prices rise more rapidly than they do in the lower priced groups. Scarce stamps, in fine condition, are undoubtedly the best philatelic investment, and many wealthy men have put large sums of money into such property. Not all have made a profit, but the majority will be able to say that they have more to show for their money than they would have had if it had been put into stocks and shares during these unsettled times.

The collector of limited means cannot hope to buy many fine and rare stamps, and, from the investment point of view, even if he does, he may select some which do not rise in value. Is there any way by which he can hope to profit?

'Money breeds money' in stamps as in most other departments of life, but there is another thing which produces money and that is hard work. The collector with a small purse, who will take up a country not in too keen demand at the moment, who will study its stamps intensively, make them his pet subject, know where to find the bargains, and when to avoid pitfalls, and who will do judicious propaganda work on behalf of its stamps by writing in the Philatelic Press concerning his discoveries, will, in many cases, find that he can sell his collection eventually at a profit. Not in all cases, for a country may be so 'dead' that nothing will revive it within a single lifetime, but it is a fact that, apart from the wealthy buyers of philatelic gems, the keenest students of stamps have been the most fortunate financially. As philatelic study is open to all, there is thus hope for every collector.

Profits are sometimes made by collectors who take up a new stamp-issuing country from the start, and follow its stamps closely. If a 'boom' starts, as happened in the case of Israel and the United Nations, quick profits may be made, but only by those who pick the right country (a matter of instinct or luck) and who sell out in time, for a boom is inevitably followed by a reaction.

The best attitude for the average collector to take up in regard to the financial aspect of philately is to remember always that he is spending money on an intensely interesting hobby. He is getting more than his money's worth out of it in enjoyment alone – and no one who has collected stamps will deny this – and thus, when he sells his collection, if he ever does, any money he obtains for it is clear profit, even if it does not represent the whole of his outlay. To collect solely with the idea of making money is to place oneself outside the circle of stamp lovers, but to build up a collection with a real love for stamps and with a determination to study them and find out more about them than has yet been known, is the likeliest way to eventual profit.

PART THREE · THE HOBBY

Chapter Twenty-five

THE STAMP WORLD

THE stamp world which this chapter will describe is one into which the vast majority of collectors never enter – a small inner circle which is to some extent organized in societies or groups. Outside this central nucleus comes a larger group, or series of groups of collectors, whose only link is that they read the same stamp magazine, while beyond them again is the great army of stamp collectors, the people who collect because they love the hobby but who have never seen a stamp magazine nor heard of a stamp club or philatelic society. Though the inner and intermediate circles may from time to time do good work for the hobby, by study, by writing, or by propaganda, it is the outer ring, the host of ordinary, unorganized, unlinked collectors, which is the backbone of the game.

The germ of the present-day philatelic society will be found in the informal open-air meetings for the exchange of stamps, which took place in several European capitals in the early days of the hobby. Birchin Lane was the rendezvous in London until the police asked Philately to 'move on'. It did move on, and the consequence was the formation of societies or clubs of enthusiastic collectors for social intercourse, exchange of information and stamps, and the general cultivation of the hobby. Paris led the way in about 1865, but its first society did not have a long life, nor did the first New York society, which followed it in 1867, fare any better, though its successor, the modern Collectors' Club, ranks very high today.

Britain, a little late in the field, as she often is, was able to build on a firmer foundation, and the London Philatelic Society (now the Royal Philatelic Society), which was born in 1869, is alive and flourishing at the present day, and numbers among its past Presidents King George V who held the office when he was Prince of Wales.

There are other societies of various grades and sizes, scattered throughout England and the civilized world. Some of them cater for the young collector, while others are more concerned with advanced students of stamps. They hold regular meetings at which the members, or invited guests, show and describe their collections. Papers are read on various topics, or lectures are given on matters of interest. Many societies have their own library, of which the wiser members make full use, while nearly all have a section through which stamps may be exchanged through the post, each member contributing priced sheets of stamps to a circulating packet, only the difference between sales and purchases being settled in cash. The society usually takes a percentage on the turnover for its general funds.

It has become the practice of late years in many countries for delegates from the various philatelic societies to meet in congress each year. At such gatherings, matters of moment in connexion with the hobby are discussed in papers read before the meetings and are then debated. While not much practical result accrues from these congresses, they provide an opportunity for collectors from different parts of the country to meet socially and to widen their philatelic horizon.

To the leading philatelic societies of the world is also due the momentum and energy which has brought into being another outcome of the hobby – the stamp exhibition. Some of these are merely local shows, organized by a single society, but they have a good effect in promoting interest in

Philately and attracting recruits. The earliest philatelic exhibitions were probably similar, but they are very far removed from the great international exhibitions of the present day, in which collectors from all parts of the world display their collections in the hope of winning medals or trophies, and where stamps to the value of several million pounds may be displayed under one roof. These exhibitions draw visitors from all over the globe, and provide opportunities for intercourse in the international sphere, such as the congress offers in national circles.

In 1956 Stanley Gibbons marked the occasion of their centenary with a splendid Exhibition at the Waldorf Hotel in London, and in 1965 they held a much bigger Exhibition at the Royal Festival Hall, London, for the centenary of the Gibbons Catalogue which was first published in 1865. This magnificent show was opened by the Postmaster-General, the Right Honourable Anthony Wedgwood Benn, M.P., and some of the world's rarest stamps, including the unique British Guiana 'One Cent' black on magenta of 1856, were on show.

From the philatelic societies has also sprung the idea of honouring those who have done good work for the hobby, either by study, by writing, or in any other way. The Philatelic Congress of Great Britain is responsible for a Roll of Distinguished Philatelists, which includes the names of leading collectors of many nations, headed by that of King George V, and the Collectors' Club of New York also has a similar Roll of Honour. Medals are also given by many philatelic societies for good work done by their members, particularly in the reading of papers.

It is not a difficult matter to form a philatelic society (or perhaps the simpler title of 'stamp club' will be less suggestive of difficulty). The first essential is an extremely energetic man, very keen on the hobby, to act as secretary. Around him he should gather a small nucleus of equally enthusiastic collectors. These may meet at first in one another's houses, at not too frequent intervals – possibly once a fortnight while the first glow of pride in the society is still there, and later, when things settle down, once a month. The early meetings should consist simply of an informal interchange of experiences and a similarly informal inspection of the collections of members, with, of course, keen discussions as to the best method of causing the society to grow and prosper.

The next step, after the first nucleus has attracted to itself a rather larger membership, is to find a more permanent meeting-place. In most cases philatelic societies hold their meetings in a room at the local library or institute, and usually manage to secure the additional privilege of a lock-up cupboard for such catalogues and books as the club library may contain. In such surroundings, the meetings will become more formal, but always some portion of the time should be given up to informal chat. A programme will be drafted, and here the first great difficulty will be encountered. In a modern stamp circle, particularly if the members are adults, most of them will be specialists, collecting different countries or groups, and if they are anything like the average collector, they will find very little to interest them in the stamps owned by their fellow members. The keen secretary will do all in his power to promote mutual interest and his programme must include, in addition to formal displays of members' collections, talks on general topics interesting to all, debates, film shows, competitions, and anything he can think of to brighten the evenings. Film strips, with accompanying lectures for reading, can be borrowed for a small fee, and some of these lectures are suitable for recruiting purposes, that is to say they can be delivered publicly in a hall hired for the purpose to an audience drawn there by advertising or by the persuasion of members of the stamp club, in the hope of converting some to an appreciation of the pleasures of stamp collecting.

On all these matters and in connexion with the building up of a section for the exchange of stamps, the budding secretary will be able to take advantage of the experience of other secretaries in charge of the fortunes of established societies, most of whom are only too willing to pass on their knowledge. It is essential, however, that he should avoid copying the defects of other organizations, many of which are moribund through lack of imagination.

The outstanding drawbacks to many philatelic meetings are: unpunctual starting, uncomfortable quarters, too much unnecessary talk from the chairman and other officials, and above all (owing to the fact that so many collectors specialize in the stamps of one group or country) displays and talks which appeal to very few persons in each audience.

The main object of a stamp meeting is to see stamps or talk about them. Another object is to interest all the members all the time, not a few of the members some of the time. If the secretary interests most of his members at every meeting, the success of the society is assured.

Looking at the programmes of the philatelic societies in Great Britain, as a whole, one is struck by the fact that the majority of the meetings are occupied with papers and displays dealing with a single country. Only a genius can make a specialized paper on one country interesting to people who do not collect its stamps, and so varied are the interests of collectors that, out of any audience, it is pretty certain that at least eighty per cent will have no interest in a particular specialized display. Obviously, therefore, specialized displays of a single country are *the worst possible fare to put before philatelic meetings*.

Displays by those public-spirited 'leading philatelists' who visit so many societies each season, are even worse, if over-indulged in, for, even where the papers read are not above the heads of the audiences, the stamps shown are usually so magnificent and plentiful that they dishearten the average collector. Better by far to have two or four shorter displays in an evening, or even a series of ten-minute papers and displays. In this way variety is secured and the interest of members aroused.

If a display is properly arranged and written up, there is

really no need for a lot of talk about it, all that is necessary being a few introductory remarks after which the members present can ask questions while the stamps are being handed round. Handing round the sheets of stamps in rotation is, however, a very awkward method of conducting a display as, if the owner is reading a paper about them, only one or two members will have before them the stamps he is talking about at a particular moment. It is a good idea, if feasible, to lay the display out on the tables before the meeting is formally opened, so that those present may gain a general idea of what is going to be shown.

Where conditions permit, it is a good plan to make some of the meetings entirely informal, the members gathering round the fire and handing round a couple of pages from their collections. There are sure to be items shown which will arouse discussion and members who would not speak at a formal meeting will be tempted to give their views in conversation.

Do not think that, because the members of a society are nearly all specialists, they will not be interested in meetings of a more elementary nature. Talks dealing with the designs of stamps, if interesting, will always hold an audience, while competitions calling on members to identify parts of stamp designs, or to say which country issued a stamp with a certain inscription, have proved very popular. Competitions of this kind, if they have to be based on hand-drawn pictures of bits of stamps, are rather hard to organize, but if a film or slide projector is used, any competition can be run at a comparatively low cost. An epidiascope is even better, for then no films or slides are needed, the stamps themselves being placed in the instrument and reflected on to the screen, but the hire of an epidiascope is fairly costly. Most big schools now have them, however, and can probably be induced to lend them.

One meeting a year should be reserved for a film show of a popular nature, and if this is made an open meeting and held in a fairly large hall to which the public is invited, early in the season, it should prove a good means of obtaining recruits for any philatelic society. Another way of building up a reserve of collectors for future membership is to hold a special meeting for juniors at least once a season. They will, of course, also be invited to the film show.

Joint meetings with neighbouring societies will provide a means of widening interest and making new contacts, while some societies find at least one purely social evening per season a valuable help in creating and fostering good-fellowship.

Debates on philatelic topics of general interest will often provide good fun, especially if they are not made too formal. A conversational atmosphere is best if you wish to have the majority of those present taking part.

An evening of impromptu talks will prove very interesting if it is understood that anyone who is called upon to speak must do so. The best method of selecting speakers is for those present to draw slips of paper out of a hat, each member having to deal in a five minutes' talk with the subject written on his slip. The subjects must, of course, be of a general nature, such as 'My Favourite Stamp Design', or 'Why I like (or dislike) Commemoratives'.

Informality and ingenuity are the keys to interest. When that august body, the Royal Philatelic Society, started meetings which it described by the title of 'Tea, Toast and Talk' no doubt many grey hairs stood on end, but these informal gatherings proved most enjoyable and have become a permanent feature of the R.P.S. programmes.

Ingenuity in devising programmes need not become eccentricity, but a committee whose members have brains and a wide knowledge of the many interesting aspects of our hobby should be able to arrange competitions, surprise evenings, and other novelties in almost endless variety.

The collector who joins a philatelic society after collecting for some time in loneliness, will be surprised to find how much the social intercourse will add to his pleasure in the hobby, while his knowledge and experience will be greatly increased when he meets other collectors. He will also be able to widen his human horizon and to appreciate the value of the philatelic bond, for in the stamp clubs he will find men and women of all kinds, united in the pursuit and study of the postage stamp.

Protective work is an obvious necessity in connexion with a hobby such as stamp collecting, the mercenary aspect of which attracts many undesirables. The Expert Committees of the Royal Philatelic Society, the British Philatelic Association, and similar societies overseas are strong weapons against the forger and faker. In England, the British Philatelic Association fights rogues of all kinds, and invites the membership and support of all honest collectors and dealers.

Chapter Twenty-six

GREAT COLLECTIONS AND FAMOUS COLLECTORS

IT is no easy matter, in these days, to get together a collection of stamps which will bring fame to its owner. There are a few who have done it by taking up some freakish method of collecting, and thereby obtaining notoriety in the stamp press. There are quite a number who have achieved the same object by studying intensively the stamps of a single country until they have entered the ranks of the recognized authorities on those issues. Those who now rise to the philatelic heights in the realm of *general* collecting, must have the purse of Croesus and the energy of Hercules.

Among the early British collectors several names stand out. Sir Daniel Cooper, one of the founders of the London Philatelic Society, was a very active collector in the 'sixties and 'seventies, but afterwards sold his collection to another famous pioneer, Judge Philbrick. When the latter, in his turn, sold his stamps to M. Philippe la Rénotière of Paris, they included practically all the great rarities of those days, and in some cases quite a number of each.

M. la Rénotière is better known to collectors of the present day by the name of Ferrary. He was a very eccentric man who spent a fortune in stamps. A lover of England and a resident of France, he was technically of Austrian nationality, and after his death his wonderful collection was sold at auction on the instructions of the French Government, realizing the immense sum of over £400,000.

London stamp dealers of earlier days will remember the quaint figure of Ferrary, in a white yachting cap, always very mysterious concerning the movements of supposed enemies who he thought were on his track, but with pockets full of good British bank notes, which he handed out to his friends in the trade in solid rolls, in exchange for the stamps which then accumulated for him in the intervals between his visits. To his intimates he announced his intention to visit them by telegrams which always ended with the words 'Affectionate shake hands' for his knowledge of English was not as complete as his collection of stamps.

The late Earl of Crawford was a greater collector than Ferrary, for he studied stamps intensively, and his albums included every sort of document which could in any way throw light on the stamps and their production and history. His collections of the stamps of Great Britain and the United States were a revelation of what can be achieved by scientific study.

Another very large general collection which brought fame to its owner was that formed by the late H. J. Duveen, a member of the famous family of art experts. His collections were disposed of after his death, and brought in a sum which was probably second only to that realized by the sale of the Ferrary collection.

A book could be filled with descriptions of old-time collectors and their stamps, but we must pass on to those of more modern times.

First among these was King George V, whose place in the front rank of philatelists was due, not to his high position, but to his personal keenness and the fact that his wonderful collections of the stamps of the British Commonwealth fully entitled him to the honour.

When the Duke of Edinburgh, the uncle of King George V, opened the big London Stamp Exhibition in 1890, he remarked that his nephew, Prince George of Wales, was then starting from Chatham in command of the *Thrush* and that, as he also was a stamp collector, he hoped he would be bringing back with him many fine specimens from the countries visited during his cruise.

King George started collecting when he was a midshipman in the *Bacchante* and was mainly interested in the stamps of the British Commonwealth, though he received many gifts of stamps from foreign countries. At his death his collection filled several hundred volumes and was housed in a special room at Buckingham Palace.

In 1893, as Prince of Wales, he became Hon. Vice-President of the London (now the Royal) Philatelic Society and when he married in the same year, the Society gave him a present of more than 1,000 scarce and interesting stamps for his collection. He was also an exhibitor at a display of West Indian stamps organized by the Society.

Three years later he became President of the Society and took the chair at meetings on at least two occasions and it was due to his initiative that the London Philatelic Society was given the privilege of using the word 'Royal' in its title. After his accession, King George became Patron of the R.P.S. and each season of the Society still opens with a display of part of his wonderful collection.

King George V also allowed his name to be placed at the head of the Roll of Distinguished Philatelists, which is under the control of the Philatelic Congress of Great Britain, and inclusion on which is a coveted international honour.

The late King's many opportunities for travel enabled him to build up his remarkable collection in a way which every collector must envy, while few can emulate it. It is probably the finest general collection of British Commonwealth stamps in the world, for while his displays of some countries could be beaten by those who had devoted their energy and fortune to a single group, his collection was an all-round one, sane in plan and balanced in contents.

Though the King devoted a great deal of time and personal attention to his stamps, his field was so vast, and the correspondence which he received from all parts of the world so voluminous, that he always had to employ the services of an expert curator. The first was the late J. A. Tilleard, M.V.O., who was followed by the late Sir Edward Denny Bacon, K.C.V.O., whose work was rewarded by a knighthood in 1932. The present curator of the Royal collections is Sir John Wilson, Bart., an expert of wide knowledge and sound philatelic judgment.

Among the outstanding sections of the collection are the stamps of Great Britain, Mauritius (which includes both the 1*d*. and 2*d*. 'Post Office' rarities), British Guiana, and the West Indies, but no section of the Commonwealth's stamps is poorly represented.

Many people have suggested that perhaps philately was just a formal hobby, so far as King George V was concerned, but this was far from the truth. He was intensely keen on his stamps – indeed on the stamps of the British Commonwealth wherever they might be found – and he used to reserve as much time as he could from his official duties for the study of his collection and discussions with other philatelists.

He said once that he did not think he would ever have been able to stand the strain of the First World War had it not been for the relaxation he obtained from stamp collecting, and his personal interest in the hobby was again shown during Silver Jubilee week in 1935, at a time when the King must have been subjected to great emotional and physical strain. He did not get many moments to himself during that momentous week, but during one brief period of leisure he drove to the headquarters of the Royal Philatelic Society to inspect an exhibition of the finest stamps owned by members of the Society, which had been assembled as a tribute to their Royal patron, an exhibition which, for quality and interest, has never been surpassed.

H.M. King George VI maintained his father's collection and formed a separate collection of the issues of his own reign, which is housed in special blue albums to distinguish it from his father's famous red volumes. He gave an interview to a popular illustrated weekly and was photographed while inspecting some of his stamps. Nowadays Her Majesty maintains the collections, and has her own special albums for the stamps of her reign.

Several other European royalties, among them members of the Belgian and Italian royal families and ex-King Carol of Roumania, were stamp collectors, though not on the same scale as King George V, or the late King Fuad of Egypt, for the latter had a magnificent collection, particularly of the stamps of his own country. Several of the Indian princes were also keen collectors.

The Duke of Windsor was also at one time a general collector, though it is doubtful if the hobby ever really gripped him after he had passed the schoolboy stage.

There are many very fine collections among those owned by members of the Royal Philatelic Society, but the majority of present-day collectors prefer to confine themselves to small groups of countries, or perhaps to one country only. A few of the old-time general collections on a large scale are in the hands of some of the older collectors. That of the late T. W. Hall, a past-President of the Society, was typical. It filled many volumes and held a lavish display of rarities from all countries. Other world famous R.P.S. members who have now gone from us include W. Dorning Beckton, R. B. Yardley, and Benjamin Goodfellow.

When we turn to the United States we think of another philatelist-ruler, the late President Roosevelt, who was a keen collector on general lines. His collection, which included many interesting gifts from foreign states and rulers, was sold after his death and realized a very large sum.

The late Arthur Hind had a world-famous collection, which was dispersed at auction in New York and London in 1934 and 1935, many of his rarities fetching high prices. He will be chiefly remembered as the owner of the world's most valuable stamp (though there are many others just as scarce), the One Cent British Guiana of 1856, for which he paid over £7,000 at the sale of the Ferrary collection, and which is now valued at £200,000. There are many other wonderful collections in the United States.

To bring together a comprehensive general collection at the present day is work for a millionaire and even a successful collection of a single big country may cost the owner thousands of pounds. In its higher ranks, therefore, stamp collecting is becoming more and more the hobby of the rich, and particularly of wealthy professional and business men. Such is the elasticity of the pursuit, however, that it is still possible for the man with little to spend, to gain a measure of fame by studying the stamps of one of the (philatelically) smaller countries, and for the rest of us there is the joy of collecting and of competing among ourselves for the possession of the less valuable stamps.

Chapter Twenty-seven

THE STAMP LIBRARY

IT is not strange that a hobby so varied and complex as stamp collecting should require a literature of its own, but it is one of the most curious characteristics of stamp collectors generally that they do not, to any great extent, avail themselves of existing literature. Some may have an introductory primer to the hobby; many possess a stamp catalogue of some kind, usually several years out of date; but only here and there do we find one who has troubled to acquire the books and magazines which will help him to study his stamps in the light of the knowledge already acquired by other collectors. It is as if a student tried to pass an important examination by the light of his own unaided research, and without the use of a single text-book.

The earliest contribution to the philatelic library came from France in September 1861, where a Strasbourg printer, M. Berger-Levrault, produced for private circulation a small list of the existing postage stamps. In December of the same year this was followed by the Potiquet Catalogue, while the following year, 1862, witnessed the appearance of two English stamp catalogues, that of Mount Brown, which listed 1,200 different stamps and the Booty Catalogue, which mentioned 1,100.

In September 1862 came the first stamp magazine, the *Monthly Intelligencer*, a Birmingham publication, which was not exclusively philatelic, followed, after a short interval, by the *Stamp-Collector's Monthly Advertiser* and the *Stamp-Collector's Magazine*. The latter had quite a long and useful life.

Though albums hardly find a place in the stamp library,

it is worth noting that the first stamp album also saw the light in 1862, and again the honour goes to France, for this was the famous Lallier album.

The modern stamp library is divided into three sections, catalogues, books, and magazines. Of these, the catalogues are the most important.

If, after thirty-five years' experience as a collector and writer about stamp collecting, I were asked what is the best single piece of advice I can give the collector, I would say 'Never be without an up-to-date stamp catalogue'. It is true that some stamp albums include what may appear to be the equivalent of a catalogue, facing the squares for the stamps, but this gives nothing like the amount of information included in a stamp catalogue.

There are two general stamp catalogues published in England, both by Stanley Gibbons Ltd, the biggest firm of stamp dealers.

The Stanley Gibbons Simplified Catalogue, with over 130,000 stamps listed, pays no attention to watermarks, perfs., shades, errors, etc., and is therefore the simplest stamp catalogue in the world. It has thousands of illustrations and the stamp designs are described.

The big Stanley Gibbons Catalogue, familiarly referred to as 'Gibbons', can fairly be described as the standard reference volume for English-speaking collectors. It is published in three sections, 'British Commonwealth' and 'Foreign Countries', the latter being sub-divided into 'Europe' and 'The Rest of the World'. It is highly specialized in many sections and lists and describes many varieties which are outside the scope of other catalogues. It has illustrations of stamp designs, watermarks, and overprints, and lists and prices many thousand different stamps, a system of large and small-type entries enabling the less advanced collector to distinguish between major and minor varieties. Where the general collector will find this catalogue of the greatest interest is in the notes which it gives concerning the subjects depicted on the stamps. Once the name of the person, place, or event depicted is known, it is easy for the collector to turn to an ordinary work of reference to secure the information required for writing up his collection.

Other important catalogues published by Gibbons are the 'Elizabethan', which lists in specialized form all the stamp issues of Queen Elizabeth's reign (with prices in dollars as well as sterling) and replaces the old 'Two Reigns' catalogue, and the remarkable 'Great Britain Specialised' catalogue which is for specialists in British stamps. Volume I – Queen Victoria – gives a very thorough listing of the Penny Blacks and Reds, Twopence Blues, the Embossed, the Surface-printed, and remaining Queen Victoria issues, as well as Officials and Mulready Envelopes. Volume II covers the reigns of King Edward VII, King George V, King Edward VIII and King George VI.

In choosing a stamp catalogue, the collector should be guided by the scope of the collection he intends to form, and the very young beginner will naturally require an elementary catalogue, but the enthusiast who wants to grow in knowledge as his collection grows in size, will buy a catalogue which seems a little beyond him at first sight, for from such a catalogue he will be always learning something new.

Other countries of course have their national catalogues, France her Yvert et Tellier-Champion, Germany her Michel, and the United States her Scott and Minkus, each good in its way, and each containing information which is not be be found in other catalogues. The newest publication in this field is the Gibbons–Whitman Catalogue, first published in the United States in 1967. This combines the comprehensive Stanley Gibbons listings with the dollar pricing essential to American collectors. On the table of the advanced collector you will probably find the whole battery of them, together with some of those more highly specialized catalogues of the stamps of a single country or group, which the modern trend of the hobby has called into being. These specialized catalogues, of which a large number exist, cannot be disregarded by the serious collector, who will find a knowledge of some of the principal foreign languages necessary for their use, as many of them are published abroad.

Stamp magazines may also be grouped in three classes – those published by philatelic societies, those issued by the dealers as 'house-organs', and so-called 'independent' journals. As the latter are practically dependent on their advertisers for the means of existence, the independence is often more nominal than real, particularly in countries where the mercenary side of the hobby is strongly in evidence, and the fact that the advertisements of a particular firm appear in numerous magazines is not always a guarantee of that firm's honesty or reliability.

In Great Britain, the first class of stamp magazines is represented by the *London Philatelist*, the journal of the Royal Philatelic Society, whose contents are naturally of an advanced character, while its opposite number in the United States is the *Collectors' Club Philatelist*, the organ of the Collectors' Club of New York, published quarterly. The *American Philatelist* worthily upholds the reputation of the American Philatelic Society. The *Stamp Lover*, the magazine of the National Philatelic Society, with headquarters in London, is a popular monthly, and *Philately* is the journal published by the British Philatelic Association.

The second class – the dealers' magazines – has for British representatives *Gibbons Stamp Monthly*, a magazine which covers the whole field of the hobby and has broken all philatelic circulation records for the world; the *Philatelic Journal of Great Britain*, which is mainly a magazine for serious students of G.B. Philately; and *The Philatelist* which has a particular interest for students of postal history. There are also several smaller house-organs of a sectional nature, one at least devoted to aero-philately.

In the independent class we find the *Philatelic Magazine*, the *Stamp Magazine*, and *Stamp Collecting* and others, each having its own distinctive character.

Abroad there is a list of journals in almost every civilized language, including magazines printed in Russian, Persian,

Greek, Japanese, and Chinese. The general collector should select one magazine for regular reading, after carefully comparing those which are offered to him, choosing, of course, the one which will give him the most help in carrying on his hobby.

There is an extraordinarily wide range of books for the stamp collector to choose from, though owing to the international nature of the hobby, he will perhaps find that some of those he most wishes to read are written in a foreign language.

Reference works include bibliographies, address books, glossaries, and catalogues of all kinds.

Next come guides to the hobby, from the elementary primer at a few shillings to the technical or semi-technical work dealing with stamp production and advanced philatelic study generally. There are also books about stamp designs and the historical and pictorial aspects of the hobby.

Finally we come to the so-called 'handbooks', the use of which term has probably been one of the principal reasons for the neglect of the stamp library by collectors, for no one wants to buy a book described by such a formal name. As a matter of fact, these handbooks, which are books relating to the stamps of a single country or issue, cover a very wide range. Some of them are quite elementary in character, and form excellent guides to a collector taking up the stamps of a particular country for the first time. There are others of all kinds, up to the only ones which are really dull enough to deserve the name of handbook – the monographs published by the learned philatelic societies, in which the authors endeavour to include everything that is known about the stamps of the country they are dealing with.

The keen collector is strongly advised not to neglect the help which he can obtain from books. It is true that, in many directions, experience will prove his best guide, but if he relies on that alone, he will waste many years acquiring knowledge which others have already put on record in print. The beginner will want his general guide to the hobby and, above all, his catalogue. When the next stage is reached, and he looks about for a limited field on which to concentrate his efforts, the elementary books about the stamps of various countries will provide him with an excellent means of testing the comparative merits of those which he is considering, before he makes his selection. Finally, when he has decided to specialize in the stamps of a definite country or group, the very first thing he should do is to read and study everything that has been written in the Philatelic Press and in books, on that particular subject, unless, indeed, he is fortunate enough to find that it has been the subject of a recent authoritative book, in which case the earlier Press references can perhaps be disregarded.

The great thing is to know what others have done and discovered in connexion with particular stamps, and then the collector can proceed from that point, either adding to, or correcting, previous discoveries in the light of his own experience.

As the ordinary bookshop does not cater for the stamp collector, beyond the provision of one or two general works on the hobby, the reader who wants to know what literature exists in connexion with his particular subject should write to one of the dealers in philatelic literature, who will advise him. Apart from books still current, there will probably be some out-of-print works which he will need, while back numbers of various stamp magazines will also be necessary to complete his information in many cases. Before sending indiscriminate orders for articles on a particular country, the collector should either satisfy himself that all he is asking for are serious contributions, or reserve the right to return any which he does not find useful.

It cannot be urged too strongly upon the collector that money spent on catalogues, magazines, and books, is not wasted. Presumably he wishes to do something more than merely *collect*, and would clothe the dry bones of his stamps with a garment of fact, even if he has no ambition to be a searcher after new knowledge. It is absolutely certain that money spent on the proper kind of helpful reading matter will repay itself in interest and encouragement a thousand times over. Knowledge is power in stamp collecting as in everything else and, though we are not discussing here the more mercenary aspects of the hobby, it is most certainly the man who studies his stamps in the light of published information who makes money in the end.

Chapter Twenty-eight

BEHIND THE SCENES

STAMP collecting began, in a very casual and gradual manner, during the years immediately following the issue of the British 'Penny Black' and 'Twopence Blue', the world's first adhesive postage stamps, in 1840. People, especially young people, set aside all the stamps which came their way rather than destroy them, and the evidence of this is the fact that today there are hundreds of thousands of 'blacks', 'blues', and 'reds' still in existence. Then, in the late 1840s and early 1850s, when other countries started issuing stamps, the cult of stamp collecting became a recognized hobby. Collectors, eager to build up their collections quickly, were impatient to acquire the new stamps from distant lands and were no longer content to rely on chance acquisitions from friends and business acquaintances. Thus, through the simple laws of supply and demand, the stamp trade came into being.

At first, a few individuals in the countries where the collecting hobby was most firmly established – notably Great Britain, Belgium, France, and Germany – set themselves up as professional dealers. Their numbers increased rapidly with the fast-growing popularity and development of the hobby, however, and now there are many thousands of stamp dealers scattered all over the globe, ranging from the small, sparetime dealer to the highly professional firms with large staffs and world-wide facilities. The capital required to maintain a stamp business covering the whole field of philately has become so immense that many dealers now specialize in the stamps of one particular group or aspect of the hobby, such as British Commonwealth issues or smaller sections as, for example, the countries of the British West Indies, or in thematic subjects – flowers, sport, or the various kinds of transport.

The biggest British stamp firm, Stanley Gibbons Limited, belongs to the fast diminishing group of dealers who still try to keep in stock all kinds of postage stamps, of every country, from the most common to the most rare. To maintain such an enormous stock the firm is obliged to spend many thousands of pounds each year on stamp purchases, and of course the value of stamp sales must be substantially in excess of the outlay! Numerous other activities – auction sales, the editing and publishing of the famous Gibbons stamp catalogues, *Gibbons Stamp Monthly*, and stamp albums of all kinds, contribute to the esteem with which the name of Stanley Gibbons is held throughout the civilized world. Let us now make a tour of this long-established firm, starting with its Strand premises in the heart of London.

The firm, founded by Edward Stanley Gibbons at Plymouth, Devon, in 1856, has been at 391 Strand since 1893, shortly after Gibbons relinquished his sole ownership and it became a limited company. Since that time the building has been subjected to constant development and improvement within, while the Strand shop, the stamp-collectors' Mecca, has been greatly extended and enlarged in recent years. It is invariably full of collectors, senior and junior, eagerly looking at stamps or choosing albums. Behind the shop there is a spacious 'sales reception area' with comfortable seats and tables where collectors can examine stamps from the Gibbons stock at leisure. On the floor above is a showroom where the entire range of the firm's stamp albums, catering for every taste, is on display, also a stamp packet bar.

Behind the scenes there is tremendous activity in the hive of offices which are almost entirely devoted to the buying, stocking, and selling of stamps. There is a team of buyers, each with their specialized interest and knowledge of the different kinds of stamps. If you wish to sell your stamps, one or other of the team will examine and assess the value of your collection, whether you take it personally or send it by post. Dozens of letters are received each day, containing offers of stamps of all kinds from all parts of the world. Stocks are frequently replenished in this way, and some of the rarest stamps are acquired when big collections (i.e. collections formed by distinguished collectors) come on the market or are offered at auctions. Sometimes another dealer's entire stock is purchased to strengthen the Gibbons stock.

Sometimes, too, there is disappointment for a collector when that old schoolboy collection, just discovered in the attic at home, turns out to be no treasure trove as supposed, but merely an accumulation of the most common, every-day stamps of a bygone era, or when a number of the 'rarities' in a supposedly valuable collection are found to be forgeries, repaired stamps, and other worthless items. The blow is always heaviest when the 'valuable collection' has been regarded as a family treasure for generations. On such occasions the discretion and tact of the buying staff may be taxed to the uttermost (and they may be abused for their pains!), but there are compensations in the many, many very satisfactory transactions where collections, intelligently and discriminatingly formed, fetch much more than envisaged.

Stamp forgeries are not, these days, the menace that they used to be, nevertheless one of the firm's most useful and valuable reference collections is that of forgeries, reprints, 'doctored' stamps, and other philatelic traps for the unwary. The collection includes photographs or specimens of genuine stamps for comparison. Doubtful stamps can be checked and taken out of circulation if they prove to be duds.

One of the buying offices is entirely devoted to the purchase of new issues and it is here that literally millions of new stamps are handled each year – day by day – for distribution to the stock-rooms, the shop, and the various sales departments, and to the section operating the 'new issue service', which distributes consignments of new stamps regularly to subscribers all over the world. It is exciting to see the hundreds of sheets of mint stamps being examined and sorted for distribution. The staff have to watch carefully for errors and varieties which often occur in stamps and which may considerably enhance their value.

The stock department takes up the most part of two floors in the Strand building. The main stamp stock is housed in strong safes and fireproof cabinets, subject to the strictest security measures. Detailed records are maintained of the more expensive stamps, giving the date of purchase, cost and, if sold, selling price, date, and name of purchaser. From these records it is immediately apparent whether a stamp is in stock or out on approval to a client. Here also there are vast reserves of stamps which are 'fed' to the various sales departments as required, the stock-books used in the main order department and the extensive range of counter books used in the shop needing constant replenishment. The shop books contain a selection of the stamps of every country, just a few of each kind, unused and used, conveniently arranged in the same order as they are listed in the firm's stamp catalogues. Gibbons' customers literally order stamps by numbers!

To this busy department comes the bulk of all the new stamp purchases – the stocks of new stamps from the Crown Agents who represent the British Commonwealth territories or from the London offices of the Dominions such as Australia and New Zealand, the mint and used stamps of foreign countries which are bought from wholesale dealers, the collections, large and small, which are brought into the shop or arrive by post. What happens to all these stamps? Some of the better ones are earmarked for special customers whose requirements are indexed and tabulated, some will be sent out to clients on approval (i.e. they have the choice of buying or returning the stamps). In other words we are at the third stage of the business of buying, stocking, and selling stamps – in the sales department.

In the large ground-floor office of a building which adjoins the back of the Strand premises there is a busy staff dealing with the hundreds of mail orders for stamps which arrive each day, arranging stamps in small approval books, refilling the spaces from which stamps have been sold or speedily selecting stamps requested in 'want lists'. Stamps in sets and packets are handled by a separate section which maintains the stock and deals with the orders for them. This one office deals by post with collectors all over the world, although the actual correspondence and dispatch is handled, as we shall see, elsewhere.

The greater part of the firm's postal business comes from requests for selections of stamps on approval, and the nerve-centre of all these transactions is the office of the sales director, who controls operations like an army commander, seeking out, through his staff, the stamps that collectors want to see and buy. Records are maintained in an elaborate system of card files in which every transaction is registered on the customer's card. No matter where a collector lives – in Ashby-de-la-Zouch or Hong Kong – he can see and buy stamps selected from the Gibbons stock in the comfort of his own home. Wherever the post goes, stamps can go.

We have one last call to make in the Strand building – that is at the office of the managing director on the first floor overlooking the busy street. If he is not 'at home' then he will be abroad, visiting the store of the associate company, StanGib Limited, in New York, or participating in one of the big international stamp exhibitions in Amsterdam, Prague, or Vienna. The Gibbons business is truly international.

Now we have a five-minute walk to Drury House, a large brick building which houses the Gibbons Editorial and Publishing Division, the well-appointed sale-room of Stanley Gibbons Auctions, and the Accounts Department, supervised by the company secretary, with its clerks, book-keepers, and ledgers. Here also are the general correspondence and filing sections, postal departments and warehouse. The building is in Russell Street, off Drury Lane, facing the side of the famous Theatre Royal and on the fringe of the Covent Garden market. Formerly a paper warehouse, it was drastically transformed and modernized to provide large, spacious, well-lit office accommodation for the important complementary services of the Gibbons Group.

On the left of the entrance hall on the ground floor is the lofty auction sale-room where stamps valued hundreds of thousands of pounds change hands in the company's regular sales. At the far end, above the auctioneer's rostrum, hang photographic enlargements of some of the world's rarest stamps, and a porthole where coloured slides of rare stamps are projected during sales. On the far side of this large, open-plan area are the auction offices, while on the right of the entrance foyer is the typing pool and the trade publications counter and offices. Here all the energies of the publications sales manager and his staff are concentrated on the sale of Gibbons publications – mainly stamp albums – and accessories to trade customers in this country and overseas. Virtually every stamp shop throughout the world handles Gibbons products and a very considerable export trade is done in albums and catalogues.

Adjoining these offices is the postal packing and outwards dispatch section where literally thousands of letters and packets are prepared for posting each day. Passing through we find ourselves by the loading bays located at the Drury Lane end of the vast basement warehouse, with its regimented avenues of storage racks and packing bays where, at long tables, the packers are wrapping and crating the wholesale orders for albums and catalogues, maybe a dozen catalogues for the stamp shop in the High Street, or a hundred assorted albums for the big retail store.

Back on the ground floor, we mount the stairs and cross

a bridge to reach the first floor where, at this end, are the staff rest-rooms and facilities such as the popular press-button coffee machines. From the centre gangway which runs the entire length of this floor we see, on our left, the busy mail reception area, correspondence, magazine subscription, and filing sections. Incoming letters, arriving by the sackful each day, are opened, sorted, and distributed to the various departments. Account queries are easily handled because, on the opposite side of the gangway, are the accounts clerks with their cash-books and ledgers, adding machines and computers.

At the far end of the first floor, through the swing-doors, we enter the editorial departments – magazine, general advertising, and album production on the one hand, stamp catalogue editorial and production on the other. The editor of *Gibbons Stamp Monthly*, the popular hobby magazine issued each month by the firm, provides interesting articles and features for more than 75,000 readers throughout the world. He is also responsible for the firm's advertising and public relations, and finds time to design attractive stamp albums. Specimens of all new stamp issues are passed to the new issue editor, whose duty it is to examine and chronicle in the 'Supplement' pages of the magazine all details of new stamps. The supplementary listings find their way into the new catalogues, while the stamps themselves are mounted in the firm's permanent reference collection, after they have been passed to the catalogue editorial section for further examination.

New albums, and supplements to existing albums, are designed, planned, and produced in this department, the work entailing meticulous drawing and layout of the album pages, and the preparation of illustrations for the printer. The need for stamp illustrations in the Gibbons catalogues, magazine, albums, and advertisements involves the department very heavily with the block-makers and the consequent traffic in blocks to and from the printers, with the eventual problems of storage.

Adjoining this office is that of the company secretary, and the company's board-room, which is also the office of the publications director. He is also the managing director of another associate firm, the Letter-Filing Appliances Company of Birmingham, whose founder originated the spring-back binder and which firm has for many years produced most of the Gibbons spring-back albums.

Across the passage we meet the catalogue editor and his staff. The work of revision of the Gibbons stamp catalogues is a full-time, round-the-year occupation for them, dealing not only with the main three-volume catalogue, but also with the 'Elizabethan', the 'Simplified', the 'Great Britain Specialized', and the American 'Gibbons–Whitman' editions. Revision includes possibly the complete rewriting of a country's stamp listings, the checking of innumerable facts and figures, the massive alteration of stamp prices – usually on an upward trend – and the addition each year of thousands of new stamps and illustrations. It is not surprising, therefore, that the Gibbons Catalogue is regarded as the finest available work of reference about postage stamps, and that it is the collectors' Bible.

Stamp collecting has been described as 'The king of hobbies' and 'The hobby of kings'. That the former is true is surely proved by what we have seen in our visit to the emporium of Stanley Gibbons, and by the current boom in British stamps inspired by the post office policy of issuing attractive commemoratives. That the latter is true it is enough to mention the Royal Philatelic Collection which is unique of its kind.

Chapter Twenty - nine

TREASURE TROVE

THE keen collector is always hoping for a 'find'. The junior will be quite satisfied if he finds a stamp catalogued at a shilling in a sixpenny packet. To the adult collector, the acquisition of bargains is just as interesting and his superior knowledge often enables him to take advantage of the carelessness of dealers, or of their lack of such detailed information as he himself possesses. The man who specializes in the stamps of one or two countries nearly always knows more than the dealer who has to handle the stamps of the whole world, and there is nothing unsporting in using that knowledge to pick up minor varieties that the dealer has overlooked. (I do not, however, think that anyone is justified in taking advantage of obvious clerical errors either of dealers or collector friends, as for example when a stamp is priced at two shillings in mistake for two pounds.)

The classic example of a find at the expense of a dealer is the oft-quoted story of the famous collector who waited for a few moments in a well-known stamp shop, while the head of the firm was engaged with another customer. When the collector was at length shown into the inner sanctum, he produced from his wallet a stamp of a European country, which showed a very marked retouch, and said: 'How much will you give me for that, C.?' The dealer looked at the stamp, thought it very nice, and offered him five pounds, which was promptly accepted. When the money was safely in his hands, the collector said quietly: 'Do you know where I got that, old man?' 'No,' said the dealer, 'but it's a very nice thing.' 'Well, while I was waiting for you in the shop, I was glancing through your stock book, and found it there priced at sixpence.' (Collapse of dealer.)

As a matter of fact, dealers, and particularly those who have to employ a large staff, often give the collector the chance to make very interesting finds. Apart from mistakes, the trader simply has not got the time to sort up all his stock on the most advanced specialist lines. If he buys common stamps at so much a hundred, he is not going to waste the time of an expensive staff in putting them to search for a few minor varieties which will add a shilling or two to the value of his stamps. He will be satisfied if he gets his normal rate of profit by selling them all as standard stamps, and if the collector gets a bargain here and there, well, the dealer knows that that will be an inducement for him to return in the hope of more. Cheap approval sheets are, in many cases, prolific sources of 'finds', for the stock used for these has to be handled very quickly, and is often not sorted for varieties of perforation, watermark, or shade.

Though the stamp dealer does not mind his customers making finds, he does very strongly object to the customer who will buy from him nothing but bargains. I know men who come into dealers' shops and sit for hours looking through books of stamps in the hope of 'spotting' something, and as such luck will not come to them every day, they waste the time of the dealer's staff and give him practically no return. I wonder whether these gentry realize that they are receiving a gentle hint, when, after two or three of their time-wasting visits, every stock book they ask to see is, much to the dealer's regret, not available for inspection! Stamp dealers will do anything to help a genuine collector who does a reasonable amount of business with them, but the man who looks for bargains and nothing else is anathema to them.

The search for philatelic treasure, like the search for sunken gold, is beset with perils. Beware those (apparently) old collections which you find in junk shops, or those dusty cards of 'rare' old stamps in the windows of the same. I do not say that all old collections in second-hand shops have been planted there to trap the unwary, but some of them have, and so have some of those attractive rarities, most of which will prove to be cleaned, or repaired, or else reprints or forgeries. (I am not, of course, speaking of the cards of common stamps in newsagents' shops, which should not suggest the thought of treasure-hunting to even the most optimistic, and which are nowadays often priced at four or five times what they would cost if bought from a reputable dealer.)

In some stamp auctions, too, old collections are not always what they seem. The album may be old, it is true, but its contents, apart from just a few specimens to give 'atmosphere', are not the stamps which were in it originally, but some that have been put there to make the collector think he is buying an old untouched lot, instead of a display of modern fakes. This is not, of course, the fault of the auctioneer, but of the person selling the collection.

Wherever he goes hunting, the collector must first be sure of his own knowledge. The man who thinks he is getting bargains in old stamps because he is getting them at cheap prices has many disappointments in store, for very few people nowadays are foolish enough or ignorant enough to sell the scarce stamps of the older issues at bargain prices. The greatest benefit that this volume could bring to the enthusiast is to make him realize that the first thing that should enter his mind, when presented with what he thinks is a bargain, is *suspicion*, whether the treasure be in an apparently old collection, in a dusty shop, or on the club exchange sheet of a friend. Club exchange sheets are particularly dangerous to the inexperienced, for the overworked secretary cannot possibly guard his members against the ignorance of the majority of their friends or the roguery of those quasi-dealers who exist in very many philatelic societies and stamp clubs, and who consider their amateur friends fair game for their superior knowledge.

During the many years I have been a stamp dealer, I

have *never* seen a collection, formed on 'bargain-hunting' lines, which was worth more than a small fraction of what the owner paid for it. The ones which showed a profit were those whose owners had paid good prices for their best stamps, realizing that then they were getting what they were paying for, both as regards genuineness and condition.

My own earliest experience of treasure trove was on quite a small scale. As a junior in the stamp business I was given the task of looking through a few hundreds of the Cape provisional stamp, 1*d*. on 2*d*., bistre, of 1893. Great was my joy when I found among them one stamp with double surcharge, then listed at thirty shillings, but now selling at about twenty pounds.

Many years later, when the first Irish provisional stamps were issued, news came to me that the 2*d*. stamp was known with overprint inverted. I told my assistant to look through the envelope containing a couple of hundred used specimens on the chance that we might, by luck, be the unwitting possessors of an 'inverted'. I added, jokingly: 'If you find one, you can have an extra half-holiday next week,' never for a moment thinking she would earn it, but in a few moments she was back again with a fine specimen of the error, and not only was it the error, but the error on the 2*d*. stamp of the other die, whose existence had only been rumoured up till that time.

The most extraordinary find, however, was that made by a specialist in the stamps of Sweden, in fact it is so extraordinary that I almost hesitate to put it on paper, but he told me himself, and I have absolute faith in his veracity. He was looking for a stamp showing a small retouch, in one of the then current issue, a thing which he had discovered but which no dealer would be likely to worry about. He watched the stock books of the leading firms for weeks and then, one day, in a certain position on a certain page of the book of a big Strand firm he found what he was looking for, priced at a penny. Jubilant, he wrote off to a fellow enthusiast in Sweden to show him the stamp, and the latter replied saying how interested he was, but that up to that time he had never seen the variety – *and his letter was franked with a specimen of it!* As if this was not a sufficient straining of the long arm of coincidence, our English friend, a week or two later, was looking once more through the Strand dealer's book and in the very same spot, on the very same page, he found another stamp with the same re-entry!

All these finds I have mentioned have been comparatively unimportant though they do show that Chance, in stamp collecting, as elsewhere, is a fickle jade. Only to a few is it given to find the big treasures of Philately, and too often they do not realize their luck. Over and over again, in the course of his business, the stamp dealer comes across people who have discovered batches of old letters which must have borne scarce, if not really rare, stamps, and the finder had not realized, until too late, that the 'rubbish' he had committed to the flames in his passion for order and cleanliness, was probably worth a small fortune.

This fiery fate befell two of the famous 'Post Office' Mauritius stamps which two British officials, on leave in the south of India, had had the good fortune to discover. For safety, one of them put the stamps in the back of his watch, but the timepiece was stolen by a native during the night and the stamps went with it. When caught and questioned, the thief was surprised to find that questioning was concentrated not on the watch, whose value he appreciated, but on the stamps. 'I not keeping dirty bits of paper,' he remarked, 'I throwing them in fire so as to destroy all trace.'

More fortunate was the finder of that other 'Post Office' Mauritius, for which King George V paid £1,450 at auction in London. A gentleman was one day entertaining a friend who collected stamps and happened to mention that he had his boyhood collection upstairs. When it was examined, the rarity was found reposing there – a potential fortune which, on this occasion, *did* materialize.

Not many years ago, a philatelic treasure was unearthed which came to be known as the 'Mayfair Find', and will go down to history under that name. In the 'fifties of the last century a youth in London conceived the then very bold idea of writing to some of our Colonial post-masters, sending each of them a five pound note, and asking them, in return, to send a supply of the stamps then on sale at their respective post offices. Back came the stamps, but the youth's ardour had cooled, or else he had been called away from home. At any rate, the stamps found their way into a trunk in an attic used for lumber, and there they remained for sixty or seventy years. The surprise of the stamp world can be imagined when stamps of the 'classic' period, many of them hitherto unknown in large blocks, turned up in this way in complete sheets. The find realized several thousand pounds.

A more recent find took place during the clearance of a dealer's premises, prior to the sale of the building. He had been established there for years, and his father before him, and stamps were tucked away in all sorts of odd corners. During the removal, a sliding shelf was used to put some boxes on, and when an attempt was made to push it back into position, it jammed. A search revealed that behind it lay a roll of stamps, and when these were examined they were found to be of a catalogue value of over £1,200.

One could go on talking of stamp finds for ever, for there is a perennial fascination in the subject. One could tell of the old lady in British Guiana who was able to give £200 to her beloved church, through chancing on some early stamps of the Colony in an old work-basket, or of the lady in England who found a sheet of early British stamps in an old blotting pad, where they had rested ever since they were bought at the post office. Finds are always being made, but the reader must remember that the chances against a big find are in inverse ratio to the rarity of the stamps. The common stamps of the early days are found in collections because they were common then, but the great rarities of today were already rare then, as only a few of them ever existed.

To the inexperienced person who finds old stamps, I would offer the following advice:

(1) If the stamps are on their original envelopes, don't try and soak them off until you have taken expert advice. Many of the old stamps have greater value on their original envelopes.

(2) If the stamps are in sheets or blocks, don't take one of them off to send as a sample to anybody, or for your own collection. In the case of many old stamps, the value of a block or sheet is far more than that of the number of single stamps it contains.

(3) If the stamps or envelopes are creased or folded, don't try to straighten them out unless you are sure you can do so without further damage, or separating the stamps along the lines of perforation. Above all, if the sheets or envelopes have not been folded, do not fold them in any way, as so many people do, in order to get them into an envelope for transmission by post. The fresher the stamps or envelopes, the greater will be their value, so keep them packed flat until an expert has seen them.

(4) Do not rely on the advice of some friend who claims to know all about stamps. The more a collector claims to know, the less he usually does know. The real experts very rarely vaunt their knowledge, and you may be placing your trust in an 'amateur dealer'.

In any case of doubt, the best advice you can get is from a dealer of really high reputation. He has to maintain that reputation, which has been built up by years of straight dealing, and though he will make a profit on the sale of your stamps, he will not rob you.

Apart from the 'rarities' which are planted in shops and elsewhere for inexperienced collectors to 'find' there are plenty of chances for the enthusiast who is keen enough to acquire knowledge of stamps generally or of some particular group. Treasure-hunting nowadays is not a matter of sailing at random or digging at random, but everything is planned methodically and scientifically. It is to those who treat their stamp-hunting in the same way that the reward at length comes in the shape of a good bargain, if not an historic find.

Chapter Thirty

THE HOBBY OF A THOUSAND FACES

THE writer who, with a full knowledge of and love for the hobby of stamp collecting, attempts to bring within the covers of a single volume a description of its many attractions, must inevitably be depressed with a sense of the hopelessness of his task. There is so much to be said that a library would not suffice to tell the story, and even if the scribe were granted unlimited time and space, and could find readers willing to follow him, he might well miss conveying some of the charm of this pursuit – the sudden unexpected sidelights on history, the glimpses of human nature, the peeps into the storehouse of general knowledge.

Some attempt must be made, however, to sum up the many-sided appeal of a hobby about which so much has been and could still be written, even though cold print can never do justice to the feelings of the enthusiast.

That there is 'something in it' – for someone – the most sceptical reader must surely admit, or whence this great army of collectors, this world-wide press and trade organization, these permanent monetary values?

What that something is we must leave the reader to find out, either from what he has already learned from this volume, or from the experiments he may base upon what he has read, and certainly experiment will be a better introduction than all the writing in the world.

It may be that you collect, just because the collecting mania has bitten you. If so, it is impossible, when collecting stamps, that you should stay at that elementary stage. Sooner or later curiosity will grip you. You will want to know the meaning of this design, the circumstances under which that stamp was issued, why this overprint was applied, or how such a variation in printing occurred. Once this curiosity is aroused your permanent enjoyment of the hobby is assured, for it is above all in the arousing and satisfaction or curiosity that philately finds its attractions. Only realize what lies behind the postage stamp and it cannot fail to interest you in one way or another and what that way shall be will be decided by the bent of your own mind.

There is no doubt that the stamp collector who exercises this curiosity in the right way will eventually find himself the possessor of much knowledge of a practical kind, which will broaden his horizon and may prove of considerable value in the ordinary give-and-take of life. No one, in these days, takes pride in ignorance, and if even the time devoted to a hobby may be regarded as educationally spent, the pursuit of that hobby is in keeping with the spirit of the age. I defy any owner of a stamp collection who is once bitten by the curiosity germ, to relinquish the hobby without benefit, and that benefit, if it be by way of increase of knowledge, will come so imperceptibly, that no thought of study or task can arise in connexion with it.

What of its practical advantages? Nerve-strain is perhaps the greatest evil from which we suffer at the present day, and doctors generally are in agreement in telling us that the best remedy is to switch the mind, in leisure hours, from the ruts along which it moves in the course of the daily task, and that an absorbing hobby provides the best alternative to work. When we ask 'What hobby?' we find, marvellous to relate, that the doctors take their own prescription, and that the hobby they favour above all is stamp collecting.

Why they, and other busy professional and commercial men, choose this in preference to other hobbies, is easily discovered. Apart from its attractions as having a mental and not a purely mechanical appeal, it is a hobby which can be taken up at odd moments, which need not necessarily occupy much space, which does not require a complicated apparatus, and which is clean and does not make a mess.

Owing to their world-wide distribution, it is possible to collect stamps in almost any place on the globe. Their small size and light weight also make it easy to send stamps for exchange or sale through the post, so that collectors in out-of-the-way places are still able to keep up their hobby.

Another advantage arises from the fact that the average value of postage stamps is less than that of many other things which are collected. The stamp collector is thus able to add continually to his treasures, while other hobbyists can only make an occasional purchase after long intervals of 'saving up'. Nor is it necessary to spend large sums in order to obtain the maximum of pleasure from the hobby. The school-boy with his pence probably enjoys wilder thrills than the millionaire who spends thousands of pounds on a single stamp.

While many collectors carry on the hobby in lonely isolation, it can be made the basis of pleasant social relationships, either by correspondence or by personal touch through philatelic societies and clubs, which abound in most parts of the globe.

For many individuals, the hobby has proved a godsend. It can be pursued just as easily in the sick-room as at the outposts of civilization. It helps the sufferer to forget pain as it helps the exile to bear his loneliness.

Thus men, women, and children, of all nationalities, classes and types of mind, are united in the pursuit of the postage stamp and in love of this one universal hobby. The best that the author can wish his readers is that they are sharing or may soon come to share in the pleasures offered by it.

APPENDIX A · STAMP CURRENCIES

SINCE the two world wars the currencies of the world have been in the melting pot and their value in relation to one another has continually fluctuated. The collector who, in normal times, wishes to know what a foreign currency is worth in terms of sterling or U.S. dollars must therefore study the financial page in his daily paper where most of the important rates are given. Here we can only record the currencies in use in the various countries during the period in which they have issued stamps, and the relation of the various coins to one another, facts which will be found helpful in many ways when arranging and studying the stamps.

It should be noted that units of different countries which bear the same name are not necessarily of the same value, in fact there is often a great difference between the various dollars, pesos, francs, and other units of currency recorded in the list which follows.

Abu Dhabi	100 naye paise = 1 rupee
	1000 fils = 1 dinar
Ajman	100 naye paise = 1 rupee
Aden	As India
	100 cents = 1 shilling
Aden ('South Arabia')	1000 fils = 1 dinar
Afghanistan	12 shahi = 6 sanar = 3 abasi = 2 kran = 1 rupee
	60 paisa = 1 rupee
	100 pouls = 1 afghani (rupee)
Ajman	100 dirhams = 1 riyal
Alaouites	100 centièmes = 1 piastre
Albania	40 paras = 1 piastre (grosch)
	100 quintars = 1 franc
	100 centimes = 1 lek
	100 quintars = 10 (old) leks = 1 (new) lek
Algeria	100 centimes = 1 franc
	100 centimes = 1 dirham
Andorra	As France and Spain
Angola	As Portugal, and (later) 100 centavos = 1 angolar
Annam	100 cents = 1 piastre

263

Antigua	100 cents = 1 dollar
Argentina	100 centavos = 1 peso
Australia	100 cents = 1 dollar
Australian Antarctic Territory	100 cents = 1 dollar
Austria	60 kreuzer = 1 florin
	100 kreuzer = 1 gulden
	100 heller = 1 krone
	100 groschen = 1 schilling
Austrian Crete	100 centimes = 1 franc
Austrian Italy (Lombardo-Venetia)	100 centesimi = 1 lira
	100 soldi = 1 florin
	100 kreuzer = 1 gulden
Austrian Levant	100 soldi = 1 gulden
	40 paras = 1 piastre
Baden	60 kreuzer = 1 gulden
Bahamas	100 cents = 1 dollar
Bahrain	As India
	100 naye paise = 1 rupee
Barbados	100 cents = 1 dollar
Bavaria	60 kreuzer = 1 gulden
	100 pfennig = 1 mark
Belgium (and Colonies)	100 centimes = 1 franc
Bergedorf	16 schilling = 1 Hamburg mark
Bhutan	100 chetrum = 1 ngultrum or rupee
Bohemia and Moravia	As Czechoslovakia
Bolivia	100 centavos = 1 boliviano
	100 cents = 1 Bolivian escudo
Bosnia and Herzegovina	100 kreuzer (novics) = 1 gulden
	100 heller = 1 krone
Botswana (Bechuanaland)	Sterling
	100 cents = 1 rand
Brazil	1000 reis = 1 milreis
	1000 reis = 100 centavos = 1 cruzeiro
	100 centavos = 1000 (old) cruzeiros = 1 (new) cruzeiro
Bremen	72 grote = 30 silbergroschen = 1 thaler
British East Africa	16 annas = 1 rupee
British Honduras	12 pence = 1 shilling
	100 cents = 1 dollar
British Levant	Sterling and Turkish
British Solomon Islands	100 cents = 1 Australian dollar
Brunei	100 cents = 1 Malayan dollar
Brunswick	30 silbergroschen = 24 gutegroschen = 1 thaler
Buenos Aires	8 reales = 1 peso

Bulgaria	100 centimes = 1 franc
	100 stotinki = 1 leva
Burma	As India
	100 pyas = 1 kyat
Burundi	100 centimes = 1 franc
Cambodia	100 cents = 1 piastre
	100 cents = 1 riel
Canada	12 pence = 1 shilling (Canadian)
	= 1s. 3d. sterling
	100 cents = 1 dollar
Carpatho-Ukraine	As Czechoslovakia
Central African Republic	100 centimes = 1 franc
Ceylon	12 pence = 1 shilling
	100 cents = 1 rupee
Chile	100 centavos = 1 peso
China	100 candarins = 1 tael
	100 cents = 1 Shanghai dollar
	100 fen = 1 yuan or 'dollar'
China (Formosa)	100 cents = 1 silver yuan or 'dollar'
Christmas Island	100 cents = 1 Malayan dollar
Cilicia	40 paras = 1 piastre
Cochin	10 pies = 1 puttan (Later as India)
Colombia	100 centavos = 1 peso
(and Departments)	
Congo (ex-Belgian)	100 centimes = 1 franc
Congo (French)	100 centimes = 1 franc
Cook Islands	100 cents = 1 N.Z. dollar
Costa Rica	8 reales = 1 peso
	100 centavos = 1 peso
	100 centimos = 1 colon
Crete	100 lepta = 1 drachma
Cuba	1000 mils. de peso = 100 cents de peso
	= 1 peso
	100 cents de peseta = 1 peseta
	100 centavos = 1 peso
Cyprus	40 paras = 1 piastre. 180 piastres = £1
	1000 mils = £1
Czechoslovakia	100 heller = 1 krone
Dahomey	100 centimes = 1 franc
Danish W. Indies	100 cents = 1 dollar
	100 bit = 1 franc
Danzig	100 pfennig = 1 mark
	100 pfennig = 1 gulden
Denmark	96 rigsbank skilling = 1 rigsdaler
	100 öre = 1 krone

Dhar	4 pice = 1 anna
Dominica	100 cents = 1 dollar
Dominican Republic	8 reales = 1 peso
	100 centimos = 1 franco
	100 centavos = 1 peso
Dubai	100 naye paise = 1 rupee
	100 dirhams = 1 riyal
E. Africa and Uganda	16 annas = 1 rupee
	100 cents = 1 rupee
East Africa (Kenya, Uganda, and Tanzania)	100 cents = 1 shilling
Ecuador	8 reales = 1 peso
	100 centavos = 1 sucre
Egypt (U.A.R.)	40 paras = 1 piastre
	10 milliemes = 1 piastre
	100 piastres = £1 (Egyptian)
Eire (Ireland)	As Great Britain
Estonia	100 kopecks = 1 rouble
	100 penni = 1 mark
	100 senti = 1 krone
Ethiopia (Abyssinia)	16 guerche (or mehaleks) = 1 taler (also French currency 1904–6). As Italy, 1936–41
	100 cents = 1 Ethiopian dollar
Faridkot	1 folus = 1 paisa = ½ anna (Later as India)
Federated Malay States	100 cents = 1 Malayan dollar
Finland	100 kopecks = 1 rouble
	100 penni = 1 Finnish mark
France (French Colonies and French Community unless otherwise stated)	100 centimes = 1 franc
French P.O.s in China	100 cents = 1 piastre
French P.O.s in Egypt	As France, and 1000 millièmes = £1 (Egyptian)
French P.O.s in Morocco	100 centimos = 1 peseta
French P.O.s in Turkey	40 paras = 1 piastre
French P.O.s in Zanzibar	16 annas = 1 rupee
Fujeira	100 naye paise = 1 rupee
	100 dirhams = 1 riyal
Gaboon (Republic)	100 centimes = 1 franc
German Colonies (unless otherwise stated)	100 pfennig = 1 mark

German E. Africa	64 pesa = 1 rupee
	100 heller = 1 rupee
German P.O.s in China	100 cents = 1 dollar (Chinese)
German P.O.s in Morocco	100 centimos = 1 peseta
German P.O.s in Turkey	40 paras = 1 piastre
	100 centimes = 1 piastre
Germany	30 groschen = 1 thaler (Northern)
	60 kreuzer = 1 gulden (Southern)
	100 pfennig = 1 mark (General)
	100 (Deutsche) pfennig = 1 (Deutsche) mark (Berlin)
	100 (Deutsche) pfennig = 1 (Deutsche) mark (West Germany)
	100 (DN) pfennig = 1 (DN) mark (Deutschen Notenbank) (East Germany)
Ghana (Gold Coast)	100 pesewas = 1 cedi
Gibraltar	British and Spanish
Gilbert & Ellice Islands	100 cents = 1 Australian dollar
Great Britain (and British Colonies and Dominions unless otherwise stated)	12 pence = 1 shilling, 20 shillings = £1
Greece	100 lepta = 1 drachma
Greenland	As Denmark
Grenada	100 cents = 1 dollar
Guatemala	100 centavos = 8 reales = 1 peso
	100 centavos de quetzal = 1 quetzal
Guyana (British Guiana)	100 cents = 1 dollar
Haiti	100 centimes = 1 gourde (or piastre)
Hamburg	16 schilling = 1 mark
Hatay	100 centièmes = 1 piastre
Hawaii	100 cents = 1 dollar
Hejaz-Nejd	40 paras = 1 piastre (or guerche)
Heligoland	6 schilling = 1 mark
	100 pfennig = 1 mark
Honduras	100 centavos = 8 reales = 1 peso (lempira)
Hong Kong	100 cents = 1 Hong Kong dollar
Hungary	100 kreuzer = 1 gulden
	100 filler = 1 krone
	100 filler = 1 pengo
	100 filler = 1 forint
Iceland	96 skilling = 1 rigsdaler
	100 aur = 1 krona

India (and Indian States unless otherwise stated)	12 pies = 1 anna. 16 annas = 1 rupee
	100 naye paisa = 1 rupee
	100 paisa = 1 rupee
Indian Settlements (Fr.)	As France, and 24 caches = 1 fanon
	8 fanons = 1 rupee
Indo-China	As France, and 100 cents = 1 piastre
Indonesia	100 sen = 1 rupiah
Ingermanland	100 penni = 1 mark
Iraq	As India, and 1000 fils = 1 dinar
Israel	100 agorots = £1 (Israeli)
Italian P.O.s in Albania and Turkey	40 paras = 1 piastre
Italian P.O.s in China	100 cents = 1 Chinese dollar (and as Italy)
Italian Somaliland	4 besa = 1 anna. 16 annas = 1 rupee (and as Italy)
Italy (and Italian States unless otherwise stated)	100 centesimi = 1 lira
Ivory Coast (Republique)	100 centimes = 1 franc
Japan	10 mon = 1 rin. 10 rin = 1 sen. 100 sen = 1 yen
Jhalawar	4 paisa = 1 anna
Jordan	10 milliemes = 1 piastre. 1000 milliemes = £1 (Jordan). 1000 fils = 1 dinar
Kenya, Uganda, and Tanganyika	100 cents = 1 shilling
Kiautschou	100 pfennig = 1 mark
	100 cents = 1 Chinese dollar
Korea	10 mons = 1 poon
	100 cheun = 1 woon
	10 (old) hwan = 1 won (South)
	100 chon = 1 (new) won (North)
Kuwait	As India
	1000 fils = 1 dinar
Labuan	100 cents = 1 Malayan dollar
Laos	100 cents = 1 piastre
	100 cents = 1 kip
Latakia	100 centièmes = 1 piastre
Latvia	100 kapiekas (kopecks) = 1 rouble
	100 santimi (centimes) = 1 lat
Lebanon	100 centièmes = 1 piastre
Lesotho (Basutoland)	Sterling
	100 cents = 1 rand
Liberia	100 cents = 1 dollar

Libya	As Italy
	1000 mils = £1 (Libyan)
Liechtenstein	100 heller = 1 krone
	100 rappen (centimes) = 1 Swiss franc
Lithuania	100 skatiku = 1 auksinas
	100 centu = 1 litas
Lubeck	15 schilling = 1 mark
Luxembourg	100 centimes = 1 franc
Macao	1000 reis = 1 milreis
	100 avos = 1 pataca
Mahra (Qishn and Socotra)	1000 fils = 1 dinar
Malagasy Republic (Madagascar)	100 centimes = 1 franc
Malaya (Federation, States and Settlements)	100 cents = 1 Malayan dollar
Malaysia (Federation)	100 cents = 1 Malayan dollar
Maldive Is.	100 cents = 1 rupee
	100 larees = 1 rupee
Mali (Federation and Republic)	100 centimes = 1 franc
Manchuria	100 fen = 1 yuan
Mauritius	12 pence = 1 shilling
	100 cents = 1 rupee
Mecklenburg-Schwerin	48 schilling = 1 thaler
Mecklenburg-Strelitz	30 silbergroschen = 48 schilling = 1 thaler
Mexico	8 reales = 100 centavos = 1 peso
Monaco	100 centimes = 1 franc
Mongolia	100 cents = 1 dollar
	100 mungs = 1 tuhrik
Montenegro	100 novics = 1 florin
	100 heller = 1 krone
	100 paras = 1 krone (perper)
Montserrat	100 cents = 1 dollar
Morocco	As France
	100 francs = 1 dirham
Morocco Agencies	Spanish and British
Muscat and Oman	64 baizas = 1 rupee
Naples	3 tornese = 1 grano
Nauru	100 cents = 1 Australian dollar
Nawanagar	6 docra = 1 anna
Nepal	16 annas = 64 pice = 1 rupee
	100 pice = 1 rupee

Netherlands (and associated territories)	100 cents = 1 gulden
Newfoundland	12 pence = 1 shilling
	100 cents = 1 dollar
New Hebrides	British and French
New Zealand	100 cents = 1 dollar
Nicaragua	100 centavos = 1 peso (cordoba)
Niger (Republic)	100 centimes = 1 franc
Niue	100 cents = 1 N.Z. dollar
Norfolk Island	100 cents = 1 Australian dollar
North German Confederation	30 groschen = 1 thaler
	60 kreuzer = 1 gulden
North Mongolia	100 kopecks = 1 rouble
Norway	120 skilling = 1 rigsdaler
	100 öre = 1 krone
Oldenburg	30 silbergroschen = 1 thaler
Pakistan	12 pies = 1 anna. 16 annas = 1 rupee
	100 paisa = 1 rupee
Palestine	10 milliemes = 1 piastre. 100 piastres = £1 (Palestine)
Panama	100 centavos = 1 peso
	100 centesimos de balboa = 1 balboa
Papua and New Guinea	100 cents = 1 Australian dollar
Paraguay	8 reals = 100 centavos = 1 peso
	100 centimes = 1 guarani
Persia (Iran)	20 shahis = 1 kran. 10 krans = 1 toman
	100 centimes = 1 franc
	100 dinars = 1 rial
Peru	100 dineros = 5 pesetas = 1 peso
	100 centavos = 1 peso (sol)
Philippine Islands	8 cuartos = 1 real. 8 reales = 1 peso fuerte
	100 centimos = 1 peso
	100 centesimos = 1 escudo
	100 centimos = 1 peseta
	1000 milesimas = 100 centavos = 1 peso
Pitcairn Islands	100 cents = 1 N.Z. dollar
Poland	100 halerzy (heller) = 1 krone (Austrian districts, 1918)
	100 fenigy (pfennig) = 1 mark (German districts, 1918)
	100 groszy = 1 zloty
Portugal (and Colonies unless otherwise stated)	1000 reis = 1 milreis
	100 centavos = 1 escudo

Portuguese India	1000 reis = 1 milreis
	12 reis = 1 tanga (anna). 16 tangas = 1 rupee
Prussia	12 pfennig = 1 silbergroschen. 30 silbergroschen = 1 thaler
	60 kreuzer = 1 gulden
Puerto Rico	100 centimos = 1 peseta
	1000 milesimas = 100 centavos = 1 peso
Qatar	100 naye paise = 1 rupee
	100 dirhams = 1 riyal
Ras al Khaima	100 naye paise = 1 rupee
	100 dirhams = 1 riyal
Romagna	100 bajocchi = 1 scudo
Roman States	100 bajocchi = 1 scudo (and as Italy)
Ross Dependency	100 cents = 1 N.Z. dollar
Roumania	40 paras = 1 piastre
	100 bani = 1 leu
Russia (with Armenia, Azerbaijan, Batum, and Georgia)	100 kopecks = 1 rouble
Rwanda Republic	100 centimes = 1 franc
Ryukyu Islands	100 sen = 1 yen
	100 cents = 1 U.S. dollar
Saar	As Germany and France
Sabah (North Borneo)	100 cents = 1 Malayan dollar
St Kitts-Nevis	100 cents = 1 dollar
St Lucia	100 cents = 1 dollar
St Vincent	100 cents = 1 dollar
Salvador	8 reales = 100 centavos = 1 peso
	100 centavos = 1 colon
Samoa	100 sene (cents) = 1 tala (N.Z. dollar)
San Marino	100 centesimi = 1 lira
Saudi Arabia	40 paras = 1 piastre = 1 guerche
	110 (later 880) guerches = 1 gold sovereign
	800 piastres = 1 gold sovereign
Sarawak	100 cents = 1 Malayan dollar
Schleswig-Holstein	16 schilling = 1 mark
Senegal (Republic)	100 centimes = 1 franc
Serbia	100 paras = 1 dinar
Seychelles	100 cents = 1 rupee
Shanghai	16 cash = 1 candareen. 100 candareens = 1 tael
	100 cents = 1 Chinese dollar

Sharjah and Dependencies	100 naye paise = 1 rupee
	100 dirhams = 1 riyal
Sicily	100 grana = 1 ducat
Sierra Leone	100 cents = 1 leone
Singapore	100 cents = 1 Malayan dollar
Slovakia	As Czechoslovakia
Somalia Republic	100 cents = 1 Somali shilling
South Africa	100 cents = 1 rand
South Arabian Federation	100 cents = 1 shilling
	1000 fils = 1 dinar
South West Africa	100 cents = 1 rand
Spain	8 cuartos = 1 real
	1000 milesimas = 100 centimos = 1 escudo
	100 centimos = 1 peseta
Spanish Colonies and P.O.s (unless otherwise stated)	100 centimos = 1 peseta
Sudan	10 milliemes = 1 piastre
Swaziland	Sterling
	100 cents = 1 rand
Sweden	48 skilling banco = 1 riksdaler
	100 öre = 1 riksdaler (krona)
Switzerland	100 rappen (centimes) = 1 franc
Syria	40 paras = 10 milliemes = 100 centimes (later centièmes) = 1 piastre
Tanzania (Tanganyika)	100 cents = 1 rupee
	100 cents = 1 shilling
Thailand (Siam)	1 salung = 4 sik = 8 sio = 16 atts = 32 solots
	64 atts = 1 tical
	100 satangs = 1 tical (or baht)
Timor	1000 reis = 1 milreis
	100 avos (cents) = 1 pataca (dollar)
Togo (Republic)	100 centimes = 1 franc
Tokelau Islands	100 cents = 1 N.Z. dollar
Tonga	100 seniti = 1 pa'anga
Travancore	16 cash = 1 chuckram. 28 chuckrams = 1 rupee
Trinidad	As Great Britain, and 100 cents = 1 dollar
Tunisia	As France
	1000 milliemes = 1 dinar
Turkey	40 paras = 1 piastre (later called grouch and then kurus)

Tuscany	60 quattrini = 20 soldi = 12 crazie = 1 lira
Uganda	1000 cowries = 2 rupees 16 annas = 1 rupee 100 cents = 1 shilling
Ukraine	100 kopecks = 1 rouble 100 schagiv = 1 grivni
Umm al Qiwain	100 naye paise = 1 rupee 100 dirhams = 1 riyal
United Nations	100 cents = 1 U.S. dollar
United States (and Canal Zone)	100 cents = 1 dollar
Uruguay	100 centavos = 1 real 1000 milesimos = 100 centesimos = 1 peso
Vatican City	100 centesimi = 1 lira
Venezuela	100 centavos = 8 reales = 1 peso 100 centimos = 1 venezolana (later = 1 bolivar)
Viet-Nam (South)	100 cents = 1 piastre
Viet-Nam (North)	100 xu = 1 (new) dong
Virgin Islands	100 cents = 1 U.S. dollar
Wurtemburg	60 kreuzer = 1 gulden 100 pfennig = 1 mark
Yemen	40 bogaches = 1 imadi
Yugoslavia	100 filler (heller) = 1 krone 100 paras = 1 dinar
Zanzibar	16 annas = 1 rupee 100 cents = 1 rupee 100 cents = 1 shilling

APPENDIX B · PHILATELIC TERMS IN THREE LANGUAGES

The collector who is really keen to learn all he can about stamps is certain, at one time or another, to need to use catalogues or books in other languages, especially French and German, in which languages there is a valuable literature on philatelic subjects.

INTERNATIONAL PHILATELIC GLOSSARY

Including the 100 colour names shown in the Stanley Gibbons Colour Guide

ENGLISH	FRENCH	GERMAN
Agate	Agate	Achat
Air stamp	Timbre de la poste aérienne	Flugpostmarke
Apple-green	Vert-pomme	Apfelgrün
Barred	Annulé par barres	Balkenentwertung
Bisected	Timbre coupé	Halbiert
Bistre	Bistre	Bister
Bistre-brown	Brun-bistre	Bisterbraun
Black	Noir	Schwarz
Blackish Brown	Brun-noir	Schwärzlichbraun
Blackish Green	Vert foncé	Schwärzlichgrün
Blackish Olive	Olive foncé	Schwärzlicholiv
Block of four	Bloc de quatre	Viererblock
Blue	Bleu	Blau
Blue-green	Vert-bleu	Blaugrün
Bluish Violet	Violet bleuâtre	Bläulichviolett
Booklet	Carnet	Heft
Bright Blue	Bleu vif	Lebhaftblau
Bright Green	Vert vif	Lebhaftgrün
Bright Purple	Mauve vif	Lebhaftpurpur
Bronze-green	Vert-bronze	Bronzegrün
Brown	Brun	Braun
Brown-lake	Carmin-brun	Braunlack
Brown-purple	Pourpre-brun	Braunpurpur
Brown-red	Rouge-brun	Braunrot
Buff	Chamois	Sämisch

ENGLISH	FRENCH	GERMAN
Cancellation	Oblitération	Entwertung
Cancelled	Annulé, oblitéré	Gestempelt
Carmine	Carmin	Karmin
Carmine-red	Rouge-carmin	Karminrot
Centred	Centré	Zentriert
Cerise	Rouge-cerise	Kirschrot
Chalk-surfaced paper	Papier couché	Kreidepapier
Chalky Blue	Bleu terne	Kreideblau
Charity stamp	Timbre de bienfaisance	Wohltätigkeitsmarke
Chestnut	Marron	Kastanienbraun
Chocolate	Chocolat	Schokoladen
Cinnamon	Cannelle	Zimtbraun
Claret	Grenat	Weinrot
Cobalt	Cobalt	Kobalt
Colour	Couleur	Farbe
Comb-perforation	Dentelure en peigne	Kammzähnung, Reihenzähnung
Commemorative stamp	Timbre commémoratif	Gedenkmarke
Crimson	Cramoisi	Karmesin
Deep Blue	Bleu foncé	Dunkelblau
Deep Bluish Green	Vert-bleu foncé	Dunkelbläulichgrün
Design	Dessin	Markenbild
Die	Matrice	Urstempel, Type, Platte
Double	Double	Doppelt
Drab	Olive terne	Trüboliv
Dull Green	Vert terne	Trübgrün
Dull Purple	Mauve terne	Trübpurpur
Embossing	Impression en relief	Prägedruck
Emerald	Vert-émeraude	Smaragdgrün
Engraved	Gravé	Graviert
Error	Erreur	Fehler, Fehldruck
Essay	Essai	Probedruck
Express letter stamp	Timbre pour lettres par exprès	Eilmarke
Fiscal-postal	Timbre fiscal-postal	Stempelmarke als Postmarke verwendet
Fiscal stamp	Timbre fiscal	Stempelmarke
Flesh	Chair	Fleischfarben
Forgery	Faux, Falsification	Fälschung
Frame	Cadre	Rahmen

ENGLISH	FRENCH	GERMAN
Granite paper	Papier avec fragments de fils de soie	Faserpapier
Green	Vert	Grün
Greenish Blue	Bleu verdâtre	Grünlichblau
Greenish Yellow	Jaune-vert	Grünlichgelb
Grey	Gris	Grau
Grey-blue	Bleu-gris	Graublau
Grey-green	Vert-gris	Graugrün
Gum	Gomme	Gummi
Gutter	Interpanneau	Zwischensteg
Imperforate	Non-dentelé	Geschnitten
Indigo	Indigo	Indigo
Inscription	Inscription	Inschrift
Inverted	Renversé	Kopfstehend
Issue	Emission	Ausgabe
Laid	Vergé	Gestreift
Lake	Lie de vin	Lackfarbe
Lake-brown	Brun-carmin	Lackbraun
Lavender	Bleu-lavande	Lavendel
Lemon	Jaune-citron	Zitrongelb
Light Blue	Bleu clair	Hellblau
Lilac	Lilas	Lila
Line perforation	Dentelure en lignes	Linienzähnung
Lithography	Lithographie	Steindruck
Local	Timbre de poste locale	Lokalpostmarke
Lozenge roulette	Percé en losanges	Rautenförmiger Durchstich
Magenta	Magenta	Magentarot
Margin	Marge	Rand
Maroon	Marron pourpré	Dunkelrotpurpur
Mauve	Mauve	Malvenfarbe
Multicoloured	Polychrome	Mehrfarbig
Myrtle-green	Vert myrte	Myrtengrün
New Blue*	Bleu ciel vif	Neublau
Newspaper stamp	Timbre pour journaux	Zeitungsmarke
Obliteration	Oblitération	Abstempelung
Obsolete	Hors (de) cours	Ausser Kurs

* 'New Blue' is a colour name introduced in the Stanley Gibbons Colour Guide to describe a colour used in the modern issues of Germany, Poland, Switzerland, etc.

ENGLISH	FRENCH	GERMAN
Ochre	Ocre	Ocker
Official stamp	Timbre de service	Dienstmarke
Olive-brown	Brun-olive	Olivbraun
Olive-green	Vert-olive	Olivgrün
Olive-grey	Gris-olive	Olivgrau
Olive-yellow	Jaune-olive	Olivgelb
Orange	Orange	Orange
Orange-brown	Brun-orange	Orangebraun
Orange-red	Rouge-orange	Orangerot
Orange-yellow	Jaune-orange	Orangegelb
Overprint	Surcharge	Aufdruck
Pair	Paire	Paar
Pale	Pâle	Blass
Pane	Panneau	Gruppe
Paper	Papier	Papier
Parcel post stamp	Timbre pour colis postaux	Paketmarke
Pen-cancelled	Oblitéré à plume	Federzugentwertung
Percé en arc	Percé en arc	Bogenförmiger Durchstich
Percé en scie	Percé en scie	Bogenförmiger Durchstich
Perforated	Dentelé	Gezähnt
Perforation	Dentelure	Zähnung
Photogravure	Photogravure, Heliogravure	Rastertiefdruck
Pin perforation	Percé en points	In Punkten durchstochen
Plate	Planche	Platte
Plum	Prune	Pflaumenfarbe
Postage Due stamp	Timbre-taxe	Portomarke
Postage	Timbre-poste	Briefmarke, Freimarke, Postmarke
Postmark	Oblitération postale	Poststempel
Printing	Impression	Druck
Proof	Épreuve	Druckprobe
Provisionals	Timbres provisoires	Provisorische Marken Provisorien
Prussian Blue	Bleu de Prusse	Preussischblau
Purple	Pourpre	Purpur
Purple-brown	Brun-pourpre	Purpurbraun
Recess-printing	Impression en taille douce	Tiefdruck
Red	Rouge	Rot

ENGLISH	FRENCH	GERMAN
Red-brown	Brun-rouge	Rotbraun
Reddish Lilac	Lilas rougeâtre	Rötlichlila
Reddish Purple	Pourpre-rouge	Rötlichpurpur
Reddish Violet	Violet rougeâtre	Rötlichviolett
Red-orange	Orange rougeâtre	Rotorange
Registration stamp	Timbre pour lettre chargée (recommandée)	Einschreibemarke
Reprint	Réimpression	Neudruck
Reversed	Retourné	Umgekehrt
Rose	Rose	Rosa
Rose-red	Rouge rosé	Rosarot
Rosine	Rose vif	Lebhaftrosa
Roulette	Perçage	Durchstich
Rouletted	Percé	Durchstochen
Royal Blue	Bleu-roi	Königblau
Sage-green	Vert-sauge	Salbeigrün
Salmon	Saumon	Lachs
Scarlet	Ecarlate	Scharlach
Sepia	Sépia	Sepia
Serpentine roulette	Percé en serpentin	Schlangenlieniger Durchstich
Shade	Nuance	Tönung
Sheet	Feuille	Bogen
Slate	Ardoise	Schiefer
Slate-blue	Bleu-ardoise	Schieferblau
Slate-green	Vert-ardoise	Schiefergrün
Slate-lilac	Lilas-gris	Schieferlila
Slate-purple	Mauve-gris	Schieferpurpur
Slate-violet	Violet-gris	Schieferviolett
Special delivery stamp	Timbres pour exprès	Eilmarke
Specimen	Spécimen	Muster
Steel Blue	Bleu acier	Stahlblau
Strip	Bande	Streifen
Surcharge	Surcharge	Aufdruck
Tête-Bêche	Tête-Bêche	Kehrdruck
Tinted paper	Papier teinté	Getöntes papier
Too-late stamp	Timbre pour lettres en retard	Verspätungsmarke
Turquoise-blue	Bleu-turquoise	Turkisblau
Turquoise-green	Vert-turquoise	Turkisgrün
Typography	Typographie	Buchdruck
Ultramarine	Outremer	Ultramarin

ENGLISH	FRENCH	GERMAN
Venetian Red	Rouge-brun terne	Venezianischrot
Vermilion	Vermillon	Zinnober
Violet	Violet	Violett
Violet-blue	Bleu-violet	Violettblau
Watermark	Filigrane	Wasserzeichen
Watermark sideways	Filigrane couché	Wasserzeichen liegend
Wove paper	Papier ordinaire, Papier uni	Einfaches papier
Yellow	Jaune	Gelb
Yellow-brown	Brun-jaune	Gelbbraun
Yellow-green	Vert-jaune	Gelbgrün
Yellow-olive	Olive jaunâtre	Gelboliv
Yellow-orange	Orange jaunâtre	Gelborange
Zig-zag roulette	Percé en zigzag	Sägezahnartiger Durchstich

APPENDIX C · STAMP INSCRIPTIONS TRANSLATED

As we have seen in Chapter Nine, the inscriptions (wording) on postage stamps cover a great variety of subjects and often help the collector to identify a stamp, to understand the reason for which it was issued or to appreciate the subject of its design. The following list includes translations of some typical or frequently used foreign inscriptions which may assist the collector to understand others.

Where an inscription indicates the purpose of a stamp, e.g. for 'postage due', that purpose is given in the English form, though the literal translation might be 'To pay', 'Collect from addressee', 'Fine', etc. according to the practice of the country concerned.

A study of this list may serve to indicate the wide scope and interest of stamp inscriptions and to whet the appetite of the reader for a deeper study of them.

Afrique Equatoriale Française (Fr.)	*French Equatorial Africa*
Afrique Occidentale Française (Fr.)	*French West Africa*
Amtlicher Verkehr (Ger.)	*Official communication*
Aniversario de la Asociacion de la Prensa de Madrid (Span.)	*Anniversary of the Press Association of Madrid*
Aniversario del Apertura del Canal de Panama (Span.)	*Anniversary of the Opening of the Panama Canal*
Anno Santo (It.)	*Holy Year*
A payer (Fr.)	*Postage Due*
A percevoir (Fr.)	*Postage Due*
Assistencia (Port.)	*Assistance*
Avisporto (Danish)	*Newspaper postage*
Bandera de la Raza (Span.)	*Flag of the Race*
Bicentenario do Caffeiro (Brazil)	*Bicentenary of Coffee*
Bollo della Posta di Sicilia (It.)	*Sicilian Postage Stamp*
Bollo della Posta Napoletana (It.)	*Postage Stamp of Naples*
Caisse d'Amortissement (Fr.)	*Sinking Fund*
Caritas (Lat.)	*Charity*
Centenario Azucar Cana (Span.)	*Centenary of the Sugar Cane*
Centenario Dantesco (It.)	*Dante Centenary*

Centenario de Independencia (Span.)	*Centenary of Independence*
Centenario de la Fundacion de la Ciudad de Lima (Span.)	*Centenary of the Foundation of the City of Lima*
Centenario de la Incorporacion del Partido de Nicoya (Span.)	*Centenary of the Incorporation of the Province of Nicoya*
Centenario del Cultivo del Cafe (Span.)	*Centenary of the Cultivation of Coffee*
Centenario del Descubrimiento del Mar del Sur (Span.)	*Centenary of the Discovery of the Southern Sea (Pacific Ocean)*
Centenario dell Medaglie al Valore Militare (It.)	*Centenary of the Military Medal for Valour*
Centenario Visita Darwin (Span.)	*Centenary of Darwin's Visit*
Certificado (Span.)	*Registered*
Chemins de Fer (Fr.)	*Railways*
Cinquantenario del Regno d'Italia (It.)	*Fiftieth Anniversary of the Kingdom of Italy*
Clarior e Tenebris (Lat.)	*Light from Darkness*
Conference du Desarmement (Fr.)	*Disarmament Conference*
Congreso Internacional del Frio (Span.)	*International Refrigeration Congress*
Correio (Port. and Brazil)	*Post*
Correo Aereo (Span.)	*Air Post*
Correos (Span.)	*Post*
Correos Nacionales (Span.)	*National Post*
Correos y Telegrafos (Span.)	*Posts and Telegraphs*
Correspondencia Oficial (Span.)	*Official Correspondence*
Correspondencia Urgente (Span.)	*Urgent Correspondence (i.e. Special Delivery)*
Croce Rossa (It.)	*Red Cross*
Croix-Rouge (Fr.)	*Red Cross*
Cruz Roja (Span.)	*Red Cross*
Cruz Vermelha (Port.)	*Red Cross*
Damus Petimusque Vicissim (Lat.)	*We give and we ask in turn*
Danzig ist Deutsch (Ger.)	*Danzig is German*
Das Braune Band von Deutschland (Ger.)	*The Brown Ribbon (Horse-Racing Prize) of Germany*
Deficit (Span.)	*Postage Due*
Deutsche Nationalversammlung (Ger.)	*German National Assembly*
Dienstmarke (Ger.)	*Official Stamp*
Die Saar Kehrt Heim (Ger.)	*The Saar Returns Home*
Dios, Patria, Libertad (Span.)	*God, Fatherland, Liberty*
Doplata (Polish)	*Postage Due*
Doplatit or Doplatne (Czech)	*Postage Due*

Drijvende Brandkast (Dutch)	*Floating Safe*
Duc. di Parma (It.)	*Duchy of Parma*
E.E.F.	*Egyptian Expeditionary Force*
Eendragt Maakt Magt (Dutch)	*Unity is Strength*
EE. UU. (or Estados Unidos) de Colombia (Span.)	*United States of Colombia*
Efterporto (Dan.)	*Postage Due*
Eilmarke (Ger.)	*Express Stamp*
Ein Reich, Ein Volk, Ein Gott (Ger.)	*One State, One People, One God*
Ein Volk, Ein Reich, Ein Führer (Ger.)	*One People, One State, One Leader*
Encomendas Postais (Port.)	*Parcel Post*
Encomiendas (Span.)	*Parcels*
Entrega Especial (Span.)	*Special Delivery*
Entrega Inmediata (Span.)	*Express Delivery*
Escuelas (Span.)	*Schools*
Espresso (It.)	*Express (Delivery)*
Estados Unidos de Nueva Granada (Span.)	*United States of New Granada (Colombia)*
Exposicion Nacional (Span.)	*National Exhibition*
Exposition Internationale des Arts Decoratifs Modernes (Fr.)	*International Exhibition of Modern Decorative Arts*
Expulsis Piratis Restituta Commercia (Lat.)	*Pirates Expelled Commerce Restored*
Flugpost (Ger.)	*Air Post*
Fondul Aviatiei (Roumanian)	*Aviation Fund*
Francobollo di Stato (It.)	*State Postage Stamp*
Franco Bollo Postale (It.)	*Postage Stamp*
Franqueo Deficiente (Span.)	*Postage Due*
Franqueo Oficial	*Official – Free*
Freie Stadt Danzig	*Free City of Danzig*
Frimarke (Swedish)	*Postage Stamp*
Fue la Mas Grande Entre las Poetisas de Todos los Tiempos (Span.)	*Was the greatest poetess of all time (on a Cuban stamp)*
Fuerstentum Liechtenstein (Ger.)	*Principality of Liechtenstein*
Fur Alters und Kinderhilfe (Ger.)	*For the Help of the Aged and Children*
Gebyrmærke (Danish)	*Fee stamp (for special postal services)*
Homenaje (Span.)	*Homage*
Honor, Libertad (Span.)	*Honour, Liberty*
Hugenote Gedenkfees (Afrikaans)	*Huguenot Commemoration*

Impresos (Span.)	*Printed Matter*
Impuesto de Guerra (Span.)	*War Tax*
Inauguracion de la Casa de Correos de Quito (Span.)	*Inauguration of the Quito Post Office*
Indus Uterque Serviet Uno (Lat.)	*The Indians Twain Serve One (Lord)*
Jeugdzorg (Dutch)	*Child Welfare*
Jornaes (Brazil)	*Newspapers*
Jubileo Cuerpo de Bomberos (Span.)	*Fire Brigade Jubilee*
Juegos Olimpicos (Span.)	*Olympic Games*
La Ley (Span.)	*The Law*
La Radio aux Aveugles (Fr.)	*Wireless for the Blind*
Leger des Heils (Dutch)	*Salvation Army*
Lösen (Swedish)	*Postage Due*
Luchtpost (Dutch)	*Air Post*
Luchtpostzegel voor Bizonderevluchten (Dutch)	*Air Post Stamp for Special Flights*
Luftpost (German and Scandinavian)	*Air Post*
Lugpos (Afrikaans)	*Air Post*
L'Union fait la force (Fr.)	*Unity is Strength*
Maaka te atua Karinea te uea (Gilbert Is.)	*Fear God; honour the King*
Mataku i te atua Fakamamalu ki te tupu (Ellice Is.)	*Fear God; honour the King*
Mensajerias (Span.)	*Special Delivery*
Multa (Span.)	*Postage Due*
Multada (Span.)	*Postage Due*
Muttertag (Ger.)	*Mother's Day*
Ne pas livrer le Dimanche (Fr.)	*Do not deliver on Sunday*
Niet bestellen op Zondag (Flemish)	*Do not deliver on Sunday*
Nothilfe (Ger.)	*Help (of the needy)*
Nov. Bruns. Sigill. Provinciæ (Lat.)	*Seal of the Province of New Brunswick*
Olympische Spiele (Ger.)	*Olympic Games*
Omnia Juncta in Uno (Lat.)	*All Joined in One*
Oro Pastas (Lithuanian)	*Air Post*
Orphelins de la Guerre (Fr.)	*War Orphans*
Pacchi Postali (It.)	*Parcel Post*
Padroes da Grande Guerra (Port.)	*Comrades of the Great War*
Para os Pobres (Port.)	*For the Poor*
Pax et Justitia (Lat.)	*Peace and Justice*

Pergo et Perago (Lat.)	*I proceed and I accomplish*
Pjonustu Frimerki (Iceland)	*Official Stamp*
Porteado (Port.)	*Postage Due*
Porto (Danish)	*Postage Due*
Portomarke (Ger.)	*Postage Due*
Posseel (Afrikaans)	*Postage Stamp*
Posta Aerea (It.)	*Air Post*
Posta Aerore (Albanian)	*Air Post*
Poste Aérienne (Fr.)	*Air Post*
Postes Persanes (Fr.)	*Persian Posts*
Postluchtdienst (Flemish)	*Air Post Service*
Postzegel (Dutch)	*Postage Stamp*
Pour les Chomeurs Intellectuels (Fr.)	*For the Unemployed Intellectuals*
Pour les Mutilés (Fr.)	*For the wounded*
Prædicate Evangilium omni Creaturæ (Lat.)	*Preach the Gospel to all Creatures*
Principauté de Monaco (Fr.)	*Principality of Monaco*
Pro Juventute (Lat.)	*For the Children*
Protección al Anciano (Span.)	*Protection for the Aged*
Proteja a la Infancia (Span.)	*Protection of Children (Child Welfare)*
Pro Tuberculatis Belli (Lat.)	*For the Fight against Tuberculosis*
Provincie Modonesi (It.)	*Province of Modena*
Rere vaka na Kalou ka doka na Tui (Fiji Is.)	*Fear God; honour the King*
Retardo (Span.)	*Too Late*
Roode Kruis (Dutch)	*Red Cross*
Secours International aux Intellectuels (Fr.)	*International Relief for Intellectuals*
Segnatasse (It.)	*Postage Due*
Segundos Juegos Deportivos Centro Americanos (Span.)	*Second Central American Games*
Seid Einig, Einig, Einig (Ger.)	*Be one, one, one*
Séptimo Congreso Panamericano del Niño (Span.)	*Seventh Panamerican Child Congress*
Service de l'Etat (Fr.)	*State Service*
Service Postal Aérien (Fr.)	*Air Post Service*
Servicio Aereo (Span.)	*Air Service*
Sigill. Inss. Antiguæ et Barbudæ (Lat.)	*Seal of the Islands of Antigua and Barbuda*
Sigillum Nov. Camb. Aust. (Lat.)	*Seal of New South Wales*
Sobreporte (Span.)	*Postage Due*
Sobreporte Aereo (Span.)	*Air Surtax*
Sobretasa Aerea (Span.)	*Air Surtax*
Spoorwegen (Flemish)	*Railways*

Staatsmarke (Ger.)	*State Stamp*
Statio Haud Malefida Carinas (Lat.)	*No harbour for disloyal ships*
Stati Parm (ensi) (It.)	*Parma State*
Stella Clavisque Maris Indici (Lat.)	*The Star and Key of the Indian Ocean*
Sub Umbra Floreo (Lat.)	*I flourish in the shade*
Tasa por Cobrar (Span.)	*Postage Due*
Taxa de Plata (Roumania)	*Postage Due*
Taxa Devida (Brazil)	*Postage Due*
Te Betaal (Afrikaans)	*Postage Due*
Te Betalen (Dutch)	*Postage Due*
Timbru Oficial (Roumania)	*Official Stamp*
Tjenstefrimarke (Swed.)	*Official Stamp*
Tuberkulosis Woche (Ger.)	*Tuberculosis Week*
Ultramar (Span.)	*Overseas*
Unie van Zuid Afrika (Dutch)	*Union of South Africa*
Union Postal Universal (Span.)	*Universal Postal Union*
Varldpost-Kongressen (Swed.)	*Postal Union Congress*
Volkshilfe (Ger.)	*People's Help (i.e. relief)*
Vom Empfänger Einzuziehen (Ger.)	*Postage Due*
Voor Het Kind (Dutch)	*For the Children*
Voortrekker Herdenking (Afrikaans)	*Voortrekker Commemoration*
Wereld Jamboree (Dutch)	*World Jamboree*
Winterhilfe (Ger.)	*Winter Help*
Winterhilfswerk (Ger.)	*Winter Help Work*
Zeitungsmarke (Ger.)	*Newspaper Stamp*
Zeitungs Stempel (Ger.)	*Newspaper Stamp*
Zona Franca del Puerto de Matanzas (Span.)	*Free Zone of the Port of Matanzas*

APPENDIX D · THE MEANING OF OVERPRINTS

THE list that follows is not intended to be exhaustive but merely to give the meaning of the overprints that are most likely to puzzle the collector, or which are of particular interest. Too many collectors do not trouble to think that an overprint must have a meaning or a purpose, and it is only by understanding what the meaning is that the full interest of stamps is brought out.

Overprints which represent the names of countries are only given here when they have not already been included in the identification lists in Chapter Eighteen.

OVERPRINT	COUNTRY	MEANING
A & T		*Annam and Tonquin*
A H P D	On Azores	*Angra, Horta, Ponta Delgada*
A M	Greece	*Value in gold*
A R	Various Spanish-American	*Aviso de Recepcion (Acknowledgment of Receipt)*
Armenwet	Netherlands	*Poor Law*
Assistencia	Portugal, etc.	*Assistance*
B.C.A.		*British Central Africa*
B.I.T.	Belgium	*Bureau International du Travail (International Labour Bureau)*
Buiten Bezit.	Netherlands Indies	*Outlying possessions (i.e. islands other than Java and Madura)*
Cabo	Nicaragua	*District of Cabo Gracias a Dios*
Caritas	Luxemburg	*Charity*
Cave	Ceylon	*A firm's name (Not an official overprint)*
C. Ch.	Cochin-China	*Cochin-Chine*
Centenario de las instrucciones	Uruguay	*Centenary of the Instructions (to declare the independence of the country)*
Centenario de S. Antonio	Portuguese Colonies	*Centenary of St Anthony (of Padua)*

OVERPRINT	COUNTRY	MEANING
C.G.H.S.	Silesia	*Commission du Gouvernement Haute-Silesie. (Governing Commission, Upper Silesia)*
C.I.H.S.	Silesia	*Commission Interalliée Haute-Silesie. (Interallied Commission, Upper Silesia)*
Costantinopoli	Italy	*Constantinople*
Corps Expeditionnaire Franco-Anglais, Cameroun	Cameroons	*Franco-English Expeditionary Force, Cameroons*
Correo Español Marruecos	Spanish Morocco	*Spanish Post, Morocco*
Costituente Fiumana	Fiume	*Fiume Constitution*
Cour permanente de Justice Internationale	Netherlands	*Permanent Court of International Justice (at The Hague)*
D.	Netherlands Indies	*Dienst (Service)*
D.B.P.	Far East Republic	*Initials of Russian words meaning Republic of the Far East*
Desmit Rubli	Latvia	*Ten roubles*
Dienst	Netherlands Indies	*Service*
Dienstmarke	Germany	*Service stamp*
Diwi Rubli	Latvia	*Two roubles*
E	Bavaria	*Eisenbahn (Railway)*
E C	Mexico	*Ejercito Constitucionalista. (Constitutional Army)*
E.E.F.	Palestine	*Egyptian Expeditionary Force*
E.F.O.	Oceanic Settlements	*Établissements Françaises de l'Oceanie*
Egeo	On Italian	*Aegean (Islands)*
E.R.I.	Orange Free State and Transvaal	*Edwardus Rex Imperator. (Edward, King, Emperor)*
E.S.	Mexico	*Estado Sonora. (State of Sonora)*
Espresso	Italy, etc.	*Express*
Estero	On Italy	*Foreign (or abroad)*
Feliz Año Nuevo	Paraguay	*Happy New Year*
Flugpost	Memel, etc.	*Air post*
F.M.	France	*Franchise Militaire*

OVERPRINT	COUNTRY	MEANING
Franqueo Oficial	Ecuador, etc.	*Official postage*
Fuera de Hora	Paraguay	*Too late (Actually a postmark, not an overprint)*
Gab.		*Gaboon*
Gbno. Const.		*Gobierno Constitucionalista (Constitutional Government)*
G.C.	Mexico	
G.C.M.		*ditto (with Mexico added)*
Gerusalemme	On Italian	*Jerusalem*
G.F.B.	Tonga	*Gaue Faka Buleaga. (On Govt. Service)*
GL.O.Z.	Hayti	*General Orestes Zamor*
Gob(ierno) Const (itucionalista)	Mexico	*Constitutional Government*
G.P. de M.	Mexico	*Provisional Govt. of Mexico*
G.R.I.	On German Cols.	*Georgius Rex Imperator. (George, King, Emperor)*
Gt. Pre.	Hayti	*Provisional Government*
Guy. Franc.	French Guiana	*Guyane Française*
G.W.	On Cape	*Griqualand West*
Habilitado	Spanish speaking countries	*Authorized*
H.P.N.		
Habilitado por la Nacion	Spain and Cols.	*Authorized by the Nation*
Hochwasser	Austria	*Flood (lit. high-water)*
I.A.A.	Germany	*Internationales Arbeits Amt. (International Labour Bureau)*
I.E.F.	On India	*Indian Expeditionary Force. (In War of 1914–18)*
I GILDI	Iceland	*Valid*
Impuesto de Guerra	Spain and Cols.	*War Tax*
Industrielle Kriegswirtschaft	Switzerland	*War Trade Board*
I Polska Wystawa Marek	Poland	*First Polish Philatelic Exhibition*
I.R. Official	Great Britain	*Inland Revenue Official*
Jornaes	Portugal and Cols.	*Journals (i.e. printed matter)*

OVERPRINT	COUNTRY	MEANING
Kans.	U.S.A.	*Kansas*
Kärnten Ab-stimmung	Carinthia	*Carinthia Plebiscite*
Kemahkotaan	Johor	*Coronation*
Koztarsasag	Hungary	*Republic*
Kraljevina	Jugoslavia	*Kingdom*
Kraljevstvo S.H.S.	Jugoslavia	*Kingdom of the Serbs, Croats, and Slovenes*
Kriegsbeschä-digte	Bavaria	*War-injured*
K.u.K. Milit. Verwaltung	On Austrian Military Post	*Imperial and Royal Military Administration*
L.F.F.	Liberia	*Liberian Frontier Force*
Luchtpost	In Dutch	*Air Post*
Luftpost	In German	*Air Post*
M.A.	Argentina	*Ministerio de Agricultura (Ministry of Agriculture)*
Magyar Nem-zeti Kor-many Szeged	Hungary	*Hungarian People's Govt., Szegedin*
Magyar Tanacs Koztarsasag	Hungary	*Hungarian Soviet Republic*
M.G.	Argentina	*Ministerio de Guerra (Ministry of War)*
M.H.	Argentina	*Ministerio de Hacienda (Ministry of Finance)*
M.I.	Argentina	*Ministerio del Interior (Ministry of the Interior)*
M.J.I.	Argentina	*Ministerio de Justicia y Instruccion (Ministry of Justice and Educa-tion)*
M.M.	Argentina	*Ministerio de Marina (Ministry of Marine)*
M.O.P.	Argentina	*Ministerio de Obras Publicas (Ministry of Public Works)*
MQE		*Martinique*
M.R.C.	Argentina	*Ministerio de Relaciones Exteriores y Culto (Ministry of Foreign Affairs and Religion)*
Muestra	In Spanish	*Specimen (lit. sample)*
M.V.i.R.	On Germany	*Militar. verwaltung in Rumanien. (Military administration in Roumania)*

OVERPRINT	COUNTRY	MEANING
Nebr.	U.S.A.	*Nebraska*
O.B.	Philippine Is.	*Official Business*
O.H.E.M.S.	Egypt	*On His Egyptian Majesty's Service*
O.H.H.S.	Egypt	*On His Highness' Service*
O(n) H.M.S.	India	*On Her (or His) Majesty's Service*
O.M.F.	Cilicia and Syria	*Occupation Militaire Française. (French Military Occupation)*
On C.G.S.	Cochin	*On Cochin Govt. Service*
On K.D.S.	Kishengarh	*On Kishengarh Durbar Service*
On S.S.S.	Sirmoor	*On Sirmoor State Service*
O.P.S.O.	New Zealand	*On Public Service Only*
O.S.	Various	*On Service*
O.S.G.S.	Sudan	*On Sudan Govt. Service*
O.W. Official	Great Britain	*Office of Works Official*
P.G.S.	Perak	*Perak Govt. Service*
Pjonusta	Iceland	*Official*
Poste par Avion	Syria, etc.	*Air post*
POSTFÆRGE	Denmark	*Ferry post*
Postgebiet Ob. Ost.	On Germany	*Postal area of the Eastern Commander-in-Chief*
Pre	Turkey	*Piastre*
Prir	Iceland	*Three*
Pro combattenti	San Marino	*For the troops*
Pro desocupados	Peru	*For the unemployed*
R	Various	*Reunion*
R	(on registration stamps)	*Recomendada (registered)*
R de C.	Nicaragua	*Recargo de Construccion (Extra charge for construction)*
Repulo posta	Hungary	*Air post*
Retardo	Spanish-American countries	*Delay (too late stamps)*
R. H. Official	Great Britain	*Royal Household Official*
R.O.	On Turkey	*Roumelie Orientale (Eastern Rumelia)*
Saggio	Italy	*Specimen*
Salonicco	On Italy	*Salonika*
Salonique	On Russia	*Salonika*
Sarkari	Soruth	*Official*

OVERPRINT	COUNTRY	MEANING
S.d.N. Bureau International du Travail	On Switzerland	*League of Nations, International Labour Bureau*
Secours aux Refugies	Syria, etc.	*Help for Refugees*
S.F.	Denmark	*Soldater Frimærke (Military Frank Stamp)*
Shkodres	Albania	*Scutari*
S.H.S.	Jugoslavia	*Srba, Hrvatska, Slovenska (Serbs, Croats, Slovenes)*
Smirne	On Italy	*Smyrna*
S.O.	Hong Kong	*Stamp Office*
S.O. 1920	Silesia	*Silesie Orientale, 1920 (Eastern Silesia)*
Sociedad de las Naciones LV Reunion del Consejo, Madrid	Spain	*League of Nations, 55th Meeting of the Council, Madrid*
Société des Nations	On Switzerland	*League of Nations*
S.U.		*Sungei Ujong*
T.	Various	*Taxe (Postage Due)*
Te Betalen	Dutch	*To pay*
T.E.O.	Cilicia and Syria	*Territoires Ennemis Occupées*
T-L	Tonga	*Taufa'ahau and Lavinia. (Names of royal bride and bridegroom)*
Veertig	Holland	*Forty*
Volkstaat Bayern	Bavaria	*Bavarian Republic*
V.R.I.	Orange Free State and Transvaal	*Victoria, Regina, Imperatrix (Victoria, Queen, Empress)*
Weens rubli	Latvia	*One rouble*
Winterhilfe	Austria	*Winter help*
Witwen und Waisenwoche	Bosnia	*Widows' and orphans' week*
Z.A.R.	Transvaal	*Zuid Afrikaanische Republiek (South African Republic)*
Zestig	Holland	*Sixty*

Accessories, 148

Acknowledgment of receipt stamps, 24

Adhesive stamps, adoption of, 16

Advantages of stamp collecting, 260

Advertisements, attached to stamps, 121; booklet, 118, 121; meter franks, 132; postmark, 133; sheet marginal, 119; stamp backs, 120

Aeroplanes on stamps, 212

Air cards, 211

Air covers, 213

Air labels, 211

Air posts, 211

Air stamps, 25, 211; of companies, 213

Albums, 146; blank loose-leaf, 147, 174; mechanism, 148; printed, 146, 173

Alphabets, foreign, on stamps, 170

American Philatelist, 240

Ampère, 197

Approval selections, 157, 219, 248

Arabic inscriptions, 171

Architecture on stamps, 192

Arc roulette, 55

Argentina, 27

'AR' on stamps, 24

Arranging a collection, 173; book on, 181

Arrival postmarks, 124

'Arrow block', 117

Arrows indicating varieties, 178

Artists' mistakes, 69; sketches, 42

Art on stamps, 196

Augustus, 190

Australia, Commonwealth postmarked sets, 130

Automatic franking, 132

Automatic machines, perforations, 58; rolls, 118

Aviso de Recepcion, 24

Babylonian posts, 8

Bach, 197

Backs of stamps, 120

Backstamp, 124

Bacon, Francis, 196

Bacon, Sir Edward D., K.C.V.O., 233

Badly centred stamps, 82, 160

Balboa, 194

Balloon posts, 211

Bank notes, stamps printed on, 47, 121

Bargains, warning *re* alleged, 143, 253

Bâtonné paper, 46

Beethoven, 197

Belgium, stamp advertisements, 121

Benzine, for detecting watermarks, 51; repaired stamps, 142; storage of, 149

Berger-Levrault Catalogue, 237

Berlioz, 197

Berthelot, 197

Biblical scenes on stamps, 197, 198

Birchin Lane stamp exchange, 223

Björnson, 195

Blank albums (*see* Loose-leaf albums)

Blanket prints, 74, 93

Bleuté paper, 49

Blind perforations, 81

Blued paper, 49

Bogus stamps, 135

Bolivia, 'Sun Gate' stamps, 136

Booklets, 117; inverted watermarks in, 84

Books on the hobby, 237

'Boom' countries, 222

Booty Catalogue, 237

Botany on stamps, 191

Branco, 195

British Commonwealth independent territories, 106

British Guiana, rarest stamp, 225, 235

British Philatelic Association, 143, 230

British stamps used abroad, 124

Broken letters in overprints, 93

Bruckner, 197

Brunei, bogus issue, 135

Building a collection, 153

Buying stamps, 143, 153, 216, 247

Cabot, 194

'Cachets', 211, 214

Camoëns, 195

Cancellations (*see* Postmarks)

'Cancelled to Order', 129, 130

'Carmen Sylva', 196

Carton Paper, 47

Catalogue of stamps, general, 146; need for, 238; prices, 217; specialist, 239

'Cave' overprints, 95

Centring, 82, 160

Centre, double, inverted, etc., 75

'Centre line block', 117

Cervantes, 195

Chalk-surfaced paper, 48; floating stamps on, 162

Changelings, 77, 108

Charity overprints, 90

Charity stamps, 34

China, treaty port locals, 22

Chinese inscriptions, 171

Choosing a country to collect, 182

Chopin, 197

Christianity on stamps, 197

Churchill, Sir Winston, 38, 195

Clean-cut perforations, 81

Cleaned stamps, detected by colour, 107; object, 138; protection against, 48; quartz lamp, 141

Cleaning stamps for collections, 162

Cleopatra, 190

Clichés, 64

Climate, effect on colour, 109

Clipperton Island, 135

Cochrane, Admiral, 194

Codrington, Sir E., 106, 194

Coils, stamp, 118

Coinages used on stamps, 263

Collectors' Club, New York, 224, 225

Collectors' Club Philatelist, 183, 240

Collectors, famous, 231

Colonial dies, 70

Coloured papers, 49

Coloured postmarks, 125, 127

Colour Guide, 110

Colour proofs, 44

Colour trials, 44

Colours, stamp, 107; changelings, 77, 108; detection of forgeries, etc., by, 107; difficulties, 107; errors, 76; fakes, 110, 138; guide to, 110; naming of, 110; variations, 77, 108

Columbus, 193, 194

Comb perforation, 57, 80

Commemoratives, overprints, 90; stamps, 28, 'omnibus' issues, 38

Common stamps, unprofitable, 220

Competitions, philatelic, 228

Compound perforations, 150

Condition of stamps, 160

Control numbers, 116

Control overprints (marks), 89

Cook, Captain, 194

Cooper, Sir Daniel, 231

Copernicus, 197

Counts of Thurn and Taxis, 11

Courier posts, 12

Covers, air, 213; stamps on, 162, 258

Crawford, Earl of, 232

Creased paper, freaks, 78, 83

Creases, removal of, 162

Currencies on stamps, 263

Current numbers, 115

'Cut-squares', 21
Cylinder number, 116

Daguerre, 197
Damaged plate, 70
Damaged stamps, 160
Damaged transfer, 65, 72
Dandy roll, 50
D'Annunzio, 195
Dante, 195
Danube Steam Navigation Co., 22
Darius, 190
Date cuts, 116
Dated postmarks, 124
Daudet's Mill, 195
Dealers' guarantee, 143
Dealer service, value of, 219
Debussy, 197
Defective watermarks, 87
Definitive issues, 23
Departmental stamps, 26
Departure postmarks, 124
Descriptive notes in collections, 178
Designs of stamps, 42, 96
De Villayer's Paris post, 12
Dickinson silk-thread paper, 47
'Dictionary' collection, 210
Die, preparation of, 43, 62; variations in, 69
Die proofs, 43
Die-stamped album headings, 152
Dockwra's post, 13
'Doctor' knife, 78
Don Quixote, 195
Double centre, 75
Double frame, 75
Double overprint, 92
Double paper, 48
Double perforation, 81
Double print, 73
Double surcharge, 92
Double watermark, 84
Dropped letters, 94
Dry process (recess printing), 71
Duke of Edinburgh, 232
Duke of Windsor, 235

Duplicate books, 149
Duplicates, 153, 155
Duty plate, 66
Duveen, H. J., 232
Dvorak, 197
Dyckmans, 196

Earliest stamps, 17
'Electronic Eye', 57
Electrotyping, 64
Elizabethan Catalogue, Gibbons, 239, 251
Embossing, 66
Enamel paper, 48
En épargne, engraving, 64
Engineering on stamps, 192
Engraving, in recess, 60, 61; *en épargne*, 64
'Entires', 21
Envelope stamps, 21
Epidiascope, 228
Errors, 69; artists', 69; bi-coloured stamps, 74; colours, 75; engraving, 70; intentional, 76; 92; issue of, 76; leakage of, 76; overprints, 91; of paper, 78; perforations, 79; printing, 73; spelling, 69; surcharge, 91; watermarks, 83
Esperanto on stamps, 105
Essays, 42, 185
Exchange clubs, 224
Exhibition stamps, 33
Exhibitions, stamp, 224
Expert Committees, 143, 230
Express letter stamps, 25
Express stamps for newspapers, 25

'Facing' machines, 67
Faked imperforate stamps, 79
Fakes, 138; cleaned stamps, 138; colours, 110, 139; repainted, 139; repaired, 138; re-perforated, 139; watermarks, 139
'False' watermarks, 53
Famous collectors and collections, 231

Farmers' parcel stamps, 25
Farragut, 194
Ferrary collection, 231
Field sports on stamps, 198
Fiji, 'V.R.' overprint, 89
Film shows, 226
Finance of philately, 216, 252
Finland, mourning stamp, 135
Firms' initials, 95
First day covers, 133
First flight covers, 213
Fiscal cancellations, admission to collections, 127; penmarks, 127; violet, 127
Fiscal stamps, 20
Fiume, stamps printed on back, 120
Flight in stamp designs, 212
Floating (soaking) stamps, 161
Folded paper freaks, 78, 83
Folded transfer, 65, 72
Forged postmarks, 140
Forgeries, 126; detection of, 107, 137, 246; overprints and sur- charges, 141; protection against, 143; value of, 136
Forming a stamp club, 225
Fragonard, 196
Frame, double, 75; inverted, 75
France, Anatole, 195
France, stamp coins, 122
Franking letters, 15
Franks, Government, 132
Frank stamps, 27
Freaks, due to creased paper, 78, 83; of impression, 78; of per- foration, 81
French philatelic terms, 274
Fugitive inks, 162

Galvani, 197
Gauges of perforation, 58; measurement of, 149
'Gebyr', 25
Geography from stamps, 190
German Occupied Zones, 37
German philatelic terms, 274

Gibbons' Stamp Monthly, 240, 245, 250
Gibbons-Whitman Catalogue, 157, 239, 251
Go-as-you-please collecting, 210
Goethals, General, 192
Goethe, 195
Gorky, Maxim, 195
Granite paper, 46
Grant, General, 194
Graphite-lined stamps, 68
Grease spots, removal of, 162
Great Britain, 1½d. *tête-bêche*, 118; used abroad, 124
Greece, 'Sir Codrington' error, 106
Greek inscriptions, 171
Guarantees, dealers', 143
Guillotine perforation, 56
Gum, 44; test for forgeries, etc., 141; variations, 45
Gum 'watermark', 54
'Gutters', 114

Hall, T. W., 235
Hand-made paper, 46
Hand-painted background, 75
Hans Andersen, 195
Harrow perforation, 56
Haydn, 197
Heading blank album pages, 152, 178
Head-plate, 66
Henry VIII, postal system, 12
Heraldic designs, 198
Herm, 22
Hill, Rowland, 17
Hind, Arthur, 235
Hinges, 145; use of, 176
Historical interest of stamps, 189
Holland (*see* Netherlands)
Holy Year stamps, 197
Honours for stamp collectors, 235
Horizontally-laid paper, 46
Horse posts, 8
Hugo, Victor, 195

Ibsen, 195
Identifying stamps, 163
Imperforate between, stamps, 80
Imperforate margins, sheets, 80
Imperforate stamps, 55; errors,
    79; fakes, 79
Impressed stamps, 21
Impressed watermark, 53
Industries on stamps, 191
Inks, 44, 76
Inscriptions, stamp, 42, 105;
    changes in, 105; foreign alpha-
    bets, 170; identification by, 170;
    mistakes in, 106; translated, 280
'Instanta' Perforation Gauge, 151
Intaglio printing (*see* Line-
    engraving)
Intentional 'errors', 76, 92
Interleaved albums, 175
Intermediate perforation, 81
Interrupted perforation, 58
Inverted centre, 75
Inverted overprint, 92
Inverted watermark, 84
I Promessi Sposi, 196
Iran (*see* Persia)
Irregular perforations, 150

James I, 196
Japanese inscriptions, 171
Jokai, Maurus, 195
Jubilee lines, 115
Julius Caesar, 190, 195

Kansas overprint, 89
Kant, 195
Kennedy, President, 195
Key-type designs, 164, 191
'Killer', 124
King George V collection, 233
King George VI, 234
King John's post, 12
'Kiss' stamp, 117
Kohl Handbuch, 183

Labels, 19, 135
Labuan, cancelled to order, 129
Laid paper, 46; how made, 50

Lallier album, 238
La Perouse, 194
La Rénotière (Ferrary), 231
Late fee stamps, 24
Latvia, 46
Lettering for album pages, 179
Light and colour, 107
Line-engraving, 59; characteris-
    tics, 60; example, 61; methods,
    62
Linen-hinged album leaves, 174
Line perforation, 56; errors, 79
Literature in stamp designs, 195
Literature, philatelic, 237
Lithographic stone, 64
Lithographic transfers, 65
Lithography, 59; characteristics,
    60; examples, 61; methods, 65;
    types, 72
Lithuania, 47, 121
'Local Carriage Labels', 22
Local stamps, 21
Lombardy-Venetia postmarks, 133
London Philatelic Society, 224
London Philatelist, 240
Loose-leaf albums, 148, 174
Loose type, 93
Louis XI, posts, 11
Lozenge, perforation, 56
Lundy, 22

Machine-made paper, 46
Magazines, stamp, 237, 240
Magellan, 194
Magnifying glasses, 148
Major varieties, 69
Making money from stamps, 216
Manzoni, 196
Maps, stamps printed on, 47, 121
Map stamps, 192
Marginal watermarks, 86
Margins, 114; information on,
    114; wide, 82; wing, 83
Marie of Roumania, Queen, 196
Marx, Karl, 195
Mauritius, King George's col-
    lection, 234, 256

'Mayfair find', 256
Metallic inks, 44
Meter franks, 132
Michelangelo, 196
Michel Stamp Catalogue, 239
Miniature sheets, 54
Minkus Catalogue, 239
Minor varieties, 69
Misplaced centre, 75
Misplaced overprint, 92
Misplaced perforations, 83
Mixed perforations, 83
Money stamps, 122
Monthly Intelligencer, 237
Moresnet, imaginary issue, 135
Mother die, 62
Moulds for stereotyping, 64
Mount Brown Stamp Catalogue, 237
Mounts (hinges), 145, 176
Mounting stamps, 176
Mozart, 197
'Muestra', 91
Mulready, William, 17, 47, 239
Multicoloured stamps, 66, 77
Multiple comb perforator, 57
Multiple watermarks, 53
Music on stamps, 196
'Muster', 91
Mythology on Stamps, 197

Names of countries (gummed), 152, 178
Native races on stamps, 191
Nebraska overprint, 89
Nelson statue, 194
Netherlands, interrupted perforations, 58; stamps postmarked in bulk, 131
New Europe, stamps of, 37
Newspaper stamp, 25
New York Philatelic Society, 224, 225
New Zealand, lithographed watermarks, 120; stamp advertisements, 121

Nicaragua, stamps overprinted on back, 122
North Borneo, cancelled to order, 129
'No watermark' varieties, 85
Numbered cancellations, 124

Obliterations (*see* Postmarks)
Occupation stamps, 36
Offers from dealers, 218
Official reprints, 137
Official stamps, 26
Offset impression, of overprint, 93; of stamp, 65, 74
Offset printing, 65
Old collections, value of, 218
Olympic Games stamps, 34, 198
Omitted centre, 76
Omitted frame, 76
'One-colour' collections, 209
Outfit, philatelic, 145
Overprints, 88; distinguishing forgeries, 94, 141; errors, 91; meaning of, 286; measurement of, 151; misplaced, 92; reasons for, 88; settings, 93; 'SPECIMEN', 91; varieties, 92
Oxydization, 110; removal of, 162

Pacific Steam Navigation Co., 22
Packets of stamps, 154
Paderewski, 197
Palestine, tri-lingual inscriptions, 105
Panes, 114
Paper, coloured, 49; errors of, 78; folds in, 78; how made, 50; kinds of, 46; protective, 48; shrinkage, 71; thickness of, 47; watermarked, 50
Paper-maker's watermark, 51
Parcel Postage Due stamps, 26
Parcel stamps, 25
Paris Philatelic Society, 223
Pasteur, 197
Pears' Soap stamps, 121

Pelure paper, 47

Penmarks, 127, 138

Penny Post, 16

Peonias, 196

Percé en arc, 55; *en lignes*, 55; *en scie*, 56

Perforated initials, 94

Perforation, 56; clean-cut and rough, 81; errors of, 79; faked, 139; freaks of, 83; gauges of, 81, 149; measuring, 149; omitted, 79; types of, 57

Perforation gauge (instrument), 149

Peroxide of hydrogen, 162

Persia, control marks, 89; obliterated Shah's portrait, 193

Personal Delivery Stamps, 27

Peru, portrait overprint, 90

Petofi, 195

Philatelic congresses, 224

Philatelic exhibitions, 224

Philatelic Journal of Great Britain, 240

Philatelic literature, 183, 237

Philatelic Magazine, 240

Philatelic societies, 224; visitors to, 184

Philatelic terms, French, German, 274

Philatelist, essential qualifications, 39

Philatelist (magazine), 240

Philately (magazine), 240

Philately, meaning of, 39, 183

Philbrick, Judge, 231

Phosphor-paper stamps, 68

Photogravure process, 65, 67

Pigeon posts, 9

Pin-perforation, 56

Pizarro, 194

Plate, electrotyped, 64; foreign matter on, 77; line engraved, 62; re-entry, 63; re-engraving, 62; retouching, 63; stereotyped, 64; typographic, 64

Plate numbers, 115

Plate proofs, 43

Plating of stamps, 186

Plebiscite stamps, 37

Pneumatic post stamps, 25

Political changes shown by stamps, 105

Popov, 197

Portrait stamps, 96

Portugal, St Anthony issue, 120

Post, history of, 8

Postage Due stamps, 23

Postage stamp, basis of cataloguing, 31; classes of, 20; definition, 15; forerunners, 15; multiple uses, 23; reason for issue, 41; used fiscally, 20

Postal Congress issues, 33

Postal-fiscals, 20

Postal history, 40, 183

Postally used forgeries, 136

Postal methods illustrated on stamps, 9

Postal monopolies, 13

Postal-telegraphs, 20

Postcard stamps, 21

Postmarks, advertising, 132; automatic, 132; cancelled to order, 129; definition, 123; detection of forgeries by, 126; effect on apparent colour, 108; evidence of use, 123; faked, 140; historical interest, 125; meter franks, 132; penmarks, 127; pre-cancels, 131; pre-stamp, 123; purpose of, 123; telegraphic, 128; used abroad, 124; violet, 127

'Post Office', Mauritius stamp, 234, 256

Potiquet Catalogue, 237

Praxiteles, 196

Prayer on stamps, 120

Pre-cancels, 131

Pressure, variation during printing, 77

Pre-stamp covers, 122

Price fluctuations, 220

Printed both sides, stamps, 73
Printer's imprint, 117
Printer's waste, 67, 76
Printing, embossing, 66; essentials of good, 67; methods, 59; in two colours, 66; 'in the web', 67
Profit from stamps, 220
'*Pro Juventute*' stamps, 35
Proofs, colour, 44; die, 43; interest of, 44; plate, 43
Protecting collectors, 230
Protecting stamps in albums, 175
Protective papers, 48
'Provisionals', 23
Pulp paper, 50

Quadrillé album leaves, 175, 179
Quadrillé paper (of stamps), 46
Quartz lamp, 141
Queen Elizabeth II, 234

Raemaekers, 196
Raphael, 196
Rare stamps, best value, 218; best investments, 221
Rarest stamp, 235
Recess-printing (*see* Line-engraving)
Recorded Message Service, 27
Red Cross stamps, 36, 38
Redrawn designs, 70
Re-engraved plate, 62
Re-entry, 63
Registration dots, 116
Registration, in printing, 67; bi-coloured stamps, 74
Registration stamps, 24
Religion on stamps, 197
Remainders, 130; objections to, 130; supplemented by reprints, 137
Rembrandt, 196
Removing stamps from paper, 161
Repairing stamps, 138; how detected, 141
Re-perforated stamps, 139

Reprints, definition, 137; detection of, 107, 142; reasons for, 138; sometimes valuable, 138
Retouching, 63, 70
Revenue stamps, 20
Reversed watermarks, 84
Rhodesia, remainders, 130; stamps as money, 122
Richelieu, his post, 11
'Ripple' gum, 45
Rocket-post, 9, 215
Roller die, 62
Roll of Distinguished Philatelists, 225, 233
Rolls, sale of stamps in, 118
Roman posts, 9, 11
Romulus and Remus, 190
Ronsard, 195
Roosevelt, President, 235
Rotary photogravure, 65
'Rotogravure', 61
Rough perforation, 81
Rouletting, 55
Royal collectors, 232
Royal Philatelic Society, 143, 224, 229, 230, 233, 234, 240, 251
Russia, Esperanto stamps, 105; money stamps, 122; multi-lingual stamps, 105; '*Zemstvo*' stamps, 22
Russian inscriptions, 171

'Saggio', 91
St Andrews' Cross, 117
St Anthony, 197
St Barnabas, 198
St Benedict, 197
St Francis, 197
St Paul, 195, 198
St Publius, 198
Saints on stamps, 197
Salvador, arms overprint, 90
S.C.A.D.T.A. air stamps, 213
Schiller, 195
Schools and collecting, 190
Schubert, 197
Scientific philately, 186

Scientific progress on stamps, 197
Scott Stamp Catalogue, 239
Scout stamps, 198
Scratched plate, 72
Sculpture on stamps, 196
Sedang, 135
'Seebeck' issues, 137
Selling stamps, 218, 258
Serial numbers, 115
Service stamps, 26
Sets of stamps, 155
Settings, 72, 94
Shades, cause of, 77, 108; variations, 108
Shakespeare, 38, 195
Sheba, Queen of, 190
Sheets, size of, 54, 114; subdivisions, 114
Sheet watermarks, 52
Sideline collections, 21, 200
Sideways watermarks, 84
Sienkiewicz, 195
Silk-thread paper, 47
Simplified Stamp Catalogue, Stanley Gibbons, 190, 199, 238, 251
Single-line perforation, 56, 80
Single watermarks, 52
Sinn Fein labels, 135
'Sir Codrington' error, 106
Size of stamps, variations in, 71
Slogan postmarks, 132
Smetana, 197
Soldiers' letter stamps, 27
Solomon, King, 190, 195
Sousa, 197
'Space' stamps, 197
Spaced letters in overprint, 94
Special delivery stamps, 25
Special fee stamps, 24
Special handling stamps, 25
Specialized Catalogue, Gibbons, 239, 251
Specialist catalogues, 183, 239
Specialist collecting, 182
'Specimen' stamps, 91, 123
Speculation in stamps, 221
Sports stamps, 198

Spring-back albums, 174
Stamp albums, 146, 173
Stamp booklets, 117
Stamp catalogues, 190, 199, 238, 251
Stamp clubs, 223; formation of, 225
Stamp coins, 122
Stamp Collecting, 240
Stamp Collectors' Magazine, 237
Stamp Collectors' Monthly Advertiser, 237
Stamp dealers, visit to, 244
Stamp designs, how obtained, 42, 43
Stamp exhibitions, 224
Stamp finds, 252
Stamp hinges (*see* Hinges)
Stamp inscriptions, translated, 280
Stamp library, 237
Stamp Lover, 240
Stamp Magazine, 240
Stamp magazines, 183, 237, 240, 250
Stamp meetings, subjects for, 226, 227
Stamp meters, 132
Stamp packets, 154, 218
Stamp printing, 59
Stamp tour, 190
Stamp values, 216
Stanley Gibbons, Ltd, visit to, 244; centenary, 225; catalogue centenary, 225
Stanley Gibbons Stamp Catalogues, 190, 199, 238, 251
Stereotyping, 64
Stevenson, Robert Louis, 195
Stone, lithographic, 60, 61, 64
Straight edges, 80
Stratosphere stamps, 213
Strauss, 197
Substituted transfers, 72
'Sun Gate' stamps, Bolivia, 136
Surcharge (*see* Overprint)
Surface-coloured papers, 49

Surface-printing, 60; characteristics, 60; example of, 61; method, 64
Switzerland, children's stamps, 35
'Syncopated' perforations, 58

'T' overprint, 24
Table of inscriptions, 164
Tax stamps, 36, 37
Telegraphic cancellations, 128
Telegraph stamps, 20
Tête-bêche stamps, 73, 118
Thematic collecting, 179, 189
Thickness of paper, 47
Thurn and Taxis posts, 11, 56
Tilleard, J. A., M.V.O., 233
Tissue paper, 47
Tolstoy, 195
'Too Late' stamps, 24
Transfers, lithographic, 64
Transport, on stamps, 192
Treasury competition, 16
Triangular stamps, 209
Trinidad (S. Atlantic), 135
Tweezers, 151
Two-colour printing, 66; errors and varieties, 74
Type-collections, 200
Type-set overprints and surcharges, 93
'Typical' collection, 209
Typography (*see* Surface-printing)

Ungummed stamps, 44
United States locals, 22
Unnecessary issues, 30
Unpaid letter stamps, 23
Unwiped plates, colouring of paper, 50
Used abroad, stamps, 124

Valuation of stamps, 216, 246
Vazoff, 196
Vertically laid paper, 46
Views on stamps, 191
Violet postmarks, 127
Volta, 197

Wagner, 197
Want lists, 157, 219
Wartime forgeries, 137
War stamps, 36
War Tax stamps, 36, 37
Watermark detector, 149
Watermarks, 50; in booklets, 84; defective, 87; detection of, 50; double, 84; errors, 83; faked, 139; inverted, 84; lithographed, 120; marginal, 86; omitted, 85; reversed, 84; in rolls, 84; sideways, 84, 86
Weapons against forgers and fakers, 140
Wedgwood Benn, M.P., Rt. Hon. Anthony, (P.M.G.), 225
Wide margins, stamps with, 82
Wilson, Sir J., Bart., 234
Wolf, Hugo, 197
Wove paper, 46; how caused, 50
Wrapper stamps, 21
Writing-up collections, 179; book on, 181
Writing-up labels, 152, 178

Yugoslavia, overprint, 90
Yvert et Tellier-Champion Catalogue, 239

Zigzag roulette, 56
Zoological stamps, 191